AF505601

National Myth and Imperial Fantasy

# National Myth and Imperial Fantasy

## Representations of Britishness on the Early Eighteenth-Century Stage

Louise H. Marshall

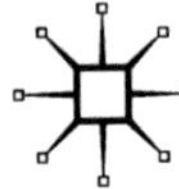



First published 2008 by
PALGRAVE MACMILLAN

Palgrave Macmillan in the UK is an imprint of Macmillan Publishers Limited, registered in England, company number 785998, of Houndmills, Basingstoke, Hampshire RG21 6XS.

Palgrave Macmillan in the US is a division of St Martin's Press LLC, 175 Fifth Avenue, New York, NY 10010.

Palgrave Macmillan is the global academic imprint of the above companies and has companies and representatives throughout the world.

Palgrave® and Macmillan® are registered trademarks in the United States, the United Kingdom, Europe and other countries.

ISBN-13: 978–0–230–57337–6        hardback

This book is printed on paper suitable for recycling and made from fully managed and sustained forest sources. Logging, pulping and manufacturing processes are expected to conform to the environmental regulations of the country of origin

A catalogue record for this book is available from the British Library.

A catalog record for this book is available from the Library of Congress.

10   9   8   7   6   5   4   3   2   1
17   16   15   14   13   12   11   10   09   08

Transferred to Digital Printing in 2010

# Contents

# Acknowledgements

To the many people who have helped me during the process of writing this book I would like to extend my thanks and gratitude. Of my colleagues and many friends at the Department of English, Aberystwyth University I would like to extend particular thanks to Dr Sarah Prescott for her invaluable help, advice, support and friendship throughout this project. Working on this book has taught me many things, not least the immeasurable value of supportive colleagues and I would like to thank Dr David Shuttleton for his unfailing enthusiasm, Dr Paulina Kewes for her incisive judgements on the early stages of this project and the many who have been subject to my persistent demands for their opinions over coffee; Becky, Caroline, Will, John, Kate, a representative but far from exhaustive list. I would like to thank my family for their endless patience, and for surviving various feats of endurance during the course of this project, seemingly unscathed. Love and appreciation also go to my parents, for everything they have done over the years and for the support they bring to everything I do. Lastly, Simon, without whom this project would have been impossible, thank you for sharing your life with it.

# Introduction: Dramatising Britain – Nation, Fantasy and the London Stage, 1719–1745

'Our Poet brings a Master-Glass to shew,
What your Sires were, and what your selves are now'
James Moore Smythe,

*The Rival Modes* (1727)

The centrality of literature to politics during the eighteenth century has been identified by modern scholarship as one of the defining characteristics of British culture from this period. 'Serious writers', Bertrand Goldgar argues, 'could not escape making political choices, for politics touched and coloured virtually every aspect of life in the world of letters, even the reception of plays or poems not overtly political.'[1] This book seeks to consider the unique contribution made by drama to a range of early eighteenth-century political discourses. Drama is often credited with a characteristic topicality, responsive to its cultural and historical place, mirroring the attitudes and ideas of its era.[2] As the prologue to James Moore Smythe's *The Rival Modes* attests, the theatre can be seen as the nation's mirror, a microcosmic version of the state.

Britain was dramatised on the early eighteenth-century London stage as a paragon state. There was seemingly little space for anything but a fanatical and fantastical representation of the nation. As the numerous prologues and epilogues dedicated to 'BRITONS' declared, the nation's glorious past must be reflected in its present. But despite the seeming robustness of such patriotic declarations multiple layers of ambiguity lie beneath these lines of nationalistic bravado. Within the confines of the theatre, itself linguistically reverberating rhetoric from the political world, modern Britain was repeatedly positioned as an echo of its own prestigious history. That is, the prologues suggest a continuation of hereditary uniqueness. They assert Britain's distinction from and superiority to her European neighbours, celebrate her unique maritime position and the tenacious independence of her people. But, in the act of gazing into a mirror does the audience see on stage a true reflection of themselves or a distorted echo, obscuring or emphasising their own flaws? The 'Master-Glass' shows the audience their past and their present in one image. But this image is no tableau; it lacks fixity and is a transient, malleable representation. Just as the prologues and epilogues presume the homogeneity of audiences by labelling them 'Britons' and assume the universality of such a term, the plays and the stories they re-tell demonstrate the endless variety of possible interpretations casting doubt over the reality and stability of such a superlative vision of the nation. In their attempts to elevate the status of audiences and evidence the great-ness of the nation prologues speculate over notions of ancestral moral connectivity between modern Britons and their ancient forebears. It is in this gap between the constructed fantasy of Britain and the realities of history, politics and culture that the early eighteenth-century plays demonstrate their interaction with politics and their interventions in political debate.

Despite this notion of an insidious nationalistic gloss the plays dis-cussed in this book also reveal the theatre's role in offering opinion and criticism as well as approbation of the current age. Folly and vice are reflected as a cathartic entertainment, prompting the voyeuristic audi-ence to self-congratulation coupled with anxiety. On stage the players represent the fears, fantasies and desires of the implied audience. In their roles the men and women on stage become representative of their fel-low Britons. The theatre audience itself becomes a miniaturised society, an imagined community whose responses to the performance empha-sise the fickle nature of public approbation, both in terms of theatrical entertainment and politics. But the theatre offered more than just the fantasies generated by the need for theatrical spectacle. The ocular fan-tasies that formed the staple material of pantomime, opera and entr'acte entertainments reflected the public spectacle, the national fantasy that was Britain and Britons. By representing audiences to themselves, the London stage is inextricably immersed in notions that permeated polit-ical, social, moral, religious and cultural debates of the period, the nature of Britain, Britons and Britishness. Of course this is not to sug-gest that the audience would 'recognize itself as a unified nation' or that 'given groups responded in simple and direct ways to dramatic repre-sentations of themselves'.[3] Beyond the simple act of looking there is no imperative to assume any further cohesive act within the transient community of the theatre audience. However, the language of the prologues and epilogues assumes not only a sense of communal experience in the act of watching the play but also a shared response to the action on stage, be it political factionalism, favouritism, usurpation or victory. 'Britons', so the texts assert will experience a unified response. Similarly the fear prompted by spectatorship theory regarding the public nature of drama assumed that 'sight creates a bond between spectator and event, which of necessity implicates the observer'.[4] If eighteenth-century anti-theatrical commentators feared that by attending plays, the audience could be wooed to the behaviours demonstrated on stage; there are clear implications for the use of drama as a vehicle for political propaganda.

It is important to remember alongside this sense of the theatre's political interventions that the activity of the London theatres was, by its very nature, commercial. Theatrical activity was driven by the needs of managers, performers and writers to make money, to capitalise on the desire of audiences to be entertained, placed on public view and to engage in social, political and communitarian activities. Just as the main piece was only one part of the evening's entertainment, the act of watching the play was only one facet of audiences' agendas. So the theatre during the early eighteenth century became a place of intertextual productivity, a location devoted to communication but subject to continual change, development and experimentation. Ideas were exchanged between an eclectic community of players and audience, managers, playwrights and critics whose response to opportunity and desire to secure commercial, aesthetic and political success was not necessarily simultaneously communicable in one theatrical product. This complex sense of continuous dialogue, the theatre's engagement with public discourse, is what this book aims to bring to life, positioning the London Stage as the respondent to, commentator on, advocate and marshal of public debates, capitulator with and demystifier of national fantasies.

The plays discussed in this book were published and performed during the period 1719–1745. They are history plays, a genre selected because of its relative abundance in the catalogue of 'new' plays during the period but also because of their engagement with recurrent contemporary political anxieties relating to nationhood and Britishness. The degree of textual engagement with politics is of course variable and differs from play to play. Interestingly however, the specific nature of British identity frequently forms the subject of prologues and epilogues irrespective of the content of the play itself. Similarly, the key terms commonly used in the rhetorical attacks that define eighteenth-century political discourse, favouritism, factionalism and patriotism are liberally scattered throughout the plays discussed, again, irrespective of any overt political content in the text itself. As a body of texts however, the wealth of political themes addressed by the plays suggests not only topicality but also an active participation in political discourse. Drama was particularly suited to the purposes of disseminating political propaganda, influencing as well as responding to political polemic.[5] I do not wish to suggest that party policy was dictated by the London stage, but rather that the texts I discuss participated in a dialogue of political ideas of which the history plays are one distinctive strand. So, despite the contrary claim arising from its economic imperative, the eighteenth-century theatre is less a barometer of public feeling, but rather a multi-faceted arena in which the instigating and sustaining of political debate was one function. The extent to which this was a two-way process, a vehicle for dialogue between public and government is an intriguing possibility. The transposition of David Armitage's account of opposition writing to Government texts, viewed alongside Government defensive reactions responding to plays such as Gays, *The Beggar's Opera* makes all the more plausible the possibility that not only does the theatre reflect political events but that the theatres and their audiences influence politics.

This reflexive dialogue between dramatic text(s) and political commentator(s) existed in part because of the ways in which plays were commissioned and written. Politicians, political commentators and, on rare occasions, the royal family all commissioned plays from known supporters. But as Brean Hammond observes, playwrights were in fact rarely commissioned to write plays.[6] Indeed texts were written uncommanded, some by party followers with a specific political purpose, whilst those aspiring to patronage penned texts aimed specifically to aid their political and or financial advancement. Playwrights sought patronage by writing what they imagined their prospective patron wanted to hear and the image they would value projected on stage. Indeed, authors clearly felt no obligation to necessarily promote their own political beliefs. Many wrote primarily from a financial perspective, choosing whichever political agenda was most likely to sell theatre tickets.[7] However, it is not simply authorial motivation that dictates the position of the dramatic text in contemporary politics. The economic significance of the demand for cheap reprints that were readily available from the 1730s demonstrates the combined need for plays to be effective on stage but also to appeal to readers.[8] The plays were subject to public consumption on multiple levels all of which involved degrees of interpretation. All of the plays discussed in this book appropriate history and it is this manipulation of largely well-known historical events rather than an individual author's political affiliations that denotes the politicisation of these texts both in their performative and documentary guises. So my focus is not the biographical accounts of playwrights or the political affiliations of theatre managers or even the imagined audiences of the various London playhouses but the discourses with which the plays themselves interact and engage. The ways in which these plays reflect, respond to, re-enact and turn against the fantasies that underpinned notions of the nation's identity and the imagined attributes of Britishness, fantasies which shored-up, linguistically if not tangibly, the stability of the nation. Despite Jacobite incursions, threats from Europe and beyond to Britain's colonial trade and endeavour, threats to commerce and the liberty of individuals from the Barbary nations, internal factionalism, political instability and the financial insecurities of a growing merchant economy the nation was strengthened and secured by a tenuous fantasy of steadfast and historically justified stability. In short, although the theatre may not have directly contributed to or significantly influenced political policy it was part of the process by which Britain's sense of stability, superiority and authority was imposed.

## Historicising identities and staging the nation's histories

During the seventeenth century and into the first half of the eighteenth century history was perceived as a form of literature aimed at the gratification as well as the education of the reader.[9] History did not exclude fictionality and the intersection between historical and fictional narratives was even more explicit on stage. The dramatisation of history was primarily an entertainment, albeit entertainment with an implicit suggestion of a didactic function. But history was not only reworked for the aesthetics of the public stage it was also plundered for its partisan political value. During the Walpole period history became an increasingly important staple of partisan discourse and as a result the people's interest in their nation's past was stirred.[10] Gerrard cites Bolingbroke's *Remarks on the History of England* (1730) as an example of 'the brand of history familiar to most readers: an interpretation of the recent and the remote past based on a sense of continuity and pride in what it meant to be a Briton'.[11] Histories were produced which positioned modern Britain as the 'necessary and healthy descendant' of the nation's own past but which simultaneously valued and celebrated that past positioning it as an exemplary heritage.[12]

During the early eighteenth century therefore, the term 'history play' could be used to refer to any text that chose an historical theme and did not apply exclusively to the dramatisation of 'events generally accepted as having actually occurred'.[13] One example of this is George Jeffrey's *Edwin* (1724) in which fact, fiction and fantasy are intimately entwined. The appropriation of history, be it British, English or foreign, allows for the re-interpretation of events to suit a specific political agenda. As D.R. Woolf suggests, 'historical interest was political interest, as usual, the past held messages for the present'.[14] Many of the plays discussed in this book present distorted or even invented histories not only in alluding to topical themes but also to market specific political propaganda. The texts are a result of the intricate relationship between history and politics during the early eighteenth century which positioned historian and reader as co-creators, an interpretive 'community engaged in a rhetorical arbitration of their own history'.[15] History was, therefore, a mode of interpretation, 'a form of spectacle designed to awaken the imagination and stimulate the sensibility'.[16] The interplay between history, theatrical performance and fantasies of nationhood becomes entwined in the concept of spectacle. Interpretation and imagination are needed to decipher and sustain these inter-related spectacles. Both author and audience were active participants in the interpretation of history plays and one important element of this interpretation was the reflection that history cast upon contemporary politics. So those eighteenth-century poets, playwrights and political commentators who wrote about Britain's past can be described as wielding 'history as a yardstick to measure the shortcomings of the present'.[17] But not only did history prove useful as a tool for emphasising the shortfall of modernity it also stood to highlight points of contact between the illustrious past and the present. History reflected the positive as well as the negative.

So, eighteenth-century history plays were particularly caught up in politics as participants in and evidence of contemporary political discourse. As Hammond suggests, 'the historian and satirist [were] joint custodians of the nation's moral and political health'.[18] What is interesting here is the suggested link between history and entertainment. By attending performances of dramatic reconstructions of history, by being entertained and morally and historically educated, the audience were actively participating in the interpretation of the relationship between history and politics, forming interpretive communities encoding the nation's identity through its history. During the early eighteenth century narrative histories were usually explicitly didactic, styled as lessons in statecraft, public conduct or the origins of the constitution.[19] In the very act of rewriting these histories therefore, playwrights were confronting political bias. Their texts offered audiences an interpretation of history from which they should 'learn' political lessons. Such bias can be identified merely by the historical subject, for example the anti-Walpole propaganda disseminated by the anonymous *The Fall of Mortimer* (1731). More often however history is malleable and its relevance to contemporary issues can be constructed by author and audience. The resultant variations in the accounts of the same history, re-appropriated and manipulated for diverse political purposes is a recurrent theme of this book.

As a literary form the narrative history became increasingly popular during the eighteenth century. Texts by diverse historians such as Knolles, Rapin, Hill and Hume were regularly reprinted to meet the demands of a growing readership. The popularity of these often conflicting versions of British and foreign histories has implications for modern narratives of emergent cultural nationalism.[20] Clearly such differing versions of English history, not necessarily written by Englishmen, or even Englishwomen, go some way towards challenging arguments for a unifying and homogenous national identity. This narrative can also be refuted by the plays discussed in this book. As historical accounts these texts engage, to varying degrees, in establishing a national identity. For many of these texts, British identity is characterised by patriotism which, in the political rhetoric of the period, is utilised cross-party to evidence the lack of patriotic conduct in partisan opponents. The popular narrative histories of the period were of course in themselves subject to political bias and often accepted or rejected by the public on this basis.[21] To return to Bertrand Goldgar's argument, considered at the beginning of this introduction, these plays are 'touched' by politics, but it is not their status as works of literature or the seriousness of their authors that dictates this relationship. It is through the dramatisation of history that these texts engage with politics. In dramatising the past early eighteenth-century history plays are touched by political discourses concerning Britishness and nationhood but, is the contact reciprocal? Are these political discourses 'touched' by the plays that dramatise them?

In many of the plays discussed, notions of identity, Britishness and nationalism are determined in direct relation to party agendas. So whilst Tory models of British identity rested on ancient democracy and agrarianism, this nostalgic version of national identity was directly opposed to the Whig model of modernity which stated liberty as modern and the result of a progressive constitution not an ancient right.[22] These versions of national identity are clearly influenced by party politics. Such diverse accounts of a constituent element of British identity suggest that versions of Britishness are, in part at least, derived from party interpretations of the foundation of British liberty. Was liberty achieved by the Glorious Revolution in 1688 and the subsequent Act of Settlement or conversely destroyed by the forced abdication of James II? Alternatively was liberty resuscitated in the recent past by the accession of William and Mary? I do not wish to deny the existence of an over-arching image of the idealised Briton. On the contrary, as Hugh Cunningham observes, eighteenth-century nationalists were convinced that, 'the English were an elect nation, that "God is English"'.[23] Indeed, the historical figures at the centre of these plays are often those English monarchs described by Christine Gerrard as 'staple icons of British national identity' – Alfred, Edward III, Henry V, and Elizabeth I.[24] However, this short list does not encompass the broad scope of iconographic representations of Britishness demonstrated in the history plays discussed in this book. Playwrights and political commentators derived examples of 'British' patriotism from Saxon, Celtic, Roman and even Islamic histories and the neat delineation between Whig and Tory interpretations of the nation's identity and the origins of British liberty are not consistently adhered to in the history plays. Given that, 'dynastic self-justification was not significantly less intense after 1714 than it had been in either the sixteenth or the seventeenth century' this broad spectrum of historical examples suggests that post-1714 commentators were searching for ways to define and, in some instances, validate the new dynasty.[25] The Hanoverian dynasty, the German foundations of which, were clearly at odds with the conventional 'staple icons' of British identity.[26]

Such expressions of British superiority are underwritten by an assumptive homogeneity that disregarded the realities of cultural difference in favour of a unified cultural self-aggrandizement. This raises a number of problems for the analysis of representations of national identity not least of which is the cultural divide between monarch and people. On a more 'domestic' front, is any distinction made between the nuances of British and English identity? Certainly many of the plays fail to differentiate between these two signifiers. How do the Scottish, Welsh and Anglo-Irish national identities impinge on the emergent 'British' model? The political implications of national diversity are overlooked in the plays, not simply as the result of a London-centric political and cultural agenda but out of the desire to appropriate the fantasy of Britishness which all of the plays, in various ways perpetuate and enlarge. Regional variation, political antagonisms and linguistic diversity all stand opposed to the notion of national unity and homogenous identity. So, Linda Colley's notion of a cohesive British identity is simultaneously upheld and destabilised by the plays.[27] Difference and diversity are effaced, not as a result of an actualised homogeneity but a fiction supporting an identity constructed on the superiority of unity over difference.

The rhetoric of patriotism formed a further barrier to the expression of cultural and regional difference within the nation. Patriotism was a key term in the description of British identity and a recurrent concern of historical drama. Emerging as a political term in the 1720s patriotism connoted 'devotion to the common good of the *patria* and hostility to sectional interests'.[28] A sense of the nation and national pride, cultural homogeneity, and fierce resistance to political factionalism were the essential markers of patriotic conduct, leaving limited space for the ethnic diversity of a conglomerate state. Such levelling of cultural diversity was not confined to opposition polemic as the association with patriotism might infer. The decidedly Tory renderings of patriotism thought of as conventional in scholarly accounts of early eighteenth-century politics are not upheld by the plays discussed in this book.[29] Patriotism and liberty were key themes in *all* of the history plays irrespective of the political agendas of individual texts. The Bolingbrokean brand of patriotism, despite its endurance, was not definitive, and the securing of the 'political liberties of the English nation' dominated the stage irrespective of the partisan agendas of playwright, audience, text, patron or theatre. Patriotism fuelled the fantasy of Britishness by imposing a common code of conduct for Britons, moving the term beyond the level of nomenclature by ascribing to it a sense of historically validated identity.

## Instability and fantasy: the politics of theatre

Underpinning the fantasy of Britishness is another persistent trope of the early eighteenth century history plays, the pursuit of political stability. Scholars broadly agree that Walpole's ministry oversaw a period of political consolidation.[30] But we should not render this period as a time of political stagnation devoid of party interaction. The very existence of a loud radical alternative to government provoked an equally vociferous conservative accord with the criticised administration.[31] Of course Tory attacks were not the only site of criticism targeting government policy. The close affiliation between the Whigs and Hanoverians was crucially effective in stabilising the relationship between the administration and monarchy, but unity within the party was far from assured. The image of stability cultivated by Walpole and so important to the self-aggrandizing rhetoric of the nationalist commentators was reliant on the industry of placemen to the extent that, 'If any of the various attempts to exclude placemen from Parliament by legislation had succeeded, the result would have been administrative anarchy.'[32] This image of a government close to crisis point as a result of internal instability contradicts assertions regarding Walpole's ministry as a source of political consolidation. One of the ways in which the period 'defended its own myths of stability against super evident threat' was through drama and the spectacle of Britishness.[33]

The strong opposition to Walpole had various consequences for dramatic production, the most obvious of which was the wealth of anti-Walpole drama produced during the minister's supremacy of which the infamous *Beggar's Opera* (1728) is but one example. Such a growth in direct and personal attacks on Walpole resulted, many scholars have argued, in the Stage Licensing Act of 1737. Goldgar contends that the Walpole administration reacted determinedly to the threat posed by opposition literature: 'the alienation of literary figures from the world of public action was well under way in the 1730s and, above all, that such alienation was encouraged and hastened by the character of the Walpole regime'.[34] However, the effect Walpole and his ministry had on the drama of this period was not entirely one of circumscription. Just as some playwrights were keen to demonstrate publicly their opposition to Walpole, others were eager to show their support. Pro-Walpole drama, written either as the direct result of patronage or created in search of favour, was frequently produced on the London stage. Much scholarly work has been carried out to uncover the extent of this literary opposition and to examine the threat this body of work posed to Walpole's power and reputation.[35] But this partisan delineation of texts and authors does not suit my own agenda because it purposefully obscures the discursive nature of the London theatres. Despite his claims for the lack of pro-Walpole literature, and the congruent sense that opposition literature received no rebuff, because it was considered politically powerless against the monolithic stability of the Walpole administration at its height of power, Goldgar makes the pertinent suggestion that 'the notion of all the wit on one side was much more politically significant and had much more political utility than any of the works of wit themselves'.[36] But unlike Goldgar I do not see 'wit' as a singularly Tory or opposition quality and certainly claims for 'wit' were made on all sides. What is important here is the notion that political instability is reflected in literary diversity and in particular dramatic diversity.

Those in opposition to Walpole repeatedly cited favouritism and the employment of parliamentary placemen as his failings. This, coupled with his resistance to war with England's traditional Catholic European enemies, provided a powerful rhetorical base for opposition to the minister. Modern scholars often identify the favourite as the antonym to the idealised patriot. The favourite is frequently portrayed in the plays discussed in this book, but, particularly given the cross-party appropriation of patriot rhetoric, it should not be assumed that the favourite is necessarily represented as an enemy to the nation. Walpole's position as a favourite of the Hanoverians created a problem for the stability and credibility of British politics requiring deft rhetorical positioning to sidestep the myriad negative associations conjured by the dual image of favourite and monarch. This endeavour to re-appropriate favouritism can be seen in a range of pro-Walpole texts with a variety of degrees of rhetorical flourish. Similarly, the effect of the preferment system is a prominent dramatic theme. This 'lynchpin' of ministerial and political power is represented in the plays in various guises.[37] Preferment is identified as detrimental to the political system in some texts yet essential to its success in others. Party factionalism and in-party opposition are seen either to destabilise parliament, leaving the government open to corruption, or are positioned as demonstrative of an appropriate and necessary challenge to government supremacy.

One of the most interesting and dynamic causes of political factionalism during the Walpole era were not the domestic issues surrounding preferment and placemen but reactions to and commentary on Britain's role as a developing colonial power. Again the history plays represent and respond to the diversity of contemporary opinion. Some writers question the validity of colonialism, others consider how far the emergent British Empire reflects an improvement both on contemporary and historic empires. Such concerns echo an earlier discomfort with the policies of the Tory regime that precipitated imperial expansion, seeking to secure parliamentary stability through politically 'unnatural' alliances.[38] Caution with regard to colonialism can therefore be represented as primarily an opposition concern transferable to whichever party was not in 'control' of this simultaneous external expansion and internal stabilisation. Such an analysis is somewhat complicated by the strong opposition to Walpole's tactical inactivity with regard to the various military threats posed to British colonial interests during his time in office. However, it should not be assumed that opposition to Britain's colonialism was restricted to opposition plays, indeed reticence concerning the nation's colonial endeavour was often impervious to political allegiance.

So, the spectres of favouritism, factionalism, placement and treaties plagued not only the Walpole administration but also dominated the theatre in its production of plays which represented the factions and favourites of Britain's past as exemplars or omens for the present.

Of course the theatre itself was subject to its own administrative factions and favourites and the faction and intrigue associated with eighteenth-century theatres has prompted many scholars to view the period as an age of 'actors rather than playwrights'.[39] Certainly there is evidence of a cult of stardom amidst accounts of contemporary performances. When Gay's *The Fortunes and Misfortunes of Three Hours After Marriage* (1717) was performed at Drury Lane the audience famously sat in awe as Wilks delivered the prologue only to erupt in vitriol at the start of the play which 'acted like a ship tost in a tempest . . . through clouds of confusion and uproar' until Oldfield rose to speak the epilogue at which, 'the storm subsided'.[40] So individual 'stars' commanded the audience but contest and faction existed between playwrights, managers, actors, actresses and theatres alike, fuelling not only the rising 'cult of stardom' but also the sense that the public theatres and their communities were a microcosm of the wrangling evident in public politics. Factionalism and favouritism in the theatre was, if contemporary periodical accounts are a reliable gauge, more salacious and more heterogeneously entertaining and the resultant instability more readily ascribed with creative dynamism than the parallel effects upon the theatre's 'serious' counterpart.

## Prohibiting the nation's commentator

Critics have argued that the Stage Licensing Act of 1737 virtually put an end to the performance of politically motivated material on the London stage a contention which clearly runs counter to the perspectives of this book. Certainly some plays were refused license, whilst others were forced to withdraw from public performance, but the true impact of the Act on the curtailment of politically motivated dramatic activity is far from clear. Henry Brooke's *Gustavus Vasa* (1739) was the first play to be banned under the directives of the new Act. Brooke claimed in his defence that he meant only to write a history play, the political analogy for which his play was condemned was, according to Brooke, unintentional. It is clear here that the act of writing history can become a foil for obscuring political comment, history is the commentator's defense. Other plays prohibited in the first years of the new Act such as, James Thomson's *Edward and Eleonora* (1739), William Paterson's *Arminius* (1740), and John Kelly's *The Levee* (1741) could not so easily adopt Brooke's defense. Perhaps the most famous example of a play prohibited from performance was John Gay's *Polly*. Intended as a sequel to *The Beggar's Opera*, *Polly* was banned from production in 1729, eight years before the Licensing Act took effect. John Loftis has linked the prohibition of

*Polly* to what he describes as a widespread clampdown by the Walpole administration on opposition literature as a way of securing opportunity for its own literary supporters.[41]

I wish to challenge recent claims by a number of critics for the cessation of political commentary through drama as a result of the Stage Licensing Act.[42] The reduction in numbers of explicitly political plays was not caused directly by the restriction on dramatic content, rather, the result of the monopoly created by the Act. The reduction in the number of licensed theatres necessitated a parallel reduction in the number of new plays produced each year. The Covent Garden and Drury Lane monopoly had a serious effect on dramatic activity post-1737. The plays discussed in this book are taken from across the divide critics have conventionally perceived between dramatic participation in politics pre-1737 and Walpole's attempts to exclude drama from the political arena. It is therefore important to stress that the production of a smaller number of new plays post-1737 is merely an indication of the necessary curtailment of theatrical productivity rather than a sudden void of political commentary in dramatic texts. In effect what the Act achieved, although not necessarily what it intended to do, was the curtailment of the theatre's dialogue with politics. The drama of the period was not de-politicised but the potential for extended political discourse was dramatically reduced.

Of course, closet drama filled some of the spaces left on the public stage by more risqué or explicitly political plays, which, even before the Stage Licensing Act may not have been either permitted public performance by the Lord Chamberlain or selected for production by theatre managers. Closet drama by its very nature could be more defamatory and explicit in its approach to political comment, particularly given the assumptions that writers could make about the shared agenda of their self-selecting readership/audience. Clearly some of the discourse between drama and politics continued in these private settings but, for the most part, closet drama is not encapsulated in the scope of this book. My interest lies in those plays selected for performance on the open stage. The public nature of these texts has significance for their contribution to political discourse and to the appropriation of these histories for propagandistic purposes. As public texts subject to public scrutiny and varied interpretation these plays become active participants in the ideological debates of the period. As public spectacles, reliant on the financial support of the paying audiences and private favour, these texts engage with and echo 'current trend[s] if not contemporary attitudes'. Public and populist fantasies are represented on stage and it is the public nature of these texts which makes them 'conspicuously sensitive to political currents' and demonstrates the theatre's intervention in politics.[43]

The five chapters of this book are organised thematically in order to read texts that engage with specific topical issues in juxtaposition. This is not to suggest that points of contact do not exist outside of this rather artificial division, or that plays addressing seemingly contrasting subjects are not engaged in a dialogue concerning a shared political discourse. This structure is rather a guide to potential rhetorical pathways, merely intended to facilitate the reader's navigation not impose an authoritative route. Thus, in 'Ancient Britons and Liberty' a group of plays that retell ancient British history are considered in relation to notions of national identity that locate the origins of contemporary Britishness in the nation's ancient ancestors. This chapter explores texts that respond to and re-appropriate established national myths regarding liberty, heroism, manliness and customs. Plays that insist on the longevity and endurance of liberty as demonstrated by Britain's ancient heroes, re-enforcing a well-worn version of Britishness and a dominant national myth that underpinned notions of British identity during the early eighteenth century. It is this myth of a heritage of carefully defended personal and national liberty that underpins the notions of national and imperial identity exploited by texts discussed in the chapters that follow.

The cluster of plays discussed in 'Kings, Ministers and Favourites' focus on favouritism, a theme that dominated British political commentary during the 1730s. Here histories that relate the threats posed to Protestant versions of the national myth of liberty by the corrupt monarchs and ministers of Britain's past are placed in context with contemporary concerns for the stability of government. Favouritism and factionalism are frequently juxtaposed in these plays, identified as interconnected threats to national liberty, itself intrinsic to nationalist notions of British superiority. In contrast to the plays discussed in chapter one, these texts are not universally triumphant in their declarations of British superiority. By focusing on ill-fated episodes from Britain's history the plays disclose the myth of national liberty and undermine the presumed supremacy of Britons over their continental neighbours. In demonstrating the fragility of a national self-image founded on such myths these plays reveal the transitory nature of the nation's moral, political and military superiority.

Adaptations of Shakespeare's English history plays are discussed in 'Shakespeare, the National Scaffold'. This chapter explores the appropriation of Shakespeare for nationalist purposes and women's role as idealised Britons within the specific context of the theatre. The adaptations document a multiplicity of political concerns, including but not limited to the threat posed by Jacobitism to the stability of the nation. The plays stress the security of British liberty despite threats from foreign powers and they construct a cross-gender model for British political virtue, the patriot character of 'true' Britons. The role of Shakespeare is important here in terms of theatre history as well as literary and social contexts. As the century progressed, Shakespeare came to represent 'English Liberty' and the works of Shakespeare were therefore relevant to modern Britons not only because playwrights adapted these texts to comment on current political crises, but also due to a developing image of Shakespeare as a national icon, a literary and political exemplar. These texts are engaged in a search for a unifying notion of British identity which gains both literary and political credence from the image of nationalism evoked by Shakespeare.

The fourth group of plays, drawn together in 'Britain, Empire and Julius Caesar', moves the discussion from issues of national myth-making to imperial fantasy and colonial ambition. This chapter discusses plays which draw parallels between contemporary Britain and ancient Rome, promoting Britain as a superior, more enlightened, emergent global power. The focus however is not to establish these plays as domestic allegory but as models for British colonial endeavour. The texts discussed in this chapter are at odds with the scholarly consensus that during the early eighteenth century, Caesar was characterised by tyranny and despotic power. These plays represent Caesar as a patriot colonialist, a model Roman and a model for modern British colonial endeavour. In creating an alternative version of Caesar, a myth reflecting Britain's own notions of liberty and superiority, these texts feed contemporary fantasies regarding the egalitarian nature of British colonial endeavour and the legitimacy of British imperialism.

The final chapter, 'Turks, Christians and Imperial Fantasy', examines texts that engage with the instability of notions of British superiority and the insecurity of empire-building based upon imperial fantasies. This chapter focuses on three plays that exploit Islamic history, drawing allegorical connections between colonial Britain and the Ottoman Empire. By representing in microcosm the downfall of the Ottoman Empire, these plays participate in the debate regarding Britain's national and increasingly imperial identity. In these plays, concerns for the costs and benefits of maintaining empire lead to questions about religious intolerance and, in common with contemporary accounts of Ottoman culture, result in unresolved contradiction. Just as favouritism and factionalism were seen to destabilise the mythologies surrounding contemporary notions of Britishness, the imperial fantasy envisioned in the Roman plays is threatened by the realities of empire represented in Ottoman history. The assumed authority legitimated by a constructed British governmental, religious and cultural superiority is undermined by the suggestion of parity of objective between Christian and Turk. These texts transpose the discussion from the notions of imperial fantasy explored in the Roman plays towards a more cautious discourse regarding the realities of empire and the threat posed by insatiable expansion, to Britain, Britishness and the liberty of Britons.

Issues of patriotism, national identity and idealism therefore connect the plays beyond their thematic focus and support the broad contention that the texts discussed are contributors to a coherent body of cross-party debate. The London theatres participated in the bolstering of a national self-image embedded in a sense of divinely ordained superiority that was not exclusive to Protestant Whig literary production. This book positions the plays and the theatres in which they were performed as part of a literary-political milieu and examines the broader cultural debates that they speak to.

Arguments for the cessation of politically relevant drama post-1737 are in part responsible for the critical neglect received by these plays. In addition, throughout the period, drama is widely perceived to have suffered an aesthetic downturn particularly in contrast to the great comedies of the Restoration period. Allardyce Nicoll for example, criticises the first fifty years of the eighteenth century for the poor quality of tragic plays during the period.[44] This book however, is not concerned with establishing the value of the individual texts discussed in relation to a canonical notion of aesthetic literary standards. Similarly, the popularity of a particular play is not taken as an indication of the critical value of an individual text. As Arthur H. Scouten and Robert D. Hume's discussion of the 'Cranky Audiences of 1697–1703' reveals, eighteenth-century audiences were fickle customers subject to a changeable and unpredictable sense of aesthetics and impervious to logical explanations or, as many a hapless theatre manager discovered, projections of their theatrical taste.[45] Some of the plays discussed in this book were very popular, others were certainly not a financial success, some not even making the customary third night benefit performance. However, neither contemporary nor modern aesthetic judgements impinge on the topicality of a text. The failure of a play or its rejection by modern critics as a 'dramatised novel' does not negate the usefulness of the text to modern scholarship in terms of tracing literary responses to politics.[46]

Despite the 1737 Act the London theatres persisted in their inhabitation of the role and position of commentator on the nation. The history plays which formed just one strand of this commentary continued to sustain, challenge and develop a fantasy of Brtishness which pervaded contemporary political rhetoric on all levels. So although the assumed position of the audience as BRITONS with its notions of a shared homogenous identity does not reflect the realities of early eighteenth-century society, the audiences nevertheless did share one agenda. One element of their identities was collective. The communal desire of the theatre audience to be 'entertained' is perhaps as close as we can come to a sense of eighteenth-century Britain as a unified nation.

# 1
# Ancient Britons and Liberty

Common Sense,
In Britain, ever may it keep Possession!
Establish'd by the Protestant Succession.
Blest in a Prince, whose high-traced Lineage Springs
From the famed Race of our Old Saxon Kings;
Our Zeal for Liberty we safely own; –
He makes it the firm basis of his Throne.
Remember, then, the Dangers, you have past: –
And, let your Earliest Virtue – be your Last.

Ambrose Philips, The Briton (1722)

'Learn hence, my Daughter, to contemn the Praise,
The Worship of self-interested Man'

William Philips, Hibernia Freed (1722)

The notion of the development of a distinctly British national identity during the eighteenth century has been something of a controversial topic for modern scholarship. It is a debate that is, particularly given its bipartite structure, not too dissimilar from the original and equally unresolved discourse that has engendered such conceptual interest and interpretive scrutiny. The suggestion that one unified vision of British identity, arising as a direct result of the 1707 Act of Union is compelling. However, significant critical resistance has challenged the imposition of such cultural unification. Particularly given that arguments in support of the homogeneity of Britain's identity are often Whig-focused and prone to interpreting the political and social landscape of the period from a perspective that asserts coherence and obscures the messiness of

Whiggish reactions to 'unification', alternative perspectives that reflect a more chaotic, less cohesive political and cultural geography, could all to easily be overlooked.[1] On the other hand, of course, clear articulations of just such a sense of national unification under the term 'British' or 'Briton' should not be underestimated, particularly when such associations are appropriated as a point of contrast; defining the nation's difference and superiority to an 'other'.

This chapter does not seek to resolve these debates, to superimpose one narrative version or identify one dominant thread. Rather, raises questions about this entanglement and what lies beneath the desire to represent national, political and cultural unification. Early eighteenth-century history plays reflect, unsurprisingly, just such a broad spectrum of attitudes towards the notion of Britishness, appropriating the term to invoke an image of cohesion or to symbolise repressive, enforced conformity as well as all the shades of grey between these two extremes. Indeed the subject matter of these plays goes some way to magnifying debates regarding national identity and the nature of Britishness, and for some texts this is the very issue dramatised. It is clear from these plays that the process of establishing British identity as a coherent political and social concept was not limited to the years immediately after 1707 and the Act of Union. The nature of Britishness was a topic contested for many decades to come and was already, by the early eighteenth century, an old debate which preceded the Act of Union by many decades, if not centuries. Some of the plays that most explicitly engage in such a dialogue are those that attempt to establish versions of British identity by reflecting on Britain's ancient history. These texts not only demonstrate the importance of Celtic or Saxon history to the nation's cultural heritage but, more importantly, identify within these histories the source of the supposed utopian democracy of modern Britain and the oft praised liberty of her people.[2]

Before exploring these issues further and examining the characteristics of Britishness represented in the ancient British history plays, it is worth considering the inherent complexities associated with any engagement with the issue of national identity during the eighteenth century. Critical arguments relating to post-1707 cohesion in terms of British identity draw upon evidence in contemporary art, literature and political commentary. This expression of a shared identity, according to scholars such as Linda Colley, united the people of the various regions of Britain through their shared Protestantism and common system of government.[3] As compelling as this notion of cultural unification appears, British identity did not completely suppress national diversity but rather acted as an establishment version of national unity. Scottish, Irish, Welsh, Catholic and Episcopalian difference were all placed in opposition to authorised versions of Britain and Britishness.[4] Commentators who promoted a unified British identity were, scholars such as Murray Pittock contend, attempting to suppress the nation's ethnic diversity. Representations of non-English Britons often did little more than re-entrench stereotyped regional characteristics. Such representations are more suggestive of exclusion than national unity, particularly given the strident differentiation between the inhabitants of the non-dominant nations and the inhabitants of London:

> Eighteenth-century Irish, Anglo-Irish, Scottish and North British identities were richly various, complex and contingent, but they had one thing in common: all of them were, in either a positive or a negative way, defined by their relationship to England and the English. The English, on the other hand, were often as indifferent as they were hostile to their 'Celtic' neighbours. It is no accident that the term 'South Britain', ridiculed by the self-proclaimed Englishman Jonathan Swift, never took hold.[5]

The plays discussed in this chapter engage in issues of national and regional identity by invoking an ancestral identity which is simultaneously cohesive and fragmentary. By offering representations of various Celtic and Saxon identities these plays are, of course, engaging with firmly entrenched regional stereotypes, particularly useful for the representation of stock characters on stage. The Caledonians in Ambrose Philips's *The Briton* (1722) are a notable example of the rather clumsy recourse to dramatic shorthand to which these plays frequently resort. However, the texts share an agenda in their desire to promote the nation's responsibility for protecting 'British' liberty, thus suggesting that Colley's assessment of a sense of Britishness emerging from these disparate representations of regional characteristics may be particularly pertinent. How were these identities configured in texts that examined the sources of cultural diversity, that is, the nation's Celtic and Saxon heritage?

Since the Glorious Revolution in 1688, political commentators had associated liberty with Britain's ancient past. The Revolution, they argued, finally restored the ancient rights of Englishmen. Political rhetoric on all sides repeatedly asserted the longevity and endurance of Britain's liberty and the importance of protecting this inherited right. The ancient Britons were not however the property of one particular party or one clearly definable community of political rhetoricians.

Tories, opposition and pro-government Whigs all attempted to appropriate British mythologies for their own political purposes.[6] Not all scholars are in agreement with regard to the extent of the longevity of this appropriation of the nation's ancient histories for the purposes of political self-justification. Many eighteenth-century writers have been represented as increasingly recalcitrant in appropriating antiquity as a precursory validation of the Revolution, a shift in rhetoric fuelled in part by the inevitable tarnishing and erosion of Revolution principles, and the rather ensconced association between pro-Revolution commentary and the glorification of Britain's ancient histories.[7] Although some political commentators were, by the 1720s, resisting evocations of Britain's ancient heritage, a number of plays that staged Britain's ancient histories were produced in London during the period 1720–40 and in these plays the association between modern politics and ancient historical figures retained a positive correlation.

This chapter focuses on a cluster of plays which uphold ancient Britons as models for political emulation, particularly in relation to the issue of protecting liberty – both the freedom of individuals and the liberty of the nation. The plays depict ancient Britons in a range of guises, pitted against an array of liberty-encroaching foes. But despite this apparent diversity in terms of the specific subjects appropriated by these texts and the varieties of historical interpretation therein, the commonality of themes is intriguing. Ambrose Philips's *The Briton* depicts ancient Britons, specifically the Welsh, resisting the incursions of Roman invaders. William Philips's *Hibernia Freed* (1722) examines a similar struggle against foreign invasion this time in first-century Ireland with Viking invaders. George Jeffreys's *Edwin* (1724) fabricates Anglo-Saxon history, telling the story of the usurpation and restoration of an ancient dynasty. Aaron Hill's *Athelwold* (1731), a revision of his earlier play *Elfrid* (1710), examines Saxon England and the treachery of the eponymous royal favourite. David Mallet and James Thomson's *Alfred* (1740), like many of these plays, merges history with fantasy. In this case the subject is Alfred the Great in a distinctly pro-Hanoverian, pro-Frederick guise.[8] All of these plays share a desire to establish authority for contemporary political policies by appropriating ancient British history. This justification is established via the connections drawn between modern political factions, ancient British predecessors and inherited or genetically guaranteed responses to liberty shared by 'true' Britons; be it simply a communal love of their right to freedom, steadfast protection of liberty or heroic acts performed in order to secure the restoration of these ancient, inherited rights.

It is clear from the span of nearly twenty years between the premières of *The Briton* in 1722 and *Alfred* in 1740 that, during this period, antiquity retained its attraction as a dramatic subject, but this should not necessarily suggest that a shared agenda can be traced between these otherwise disparate texts. Indeed, the ways in which dramatists appropriated ancient British history in order to comment on contemporary politics are varied. Some texts make use of antiquity to validate Revolution principles, others move away from such historical reflection focusing on contemporary and future political agendas, establishing antiquated models for the validation of the modern constitution and the specific activities of modern, commendable political-players. So, just as the subjects of these plays are diverse, the political purpose and the commentary that can be constructed from these simultaneously connected yet disconnected texts is equally multi-faceted. Once again, these plays share a concern with liberty and, in particular, establishing the antiquity of British liberty. In doing so, many of these texts convey a political agenda concerned with maintaining liberty in the context of eighteenth-century Britain, and read alongside contemporary commentary such as Bolingbroke's political writings and in the light of modern scholarly analysis of the formation of British identity, these plays demonstrate ways in which 'the authority of antiquity' formed a significant validation of emergent notions of national identity. Although many contemporary commentators can be seen turning from antiquity to modernity in their attempts to justify Revolution principles and the modern constitution, British 'antiquity' was nevertheless fundamental in shaping and developing contemporary ideas of what it was, or might be, to be *British*.

## The nation's ancient liberty

In his account of British antiquity in *A Dissertation upon Parties* (1736) Bolingbroke claims that, 'the ancient Britons are to us the aborigines of our island', and notes that although little is known of their history and culture, one thing is certain, 'they were freemen'.[9] *A Dissertation* is littered with evocations of the ancient Britons' tenacious protection of their liberty. He postulates that even during the darkest hours of Roman control Britons steadfastly retained their belief in constitutional liberty. For Bolingbroke this is, of course, merely the foundation upon which national integrity and superiority is based, one part of a broader heritage of which modern Britons should be proud, 'as far as we can look back, a lawless power, a government by will, never prevailed in Britain'.[10] However, tradition does not guarantee sustainability and Bolingbroke is quick to alert his readers to the notion that they will be held accountable if any of the contemporary threats to this long and salubrious tradition should succeed. Bolingbroke engages with what Roland Barthes later termed the 'ambiguous myth of human community'.[11] Bolingbroke's account of history makes assumptions regarding the linearity of community or shared experience, essentially constructing a myth that presupposes a direct and un-severable connection between Britain's past and its present. The ancient Britons laid the foundation of British liberty and for Bolingbroke this long-held, ancient tradition forms the cornerstone of the modern British national character. Thus, Bolingbroke's historical account engages directly with the myth of human community and, in so doing, becomes of and in itself a mythology, formed by the desire to simultaneously understand Britain's past and for the nation's past to inform present and future actions.

Bolingbroke's gloss on British history is important in that it is representative of a common approach to history during this period; Bolingbroke's representation of the ancient Britons is achieved by moulding limited facts into politically tantalising fictions. Bolingbroke's account of the nation's ancient liberties draws upon a heritage passed on by generations of Britons, a resistance to enslavement and the projection of an ardent defence of freedom in all its rhetorical glory. Reading through the filter of Barthes, Bolingbroke utilises historical events or episodes by making full use of 'myth's double function' – the stories he tells point out specific events, governing systems, actions from the ancient past – and then imposes meanings upon these historical episodes, investing them with national significance, encoding them as the origins of Britishness and thus creating a mythology for the nation, itself based upon a mythical notion of long-term communal human experience.[12] Bolingbroke is far from rejecting antiquity as a validation of the modern constitution, and even 'the increasingly tarnished example of Saxon antiquity' is valued as evidence of an originary British national character.[13] In relation to the Saxon kings, Bolingbroke argues that although 'the long wars they waged for and against the Britons, led to and maintained monarchical rule amongst them', the Saxons, 'persuaded, rather than commanded'.[14] Again, Bolingbroke deploys the malleability of such histories to his rhetorical advantage. Despite usurping power from the Celts, the Saxons, at least according to Bolingbroke's version, maintained the nation's political liberty; he praises the Saxons for their public assemblies and distribution of power as a form of meritocracy. Bolingbroke's argument is of course open to criticism on a number of counts, in particular his inexact representation of Saxon history. However, despite this mythologising of the past Bolingbroke does not attempt to obscure the fact that the Saxons adopted hereditary succession as their mode of government, indeed despite praising Saxon meritocracy he does not wish to discount hereditary succession as a valid mode of governance. Guarding himself against this self-evident opportunity for criticism, Bolingbroke notes that even when the Saxon kings 'for the sake of order and tranquillity' adopted birth rather than merit as the title to the throne they continued to govern Britain, 'to the satisfaction of the people':

> By what other expedient could they govern men, who were wise enough to preserve and exercise the right of electing their civil magistrates and military officers, and the system of whose government was upheld and carried on by a gradation of popular assemblies, from the inferior courts to the high court of Parliament; for such, or very near such, was the Wittena Gemote, in nature and effect, whenever the word parliament came into use?[15]

These ancient ancestors, both the 'wise' Celts and the 'persuasive' Saxons, were the original creators, and protectors, of British liberty. Bolingbroke argues that such liberty, due to its longevity and place in the nation's heritage, is the right of all modern Britons. But it is the British people themselves, like their Celtic and Saxon predecessors, who must protect their rights by monitoring and chastising their governments for any threat made to this ancient constitutional right.

There is of course a potential problem here in that Bolingbroke's manipulation of antiquity and mythologising of Britain's ancient past could be viewed as an exclusively Tory representation of liberty and its origins. Bolingbroke's *A Dissertation* is an overtly oppositional rendering of the Revolution Settlement, constructed in order to justify transfer of allegiance from the Stuarts to the Hanoverians (thus allowing the Tories some stake in contemporary politics). However, this does not preclude Whig commentators from appropriating antiquity for their own purposes, despite scholarly assertions to the contrary.[16] Certainly, Bolingbroke was not the only opposition commentator to disclose his admiration for the Saxons but this does not imply that pro-Whig commentators abandoned or rejected antiquity in favour of more 'modern' models.[17] The malleability of these ancient histories and their suitability for mythologising, as demonstrated by Bolingbroke, also made them eminently pliable for a multiplicity of political purposes.

Thomson and Mallet's *Alfred* (1740) mirrors Bolingbroke's rhetoric in *A Dissertation Upon Parties*. At a crucial moment when Alfred's waning morale looks set to fail both him and his 'nation', a hermit conjures the spirits of future monarchs in an attempt to rekindle patriotic fervour in the disconsolate king. The last in this display of conspicuously Whig heroes is William III described by the hermit as a fitting culmination in this parade of heroes, 'From before his face,/Flies Superstition, flies oppressive Power,/With vile Servility that crouch'd and kiss'd/The whip he trembled at. From this great hour/Shall Britain date her rights and laws restor'd'.[18] It is just such 'rights and laws' that the Saxon Alfred, in Thompson and Mallet's version, is fighting for, protecting his countrymen's liberty and freedom from the threat posed by Danish invaders. These rights, the Hermit's display demonstrates, are sustained throughout British history but also subject to fluctuations, waxing and waning with dynastic changes and were only finally restored by the ascension of William III and the subsequent establishment of the Hanoverian dynasty as the kings of 'Great Britain'.

Fluctuations in the stability of English liberty were, according to Bolingbroke, directly attributable to the quality of the monarch and the patriotism of his or her followers. Thus Bolingbroke apportions 'praise for monarchs attentive to populace and Parliament, and blame for ministers who usurp the power of the constitutional monarch and so undermine ancient English "liberty"'.[19] The Hermit's display clearly reflects such assertions. However, making use of Bollngbrokean rhetoric does not necessitate the promotion of his political agenda. *Alfred*, a pompous display of self-congratulatory pro-Hanoverian propaganda, merely utilises Bolingbrokean rhetoric, transposing Bolingbroke's assertions regarding the ancient lineage of British liberty on to overtly 'Whig' models of monarchy. Indeed, repeated echoes of Bolingbroke's theories regarding the relationship between history and politics are a defining characteristic of 1730's drama. This apparent slippage between, or merging of, Whig and Tory political rhetoric does not, of course, suggest total agreement amongst early eighteenth-century government, opposition Whig, and Tory commentators. However, the importance of liberty as the cornerstone of the British constitution and the ancient rights of the nation was rarely disputed. Indeed, anxiety with regard to liberty dominated political thought cross parties, well beyond the years immediately following the Revolution Settlement. It was only later in the century, as political stability in terms of dynastic certainty provided by the Hanoverians, and Jacobite defeats in 1715 and 1745 that 'the Revolution seemed secure and its constitutional gains decisive. Even then dissentient voices remained'.[20] From multivalent political perspectives, liberty was far from being a certainty, irrespective of partisan rhetorical claims to the contrary.

The Revolution had, according to its mythologised representation, secured liberty for the British people. The problem for party polemicists during the first half of the eighteenth century was not whether liberty had been salvaged but precisely who should maintain and protect it and how. For Bolingbroke, the answer to this question was simple. The ancient constitution would preserve the liberty of the people 'as long as it is respected by the government whose duty it is to put it into practice'.[21] This respect for the constitution and the liberty that it promotes repeatedly become the focus of the ancient British history plays.

Inspired by his glimpse into England's monarchical future, Alfred announces, 'If not to build on an eternal base,/On liberty and laws, the public weal:/If not for these great ends I am ordain'd/May I ne'er idly fill the throne of England'(19). In this way Thomson and Mallet establish not only the ancient origins of British liberty but also assert the role of both monarch and government as protectors of this liberty. There is no doubt that in this instance the appropriate monarch and government model for fulfilling this role are represented as a Hanoverian/Whig alliance. All of the plays discussed in this chapter are, to some extent, concerned with the loss and restoration of national liberty, but not all of the texts impose such an establishment model as the solution to the problem of protecting the nation's liberty as that found in Thomson and Mallet's play. Liberty is contested rhetorical space, a linguistic commodity not only of considerable political value but also malleable, a term, the meaning of which could be subjected to deliberate manipulation for partisan agenda but also unconscious appropriation. George Jeffreys's *Edwin*, for example, repeatedly asserts that hereditary right is paramount, 'Let Usurpation, that Eternal Slave/To Fear, the Tyrant's greater Tyrant, dy/Her thirsty Purple deep in native Blood,/The lawful Prince, by daring to forgive,/Asserts the great Prerogative of Heaven,/And proves his Claim Divine'.[22] *Edwin* not only promotes hereditary succession as the key to protecting British liberty but also makes the politically archaic claim that a good king will prove his right 'divine'. The rhetoric of liberty was appropriated for a complex variety of political agendas, from supporters of divine right to the most ardent proponents of the Glorious Revolution and the Revolution Settlement. Thus, not only were cross- and inter-party responses to the Glorious Revolution and unification messy and discordant, but the political rhetoric that underpinned these political changes was subject equally to instability.

Given the variety of political programmes which promised to protect the nation's liberty, it is important to consider the manifest complications of appropriating a term with such diverse applications. Just as Bolingbroke's rhetoric was open for appropriation and manipulation by the very party it was intended to criticise (Thomson and Mallet's *Alfred* is just one of the pro-Whig texts to echo Bolingbroke) the rhetoric of liberty could be transposed onto and subsumed by almost any political agenda. As Alexander Pettit suggests, many commentators, both contemporary and modern, assume 'a consensus about the meaning of liberty' when in fact 'liberty' was, 'an indefinable term that political writers of all sorts quarrelled about endlessly in the period'.[23] So, multiple interpretations of the term endow 'liberty' with a political pliability which makes any attempt to eschew such rhetoric to one political perspective futile. By adopting liberty as a central theme, the plays discussed in this chapter disclose an engagement with a contemporary political anxiety that crosses conventional boundaries and is inextricably associated with questions relating to national identity and British character. With this inter-related discourse in mind, one important way of examining liberty without attempting to impose static meaning upon the term is through religion, itself inextricably linked to notions of national identity.

As Pittock has asserted, 'in religious terms, eighteenth-century Britain was already a pluralist society'.[24] In the plays, a respect for liberty is repeatedly related to Protestantism. Playwrights resort to complex allegories in order to transpose contemporary religious conflicts onto ancient historical events. For example, in William Philips's *Hibernia Freed* the Pagan Danes (Catholics) are contrasted with the Christian Irish (Protestants). The Danes deride the Irish respect for liberty asserting their political ambitions as a desire to gain control rather than securing freedom; 'Why have I fought, to what has Conquest serv'd,/But for unlimited despotic Pow'r?'.[25] Protestantism is associated with liberty, Catholicism with tyranny. In Ambrose Philips's *The Briton*, Roman and British paganism are contrasted; as in *Hibernia Freed*, the religious practices of the transgressors of liberty have negative consequences. The Romans pray for success in impeding British liberty, whereas the Britons pray for the restoration of their liberty and the re-establishment of their pre-colonised status. In both of these plays, two types of religion are represented both of which fuel the oppositional characterisation of their adherents. The invaders practise a religion based upon aggression and despotism. Conversely, the native peoples practise a religion that promotes liberty and values freedom. Ambrose Philips and William Philips equate the conventional representation of Catholic states as tyrannous and despotic with a direct threat to British liberty. Protestantism, conversely, is positioned as the guardian of liberty.

Where respect for liberty is not defined in terms of religious practices, a more political definition is often proposed. For example, in Jeffreys's *Edwin* (1724), maintaining hereditary right is identified as the primary method of protecting liberty. By contrast, in *Hibernia Freed* hereditary right is openly questioned:

> How vain is the Prerogative of Birth:
> How useless to be sprung of Royal Blood;
> To have Pretence to or deserve a Crown:
> Depriv'd of Power to punish or reward!
> How soon that Pow'r is lost too well I know. (26)

Hill's *Athelwold* is perhaps the play seemingly least directly concerned with liberty. It depicts a stable Saxon Britain under the leadership of a virtuous king whose trust is misplaced. In Hill's play the abuse of trust, particularly a monarch's trust, is a key theme. Treason is the primary threat to the nation's stability, and thus the liberty of the people. Liberty is threatened not by an external aggressor, but from within. Athelwold is therefore an anti-hero, but his actions are not evil, merely misguided, as he misjudges the political ramifications of his domestic actions. As the play begins, Athelwold's character is widely perceived to be impeccable, 'Bow, but to Heaven,/That made thee not a King, to make thee more;/And stampt thy soul divinely!'.[26] He is the protector of liberty placed in opposition to the self-interested Oswald. Athelwold's 'mistake' is to fall in love and secretly marry a woman beloved by the King. This relatively minor act of 'treachery' is employed by Oswald to further his own position, and hence, indirectly, Athelwold's actions threaten the 'liberty' of the nation. In Hill's play the vulnerability of liberty is amplified. Liberty is endangered by the actions of individuals, weakened by the mistakes of just one man.

The threat to British liberty in the majority of these plays is realised through the incursions of foreign invaders. Despite the many parallels that may be drawn between these historical military threats and the fear, or anticipation, of Jacobite uprising during the first half of the eighteenth century, there was, for some commentators, a more immediate danger, the threat posed to liberty by destructive party politics. During the early eighteenth century a degree of common ground was shared by Whig and Tory commentators focusing on the ancient roots of the modern constitution. Party attention turned to the post-Revolution establishment; discord and faction no longer rested upon the need to declaim 'the nature of a desirable political establishment, but were about the forms of corruption that prevented agreed constitutional arrangements from working'.[27] In this sense, therefore, history is used to validate the importance of liberty as a broad concept, to generate mythologised versions of ancient liberty which could be transposed to the context of modern Britain. What is at stake, in political terms, is not the value of liberty as a commodity or proof that liberty is under threat and in need of a protector but rather a contest for what liberty rhetorically signifies. The ground that is fought over, or exploited, is linguistic instability, what is signified by the term 'liberty', where its meaning is located, determines which party can claim the right to protect it.

We can assert, therefore, that the construction or nature of government itself was not contested and that attention had shifted to 'the rage of party', that is, internal conflicts concerning corruption from within the government and the threat posed to the ancient constitution by such scandal-mongering.[28] Hammond suggests that cross-party appropriation of Britain's ancient constitution as a validation of contemporary party ideology resulted in a redirection of the political agenda. Concerns over the structure of the political establishment no longer dominated British politics and attention turned to identifying the party best suited as the guardians of these ancient rights. It is in this way that accusations of corruption became so potent in the rhetorical struggle for political supremacy. Bolingbroke's assertions regarding the security of British liberty uphold the constitution, but he is careful to limit the extent to which constitutional arrangements can safeguard the nation against the threat of internal corruption:

> Our constitution, indeed makes it impossible to destroy liberty by any sudden blast of popular fury, or by the treachery of a few; for though the many cannot easily hurt, they may easily save themselves. But if the many will concur with the few; if they will advisedly and deliberately suffer their liberty to be taken away by those, to whom they delegate power to preserve it; this no constitution can prevent.[29]

Unwittingly the British people could sacrifice their own liberty if not alert to the machinations of ministers keen to secure power for themselves by any means. Evidence for the type of underhand behaviour feared by Bolingbroke can be seen in the growing number of MPs offered 'preferment' since the Restoration and repeated 'demand[s] that office-holders be disqualified from parliament'.[30] Fears regarding the increase in numbers of parliamentary placemen, particularly after the ascendancy of Robert Walpole during the 1720s meant that, 'corruption came to seem the principal threat to liberty. Bribery appeared endemic to the post-Revolutionary political culture'.[31]

Bolingbroke's call to 'fence in' the British constitution and protect it 'against the beasts of the field and the insects of the earth' was not unique. However, it was not only opposition commentators who perceived party politics to pose a significant threat to the nation's liberty. As Pettit asserts, 'Revolution principles are clear and incontrovertible statements against "parties" (or for "liberty"); a true believer in the Hanoverian monarchy is perforce a believer in these principles; therefore, anyone professing support for the Hanoverian monarchy must endorse a political model founded on the absence of factious parties'.[32] It is in this way that Bolingbroke is able to uphold the principles of the 1688 Revolution yet criticise the apparently devoutly Hanoverian Walpole, who, 'by dint of his hostility to Bolingbroke's opposition, becomes the enemy of the Revolution and, even, of the Hanoverians'.[33] Therefore, just as liberty was established cross party as the fundamental right of all Britons, factionalism was unequivocally rejected, identified as the primary threat to liberty. Factions spawned self-interest, and self-interest directly apposed the notion of an all-encompassing liberty, the protection of which should concern all Britons. Factions were perceived as dangerous in their prioritising of private over public good, but also due to their potential appropriation by 'dishonest ministries' who rely on factions to forestall 'concerted criticism'.[34]

This connection between factionalism and self-interested ministries and the combined threat these pose to liberty is reflected explicitly in the ancient British history plays. In *The Briton*, Ambrose Philips depicts a country torn by internal division. The success of the Roman invaders is due entirely to disunity amongst the British clans. As Vanoc begins to unite these disparate groups against their common enemy, the Roman tribune Valens warns, 'know this strict alliance, sought by Vanoc,/Unities three bordering nations in his cause'(10). Vanoc's enemies fear that the 'Trinobants', traditional allies of the treacherous Queen Cartismande, herself allied to the Romans, will not 'stand against this formidable union' (10). In *Hibernia Freed*, the bard, Eugenius, observes, 'Fatal Disunion and intestine Strife/Have render'd us a Prey to foreign Pow'r' (2). It is not only the insatiable greed of the Danes that has led to the Viking invasion of Ireland, but the Irish people have brought subjugation upon themselves, 'The People's Crimes have drawn this Vengeance down,/Which the King's Virtue only can remove'(3). In this way these plays suggest that factionalism was responsible for these historic losses of liberty. Modern Britons should observe and take heed of these anti-faction warnings embedded in the nation's own history. Just as liberty is conceptualised in these plays in a way that mythologises it as embedded in the national political land-scape and public/private consciousness, factionalism is demonised in the role as antithesis to liberty. This dichotomy is problematised in other plays from the period but in the ancient British history plays this simplistic opposition serves to polarise ancient Briton and aggres-sor as mythical Manichean combatants, diametric pairs signifying good and evil.

Jeffreys's *Edwin* further supports the notion of factionalism as the key threat posed to national liberty. The play opens with the funeral of Cad-uan, former king of Britain whose country was torn apart by the late usurper Elfrid and the factionalism of the disloyal Tudor. The action fol-lows Edwin, as he discovers that he is *not* in fact the son of Caduan, but the son of Elfid the usurper. Edwin was swapped at birth with Leolin, Caduan's true son and the real, hereditary heir to the British throne, who at the start of the play is Edwin's prisoner. It is Tudor, whose disloy-alty to Caduan was merely a pretence designed to ensure the safety of Leolin, who eventually reveals the truth. The old King represents a lack of self-interest. In giving up his own son he prioritises the nation's future rather than his own. Caduan's actions ensure the eventual downfall of the usurper by guaranteeing the rightful succession thus demonstrating the way in which self-denial can restore liberty lost through faction. Tudor's 'false faction' ensures the success of the plan. In reality it is Tudor's loyalty to the rightful dynasty, his protection of the heir to the throne that re-establishes dynastic order and national unity. Here a faux-faction is created in order to restore liberty through peaceful means, a seemingly asynchronous validation of both hereditary succession and the Glorious Revolution, itself a manipulation of 'faction' in terms of securing an incontestable political alliance.

Aaron Hill further complicates this notion of factionalism as the threat to liberty and asserts the need not only for party unity but for patrio-tism. Writing in 1731 of his forthcoming play, *The Generous Traitor*, later renamed *Athelwold*, Hill contends:

> This being my notion of the *modern patriotism*, I am in hopes to see it set right, in some *Tragedy*; that *Legion* may be bubbled no longer, by animosity, for *public spiritedness*, on one side, – and, that *ambition*, on the other, may be taught to measure itself, and take bounds in proportion to capacity. We should, then, have *humbler factions*, and *abler administration*.[35]

Hill's text in indeed 'a tragedy' that attempts to set 'modern patrio-tism' right. Before the Saxon King, Edgar, becomes aware of Athelwold's misdemeanours he predicts:

> Statesmen shall learn, from the deserv'd Renown,
> From Honours thou shalt owe my strengthen'd Crown;
> That, where the Monarch is not blind of Heart,
> Affection is the Favourite's wisest Art:
> While, to Self-Servers, due Contempt is shown,
> Let Friends, who seek our Int'rest, find their own. (45)

The irony here is of course that Athelwold's behaviour is self-serving. Although it is in the pursuit of love rather than wealth or power, nonethe-less, he is accused by his enemies of being a self-interested favourite. Hill's play, rather than merely rejecting factionalism, addresses contemporary causes of party strife. For example, in response to opposition charges of favouritism levied against Walpole, Hill's text suggests that favouritism *is* justified, provided the right favourite is selected; an assertion which will be returned to and discussed in more detail in the chapters that follow. Countering repeated demands for an aggressive foreign policy, the play also draws upon the contention that a 'passive monarch' who safeguards his country rather than subjecting it to the ravages of war is just as worthy of the epithet 'Patriot' as a King who achieves success in glorious battle:

> Proud of Dominion, yet enslav'd to Fear,
> Kings who love Blood, thro' one long Tempest steer,
> While the calm Monarch, who with Smiles controuls,
> Roofs his safe Empire, and is King of Souls. (56)

Despite criticising contemporary party factionalism, Hill's play overtly supports both the Hanoverian dynasty and Walpole's policy of peace with Europe; provided that both 'partners' in this governmental rela-tionship demonstrate their intent to protect British liberty. However, as the century progressed and party factionalism deepened, bringing back-bench Whig and Tory rhetoric closer together, the idea of faction as a danger to liberty intensified. Not every text therefore offers a clear repre-sentation of 'who' should be the protectors of British liberty. The focus for these plays are the mythologies that endow the ancient protectors of British liberty as models for modern emulation against which contem-porary Britons could measure themselves, their peers and their betters. The concept of liberty is clearly contested political ground but close scrutiny reveals perpetually shifting sands rather than the static meaning intimated by repeated claims for the ancient origins of British liberty.

## National identity

If liberty is difficult to define due to its multivalent political appropriations, notions of British national identity, inextricably related to liberty, are, in the ancient British history plays, surprisingly homogenous. Despite the obvious tension between the desirability of homogeneity in terms of the nation's identity (particularly in relation to commercial and colonial ambitions) and the need for partisan distinction (sustaining clear party identities in relation to political ambitions), these plays are successful in utilising ancient British cultures to validate claims for a shared and authorised version of Britishness.

In *The Briton*, Yvor, described as the Prince of the Silurians, is a fiercely patriotic Welsh leader, 'He rules an untam'd, mountain race;/A nation walled, on every side, with rocks:/A fiery people; desperate foes to Rome;/Whom dangers only kindle into rage' (10). Yvor is proud of his 'native land: where Romans never enter'd' (18). Wales is depicted as 'by nature fenced; the refuge of the Britons' but, with the death of his betrothed Gwendolyn, the 'youthful progeny' imagined by Yvor to 'oppose/These strangers, who encroach upon our rights' will never be forthcoming (18–19). As the play closes, Yvor is reduced to a shadow of his initial proud, warlike self. In *Athelwold*, another Welsh prince, Leolyn, shares many of these characteristics but, just as Yvor's character is weakened by the Romans, Leolyn (like his Anglicised name) is 'tamed' by the Saxons. Hill's Leolyn is a loyal Welshman and his dress and characteristics are distinct from the Saxons who make up the remaining characters of the play.[36] The arguments used for restricting Leolyn's power are his own violence and rashness, itself directly connected to his father's act of treason against the Saxon King, Edgar:

> Proud Leolyn!
> Thy Father was a Rebel – Detected Treason
> Inverts the vanquish'd Traitor's Property.
> And he and his lost Blood are Forfeits, all.
> I love the fearless Bravery of free Spirits;
> But the blind fierceness shocks me. (32–3)

Leolyn's 'hot British blood' is restrained by the Saxons. The new 'Welsh' identity imposed by the 'English' is one of timidity, 'He sees me; now, grown tame: an humble suff'rer!/And, while he holds my lands, neglects my blood'.[37] Just as Hill's Leolyn talks in bitter tones of his subordination to Edgar, Philips's Yvor detests the attempted Roman incursion of his homeland. In Jeffreys's *Edwin*, ethnic identities are blurred. Here Leolin is the true heir, son of the deposed Saxon King, swapped at birth with the titular hero Edwin, son of the usurper Elfrid. Leolin is therefore not actually Welsh and it is merely his name that suggests his heritage rather than either his behaviour or his rhetoric. There is a distinct difference between Jeffreys's Welsh hero and the Welsh heroes of the other texts. What unites the other Welshmen is a love of their homeland. The mountains of Wales are repeatedly described with fondness and depicted as an insurmountable barrier to invaders. At no point during *Edwin* does Leolin demonstrate such ardent pride and nationalistic fervour.

Despite their overt nationalism, these Welsh princes aim to increase their power by marrying Saxon or Briton nobility. In *The Briton*, Yvor is betrothed to Gwendolen (Vanoc's daughter). In *Athelwold*, Leolyn's sister was intended as the King's bride, and Leolyn himself aims to marry the Minister of State's niece, Ethelinda. In *Edwin*, Leolin is in love with Adeliza (Tudor's daughter, also beloved by his rival Edwin). The failure of all of these love matches suggests the failure of unification between England and Wales. Eighteenth-century Britons, Pittock suggests, identified Wales as 'the original British nation' – the modern Welsh were 'the remnant of the Celtic Britons driven out of England by the Saxons'.[38] Intermarriage is not a route for the integration of national identities. However, key aspects of 'Welsh' identity are obvious elements of modern British self-perception, 'the idea of the Britishness of Wales was by no means an alien one, and indeed among the Anglophone political classes it is hard to discern the notion of Welsh national difference at all'.[39] National pride, personal integrity, and love of liberty, all clearly suggest common factors in regional versions of Britishness. The geographic object of which such pride and loyalty was the focus shifts here; the mountains of Cambria, the vales of Albion or the rugged wilds of Caledonia.

In apparent contradiction to this desire to locate the ancestral origins of Britishness, other Celtic Britons remain marginalised. Of the plays discussed here, only William Philips's *Hibernia Freed* depicts the Irish, a fact that the dedication to Henry O'Brien, Earl of Thomonde, passes comment upon, 'Tho' the Histories of Ireland are not writ in such a manner as to intice many Readers, (a Misfortune however, not particular to that Nation) yet none are ignorant that your Lordship is lineally descended from the Monarchs of it'. Philips's text works against normative literary and historical representations of the Irish as 'inferior, lazy, feckless and warlike' By the juxtaposition of Irish Christians with the barbarous heathen Danes,'what is so noble as to free one's Country from Tyranny and Invasion?' (53).[40] United against a common foe, and rising above internal factionalism, the Irish clans join to defeat the Danes. Having overthrown their invaders, the Irish are offered two versions of their future, both of which focus on colonisation. The first is declared by Turgenisis the Danish leader:

> I foretell,
> Another Nation shall revenge my Death,
> And with successful Arms invade this Realm.
> And if Hereafter be, and Souls can know,
> And taste the Pains which Mortals undergo;
> Mine shall rejoyce to see thy Land subdu'd,
> And Peasants Hands with Royal Blood embru'd;
> Then shall I laugh at Hell's severest Pain,
> And scorn the Tortures all thy Priests can feign. (57)

This apocalyptic version of the English colonisation of Ireland is countered by Eugenius's alternative vision, a re-appropriation of the story told by Turgenisis asserting the perceived benefits to Ireland of English rule:

> Another Nation, famous through the World,
> For martial Deeds, for Strength and Skill in Arms,
> Belov'd and blest for their Humanity.
> Where Wealth abounds, and Liberty resides,
> . . .
>
> They shall succeed, invited to our Aid,
> And mix their Blood with ours; one People grow. (57)

O'Brien's fatalistic acceptance of Eugenius's overtly positive premonition of an English 'invasion' at Ireland's invitation – 'Whatever Changes are decreed by Fate,/Bear we with Patience, with a Will resign'd./Honour and Truth pursue, and firmly trust,/Heav'n may at last prove Kind, it will be Just' – is suggestive of a particularly Anglo-Irish interpretation of the subjugation of Ireland (57). As Jim Smyth asserts, until the late seventeenth century the survival of Irish Protestants was dependent upon 'English connection and English identity'.[41] However, as the military threat posed by the Catholic Irish waned, a 'Protestant appropriation of Irishness' developed alongside a 'sense of a privileged joint proprietorship in unique Saxon liberties'.[42] In *Hibernia Freed*, Irish identity is not only aligned with English identity, as with the representations of the Welsh in *The Briton*, but is also manipulated to suggest an historic capitulation with English rule and cultural approbation of the subsuming of Irish identity into notations of Britishness.

This interpretation of the Irish heroes as overtly Anglo-Irish suggests that Turgenisis's version of the English subjugation of Ireland echoes Catholic interpretations of English control. Characterised by their brutality and immoral religious practices, controlled by a demonised leader with a strong desire for absolute power and no respect for his devotees, do the Danes in turn act as an allegorical representation of the degeneracy of the Catholic Irish? Philips clearly appropriates Gaelic history in order to glorify the claimed ancestor of his patron and firmly define Ancient Irish heroes as the forefathers of modern Anglo-Irish Protestants. [43] This Anglicisation of ancient Irish history echoes Pittock's assertion that 'English enthusiasm for Britain had been (and up to perhaps 1770 entirely remained) of a firmly imperialist cast, being linked to foundation-myth-derived claims of sovereignty and hegemony'.[44] In terms of a British national identity, the Anglo-Irish, like the Welsh, are represented in the plays by their desire for liberty, and sense of national pride, characteristics that can easily be attributed to an homogenous 'British' identity rather than the individualistic and often caricatured regional identities.

Perhaps surprisingly, the Scottish are further marginalised to the extent that none of these plays offer a representation of Scottish heroes. Seemingly, the only space for Scottish ancestors in articulating the roots of Britishness was to position them as distant unrelated figures. In *The Briton*, the Caledonians side with the Romans against the Britons. They are excluded from the label of 'Briton' and are represented as heathen brutes, easily overcome by the superior military skill of the Britons (clearly a somewhat barbed political point to make in 1722). Described as 'A swarm of Caledonians; huge-limb'd warriours;/Who wield, with sinewy arm, a deadly sword' (6), these men are represented in a way which closely corresponds to the stereotype commonly ascribed to their nation.[45] This raises a number of questions. Why were plays representing ancient Scottish heroes not produced on the London stage when so many plays concerning English, Welsh and, to a lesser extent, Irish history were? The simple answer may be that any positive representation of Scottish heroes would be considered by audiences (and, particularly post-1737, the censor) to demonstrate Jacobite sympathies irrespective of political or even apolitical agenda. An alternative response to this question could lie in the codification used to rhetorically negotiate the opposing interpretations of the 1707 Union, viewed in Scotland as a partnership whereas in England, the acquisition of a possession.[46] This dual interpretation could be seen as obstructive to dramatic representations of Scottish historical heroes on the London stage, a point perhaps validated by Ambrose Philips's rather historically eschewed representation of the Scottish in *The Briton*. If the English identified Scotland as a 'possession' plays which took as their focus Scottish nationalism would be somewhat misplaced on the London stage. The need for homogeneity in relation to Britishness resulted in an English-centric version of national identity that is resistant to Scottish culture yet comfortable with the sublimation of Welsh and Anglo-Irish identities into an Anglophilic Britishness. Not only were the differences between English, Welsh and Anglo-Irish identities more easily elided (in political, historical and doctrinal terms) than the contrasts perceived between the English and the Scottish, but these imagined and real points of cultural contact effectively over-wrote ideological differences, thus diminishing the notion that either Welsh or Anglo-Irish posed a tangible destabilising threat to the English centre.

Further compounding this intermingling or blending of regional identities is the fluidity of terminology that pervades a number of these texts. The terms 'Briton' and 'British' are repeatedly juxtaposed, diminishing the discrete differences between the ancient Britons performed on stage and the modern British they allegorically represent. The terms 'Briton' and 'British', their cultural, historical and political gaps, become interchangeable. In Thomson and Mallet's *Alfred*, the peasant Corin exclaims, 'just Heaven forbid,/A British man should ever count for gain,/What villainy must earn. No: are we poor?/Be honesty our riches./Are we mean,/And humbly born? The true heart makes us noble' (9). Clearly this proud characterisation of Anglo-Saxon virtues is made with explicit reference to the 'modern' Britons of the audience. Corin's sentiment is aligned with the characteristics already identified as particularly modern British: honesty, humility, nobility and an abhorrence of self-interest. His words act as a reminder to the audience of the qualities of 'Britishness' not only by demonstrating the cultural heritage, the antiquity, of such national characteristics but by explicitly conflating this stereotype with a modern term. A similar reference is made in the prologue to Jeffreys's *Edwin* written by Lewis Theobald, 'The Heroes Blood still runs in British Veins./Of Our old Virtue there we stand possest;/Brave, when most cool; unconquer'd tho' deprest'. Theobald draws a direct link between eighteenth-century Britons and the ancient Saxons of the play. In the prologue to *The Briton* the link between ancient Britons and modern Britons is made, again, not only through their shared heritage but also through equivocation, 'Britons, you'll see, when Vanoc comes before ye,/The love of Freedom is your ancient Glory'. Taken quite literally, ancient Britons will be seen on stage, demonstrating to modern 'Britons' their love of freedom and the value such audiences should place on this inherited right.

Do the representations of Welsh and Irish heroes in these texts counter critical arguments for a cohesive British identity? A number of these texts directly link positive characteristics of ancient British ancestors with models for the modern custodians of British liberty to emulate. These seemingly opposed approaches are not mutually exclusive; what is important is the proposal that all Britons play a role in safeguarding their own liberty, irrespective of the distinctions endorsed by regional and cultural identities. The nation as a whole has a shared responsibility for maintaining British liberty. For example, in *The Briton*, Philips looks beyond the history of his text and points forward to the Saxons, 'Unpolish'd – greatly Rude, Strangers to Luxury, – and Servitude,/Reviv'd the British Manliness of Soul,/That spurns at Tyranny, nor brookes Controul'. The Saxons are the 'restorers' of British liberty and revive the desire for cultural freedom, eroded from the Britons by centuries of Roman occupation. They rekindle 'British Manliness', reinstating Britishness. In these plays, the varied regional characteristics of these ancient ancestors are distinct yet conform to a broadly 'British' identity centred upon manliness. In Philips' s play this 'British' identity encompasses the Saxon and Celtic 'manliness of soul'. Is the representation of manliness as a key element of British identity echoed in other ancient British history plays?

Eighteenth-century attitudes towards manliness have been juxtaposed by scholars such as Michèle Cohen with the issue of politeness, which itself dominated sentimental discourses throughout the period. Cohen sees both politeness and conversation as necessary tools for the fashionable gentleman but these tools occupied a complex cultural space in that they were thought to be effeminising, 'not just because they could be achieved only in the company of women, but because they were modelled on the French. The question is, could men be at once polite and manly?'[47] Similar conflicts between the desire to construct dramatic heroes who demonstrate manliness and the need for these heroes to possess codes of conduct appropriate to the taste and politeness of an eighteenth-century audience can be seen in the ancient British history plays. Clearly, through their actions and military prowess, the men of these plays demonstrate the conventions of heroic manliness. But what is more significant is the way in which this manliness is characterised as particularly British, a formulation, in part, constructed by women, written into the role of linguistic civilisers. Cohen asserts, 'the English saw themselves as a nation with a sullen and uncommunicative disposition'.[48] In the plays depicting ancient British history this taciturn aspect of Britishness is tempered by the presence of women and polite conversation. Cohen observes:

> The association of politeness with France had been an abiding problem for the English, sincerity, especially unpolished, resonated with echoes of a proud national ancestry, the ancient Briton.[49]

In order to establish a clear definition of British men as inheritors of the masculine qualities of their ancient ancestors, yet demonstrating the social 'politeness' required of modern men, these plays must negotiate an appropriate level of 'polite conversation' balanced against 'manly' credentials.

Eloquence is thus a recurring theme. Athelwold's interactions with women lead the hero to practice eloquent speech as a form of persuasion, employed against the best interests of less linguistically duplicitous men and women. Indeed, Ethelinda is duped by Athelwold's false protestations of love:

> Such was the false, the artful Eloquence,
> That lur'd me to my Ruin my heart,
> Instructed by Distress, can now read Meanings.
> Who, that is new to Passion, cou'd believe,
> That this fair Picture, of thy faded love,
> But proves, thou lovs't another. (42)

Ethelinda is uneducated in such courtly arts until seduced by Athelwold. Leolyn is also exposed to such rhetoric from Athelwold and the linguistically manipulative Oswald. In fact Oswald conducts all of his business through duplicitous rhetoric. He schools Athelwold to abandon his trademark manly heroism and instead to 'Dissemble your Concern – and I will move him/To stir in your Behalf, and reconcile you/To the King's Pardon' (35). In direct contrast with Hill's earlier version of the history, Ethelinda, Athelwold's rejected lover, and Elfrid, his wife, are represented as idealistically virtuous women. Elfrid refuses Edgar's advances, vowing never to marry him, even if Athelwold should die. At no point is Ethelinda criticised for succumbing to her passion for Athelwold. It is not 'women's conversation' that has corrupted Athelwold, rather an experience for which he is unprepared, the fickleness of his own heart, 'The barb'rous Elegance of Man's soft Art,/To cheat believing Innocence! – E'er long/Thy Elfrid, the resistless Charmer! – She!/ Will hear thee poorly urge the same Excuse,/When some third Fool believes thee' (58). Women's conversation teaches Athelwold, somewhat too late, that he cannot act purely on natural instinct and retain his honour when it comes to matters of the heart. Love and war require very different codes of conduct.

In *The Briton*, Gwendolyn, another model of feminine virtue, is contrasted with Cartismande whose 'conversation' has lured first Caradoc and then Vanoc to her bed and, ultimately, destruction at the hands of the Romans. Unlike Hill's Athelwold and Leolyn, in Ambrose Philips's play the heroic Britons are already masters of 'women's conversation'. They combine politeness with manliness, demonstrating both modesty and heroism. Commending the hero Ebranc, Vanoc exclaims, 'Thy modesty shall do thee no disservice: –/It is a virtue, of the growth of Britain. – Boasters, and Sycophants, come from abroad' (21). It is the Romans who 'have the Art to glos the foulest Cause' and are portrayed as the corrupting force in terms of linguistic manipulation or 'eloquence' (34):

> Valens:   Did not the Romans civilize you?
> Vanoc:   No!
>             They brought new Customs, and new vices over;
>             Taught us more Arts, than honest Men require;
>             And gave us wants, that nature never gave
> Valens:   We found you naked: –
> Vanoc:   And you found us free! (35–6)

Whereas in *Athelwold* Saxon women are corrupted by men's manipulation of language, in *The Briton* British freedom is threatened by Roman linguistic artifice. In terms of language therefore, it is the Celts rather than the Saxons who demonstrate the moral integrity required of protectors of liberty. However, this integrity can also be read as naivety. Understanding the power of language without succumbing to such artifice is a lesson which these Britons seem yet to have mastered. They need to acquire what Michael Mangan has described as 'mercantile masculinity', a masculinity that although 'polite, civilised and socialized' retains the linguistic control required for commercial success.[50] Conversely, in *Hibernia Freed* the destructive power of language is openly demonstrated. Sabina is reprimanded for 'talking' to the Danes; her outbursts, although honest and virtuous, are a direct threat to what small degree of liberty is still enjoyed by the colonised Irish. In this instance, women's conversation is deemed inappropriately confrontational, uncontrolled and unrestrained. This is further compounded when the men dress as women in order to infiltrate the enemy camp and attack the Danish leaders. Their actions, despite being somewhat underhand, and reminiscent (to an English eye at least) of a stereotypically Celtic mode of defence, are upheld as heroic.[51] However, the ease with which the Danes are duped by the Irish clearly demonstrates the dangers of succumbing, unreservedly, to women's conversation.

National identity is therefore dependent upon a variety of influences. Regional characteristics are, in these plays, distilled to heroic manliness tempered, on occasion, by women's influence, thus making the characteristics of ancient British ancestors more palatable to a modern, 'polite' audience. With the exception of the representation of the Scots in *The Briton*, what Smyth identifies as a xenophobic prejudice towards 'domestic foreigners' and Pittock describes as a 'xenophobic hatred' more vociferously expressed by the British to 'their fellow countrymen than to the French enemy' is not discernible in these plays.[52] However, this observation is not intended to counter assertions regarding the fragmentation of British identity but rather to suggest that these texts attempt to elide this cultural division. Instead of recapitulating the established differences perceived as inherent in the various 'national' cultures of eighteenth-century Britain, these plays attempt to overcome such differences in order to create a composite British identity; an identity firmly rooted in Britain's ancient history and exemplified by the representatively British characters of these ancient national heroes. Xenophobia, however entrenched in British society, receives a gloss in these texts, which permits a universal call to modern Britons to recognise their duty to protect British liberty. This is a form of duty not merely defined in terms of moral responsibility but handed down through generations of 'Britons', the inheritance of a nation irrespective of its internal factions and divisions. This gloss is effective not only in diffusing xenophobic prejudice, but also in challenging preconceptions of gender difference; after all, it was not only men who were expected to take responsibility for their freedom. British women are important beneficiaries of this national inheritance and must play their part in its protection. Even when women's guardianship of liberty is not represented as exactly equal to that of their male counterparts, their role is nevertheless important, at least as a reminder to men of their social responsibility. Whatever gender, whatever cultural affiliation, all Britons are charged with protecting British liberty. This universal responsibility, seen by Bolingbroke as vital to the protection of liberty against the unpatriotic tactics of self-interested ministers, is somewhat fantastical, and even the most nationalistic audience members, however flattered by the notion that they, as individuals, were integral to the protection of the nation must have seen such assertions as little more than evocative fantasies. However, the concept of individual polity is not as abstract as it may initially appear and, in the early eighteenth century, such claims could be directly connected to another myth-in-the-making; the representation of Parliament as democratic representative of the people.

## Parliament as the protector of liberty

Just as Bolingbroke argued for the close link between British national identity and the nation's ancient history, this connection is given rhetorical strength by the interchangeable use of the terms 'Briton' and 'British' in the ancient British history plays. Nevertheless, although national history is important in defining national identity, links must be established between the ancient and the modern in order to blur cultural distinctions; for example, Celtic and Saxon manliness is softened and updated by the impact, sometimes positive, sometimes negative, of women's conversation. It is in this way that Bolingbroke attempted to draw parallels between modern and ancient modes of government, validating the modern by emphasising similarities with the ancient. Modern Britain's parliament, according to Bolingbroke, originates in the Anglo-Saxon Wittena Gemote.[53] Here Bolingbroke's political rhetoric, his language, has commonality with Barthes' construction of mythical speech wherein 'the signifier is already formed by the signs of the language'.[54] The parallels drawn between modern and ancient modes of government are tenuous, at best, but the connections are sustained by the meta-language of Bolingbroke's rhetoric, what Barthes terms, 'mythical speech', which makes use of existing signs to create new meanings – or more precisely, justifications – for new political orders based upon mythologised reconstructions of systems whose archaic status amplifies their linguistic instabilities.

Having argued that the ancient British history plays attempt to conceal contemporary xenophobic tensions that resided within other accounts of the composite nation, it can also be argued that the plays support assertions regarding Parliament as a cultural symbol and proponent of 'national unity'.[55] The British Parliament, idealised as a privileged inheritance from the ancient Britons, in and of itself promotes a sense of unity within the nation:

After 1707, virtually every part of the island had a nearby peer who sat in the House of Lords and/or sent representatives to the House of Commons. And though Wales, Scotland and northern England were badly under-represented in comparison with the south, in practice the system worked more equitably than it appeared. Wealthy and influential men from the less favoured regions frequently got themselves elected for seats in the more abundantly represented regions, and in this indirect way their localities obtained a voice at Westminster.[56]

So, according to this model, by ensuring that even minority voices could be heard, the British Parliament brought the nation's regional factions together, uniting the various regions of Britain under one constitution. But to what extent is this model a reflection of establishment views rather than experienced realities? Given what Colley identifies as the 'cult of parliament', an entrenched and 'increasingly important part of elite attitudes', how widespread were such notions and how significant a part did Parliament play in the image of the nation as represented on the early eighteenth-century stage?[57] One argument that would support the concept of Parliament as a symbol of national unification is its significance as proof of a clear distinction between Britain and her European counterparts, 'by the early 1700s, most comparable institutions had ceased to meet'.[58] British superiority was therefore confirmed by the unquestioned uniqueness of Britain's mode of government; commentators remarked upon its efficiency and general superiority when compared to all other contemporary models.

However, this vision of national 'unity', confirmed by the polity's superiority, is not supported by the dramatic histories of 'ancient Britain' discussed in this chapter. These texts reflect the concerns of commentators such as Bolingbroke who identified 'party politics' and its inherent factionalism as the greatest threat to Britain's political stability and to the liberty of the British people. As Blair Worden suggests, familiar seventeenth-century conflicts regarding the balance of power between Crown and Parliament did not cease during the first half of the eighteenth century.[59] Furthermore, Parliament, the supposed check on the Crown's behaviour, became perceived as its ally. Power was firmly ensconced in elitist groups courtesy of systems of patronage and the associated accusations of self-interested nepotism.

Such concerns regarding the integrity of statesmen are reflected in the ancient British history plays. In *Edwin*, Morvid, governor of Edwin's castle, observes:

> You Statesmen are so shrewd in forming Schemes!
> But often to secure some trivial Point,
> And answer ends as little wise as just!

> Such, Children are ye, busy, nice and anxious,
> To raise a Bawble, Paper Edifice,
> That by its own flight Make betray'd to Ruin,
> Wants not a Breath of Air to puff it down! (21)

One such example of a 'shrewd' statesman is Gomel, chief minister to Edwin, whose corruption and Machiavellian self-interest reveal him willing to offer his support to whichever side looks more likely to retain or regain power. His unpredictability makes him dangerous; payment or reward secure Gomel's obligation but his service is only ever for hire, never fixed. Whereas some commentators viewed reward 'as the necessary instrument of national stability', others saw such high profile 'degeneracy' and corruption as a national problem.[60] In *Athelwold*, the universality of this national problem is demonstrated by the downfall of a national hero who acts against the King, thus breaking pseudo-sacred bonds of loyalty and friendship. Athelwold, Edgar's favourite, turns against his patron and abuses his position of trust, an action both unmanly and un-British. Athelwold's conduct compares unfavourably to Bolingbroke's version of the British national character and demonstrates effectively the threat Bolingbroke imagines posed to modern Britain by corrupt ministers and complacent citizens:

> A wise and brave people will neither be cozened, nor bullied out of their liberty; but a wise and brave people may cease to be such: they may degenerate; they may sink into sloth and luxury; they may resign themselves to a treacherous conduct; or abet the enemies of the constitution, under a notion of supporting the friends of the government: they may want the sense to discern their danger in time, or the courage to resist, when it stares them in the face.[61]

The self-interested behaviour of degenerate men such as Athelwold is a direct threat to liberty and such degeneracy is, from the perspective of some eighteenth-century commentators, promoted and endorsed by Parliament and party politics.

Walpole's refusal to confront England's enemies, his preference for treaty-making and securing peace, was judged by the opposition to confirm this sense of national degeneracy, 'Corruption tyranny and weakness abroad were judged to go together'.[62] Again, this is echoed in the plays with the assertion that war is a manly, and therefore a peculiarly British pursuit. In *Edwin*, the young nobleman Albert asserts, 'War in a distemper'd State like ours / Lets out ill Blood; 'tis Exercise, 'tis Health' (8). Albert's words echo Bolingbroke's assertion that 'a free

people may be sometimes betrayed; but no people will betray themselves, and sacrifice their liberty, unless they fall into a state of universal
corruption: and when they are once fallen into such a state, they will
be sure to lose what they deserve no longer to enjoy'.[63] Liberty is to
be fought for, and any corrupt state that fails to protect its liberty,
deserves to lose it. Parliament fails to address these issues of corruption
because it was perceived to be reliant upon institutionalised dishonesty
and degeneracy. However, it was difficult for commentators to argue
against the factionalism endemic to Parliament without becoming implicated in that same supposed degeneracy. What was needed was a model
of idealised national identity for which the protection of British liberty
was paramount. This predominantly male model combined manliness
with the tempering qualities of politeness and public-spiritedness. Incor-
ruptible by the degeneracy of Parliament and immune to the lure of
preferment, this model of Britishness provided, as Worden suggests,
'legitimacy to opposition to the government':

> The term 'patriot' shifted the balance of ethical authority away from
> the Crown and court. Patriots, like the country party, represented
> the community at large: the ministries they attacked, corrupt and
> unprincipled, were the true sources of faction, division, instability.
> All definitions of patriotism agreed that the patriot was 'impartial',
> above 'party' and 'party spirit'.[64]

The patriot offered a perfect model of national identity, embodying all
of the characteristics necessary for the successful protection of national
liberty. The patriot became a significant part of Britain's new national
mythology and as such was appropriated for various political purposes
and diverse agendas. Thus evocations of the patriot are not limited to
opposition plays. As the Hermit in Thomson and Mallet's *Alfred* suggests:

> When guardian laws
> Are by the patriot, in the glowing senate,
> Won from corruption; when th' impatient arm
> Of liberty, invincible, shall scourge
> The tyrants of mankind – and when the Deep,
> Through all her swelling waves, shall proudly joy
> Beneath the boundless empire of thy sons. (17)

To some extent, by successfully restoring liberty once lost, the patriot
removes the duty from the shoulders of *all* Britons. With patriots in

Parliament, liberty was protected with the dual security of patriotism and the constitution, and could not be 'lost'. The use of the term 'patriot' in *Alfred*, an overtly pro-Whig play, of course reinforces an important point, and one that will remain under consideration throughout this book; patriot rhetoric was not limited merely to opposition tracts, patriotism was appropriated across both factions and parties.

This should not be taken as complete refutation of Colley's claims for a widespread national pride in the British Parliament. Despite 'innumerable writers' expressing concerns about ministerial corruption and seemingly insidious bribery as threats to Britain's 'balanced constitution', the plays repeatedly call on Britons to reflect on their unique position as 'free men and women'. In *The Briton*, Vanoc sets out the uniqueness of Britain as an 'elect' nation:

> From the main land, why are we set apart;
> Seated amidst the waves; high-fenced by Cliffs;
> And blest with a delightful, fertile Soil?
> But that, indulgent nature meant the Britons,
> A chosen people; a distinguish'd race;
> A nation, independent of the world:
> Whose weal, whose wisdom, it will ever be,
> Neither to conquer, nor to suffer conquest. (20)

Indeed assertions regarding the unique qualities of British liberty are not limited to the ancient British history plays. Texts reflecting upon medieval and later English history also evoke images of incursions upon and restorations of British liberty. Equally, plays concerned with foreign histories draw upon contrasts between restrictive regimes and British political freedoms or identify parallels between ancient empires and modern Britain. Almost without exception, the plays discussed in this book represent liberty as a particularly *British* privilege, a privilege that is frequently associated with the 'uniqueness' of the British constitution but also due to the British national character and its unique heritage. Of course, some scholars have adroitly asserted that the level of debate and repeated eulogising invested in the British constitution during the eighteenth century hints at an underlying anxiety regarding stability and permanence.[65] This anxiety is clearly palpable in a number of the plays discussed in this book. However, there is seemingly little room in the ancient British history plays for such unease as no matter which political agenda these texts promote, the allegories struck are clear and bold assertions regarding British supremacy and the inimitable qualities associated with British identity. In these plays, ancient Britons are representative of an idealised version of British identity. Modern patriots are the direct descendants, both in the literal sense and in terms of shared geographical and historical perspectives, of the nation's ancient fore-fathers and mothers and, therefore, the ideal protectors of a national liberty inherited by all Britons from their ancient ancestors. This mythologised version of the nation's ancient past imparts a sense of longevity and stability that deliberately overlooks the obvious disruptions to this narrative of 'liberty', obscuring the historical spaces between ancient and modern in which Britain could not be convincingly cast as 'great and free'. The patriotic conduct of ancient Britons is evoked to construct and defend what Pettit describes as the period's 'myths of stability'.[66] Indeed, within the context of this group of plays, ancient Britons and their imagined histories stand as evidence for the veracity of claims, such as that made in the epilogue to *The Briton* that, 'Britons, united, may defy the world!'(19).

# 2
# Kings, Ministers and Favourites: the National Myth in Peril

> Who Careless sits and nods upon a Throne
> Rules by the Will of Others not his own:
> Of every ill he justly hears the Blame;
> But all the Praise of God his subjects claim
> Eliza Haywood, *Frederick Duke of Brunswick Lunenburg* (1729)

> The absolute Reign of FAVOURITES is the RUIN of the State ... I could bring Numbers of Examples from History to prove it; and the Historians seem to handle no Part of it with so much Pleasure as the Fall of Favourites
> Anon., *The Norfolk Sting, or, the History and Fall of Evil Ministers* (1732)

In the English theatrical tradition, the fall of the favourite is a theme that dates back to the theatres of the 1590s.[1] Dramatic representations of history from the late sixteenth to the early eighteenth century share a pre-occupation with the favourite and a continuity of the negative language associated with favouritism.[2] The persistent presence of the favourite on stage during this period demonstrates the significance of this figure to contemporary interpretations of British history; it is a dramatic trope that occupies the negative spaces of British political histories. However, this is not merely an image utilised to demonstrate past failings. The mythological status of the favourite makes him/her the ideal allegorical vehicle with which to reflect concerns shared by contemporary audiences. Like the evil 'stepmother' of folklore, the favourite was cast as the enemy from within, an evil presence lurking in the shadows of close court culture. Repeatedly represented as ambitious political aggressors, consumed by self-interest, favourites are inevitably intent upon wresting control from the rightful patriarch, the monarch. In common with these dramatised versions, the favourite occupied a similar mythological status in political commentary, depicted as an enemy to the stability of the state, whose fall was something to be celebrated, a victory for good over evil. However, this simple construction is fractured by early eighteenth-century plays in which the function of the favourite is re-considered. This fissure is caused, in part, by contemporary political events but also by the developing mythologies surrounding Britishness, versions of British identity and, in particular, the perceived stability of the nation under Walpole and the Hanoverians. In such plays, Britain's histories are rewritten and the notion of what is signified by the term 'favourite' is re-determined. History and the nature of favouritism are represented to audiences with revised interpretations which suggest that, in the past, some favourites made good and judicious 'step-mothers' for the nation.

As part of this developing mythology favouritism, as it is represented in early eighteenth-century history plays, shares a number of points of contact with the rhetoric of patriotism. This chapter focuses on the ways in which favouritism and patriotism, myth and history, interact and coincide in these texts. The discussion is divided between two sets of plays, those that, although not exclusively concerned with favouritism, do engage with the theme and those that are specifically concerned with the fall of the favourite. Eliza Haywood's *Frederick Duke of Brunswick Lunenburg* (1729) draws on German history in depicting the difficulties of establishing a patriot government from the ruins of a ministry embroiled in favouritism and political patronage. William Havard's *King Charles the First* (1737) contrasts the monarchical favouritism of Charles with the negative effects of the favouritism of Cromwell. George Sewell's *The Tragedy of Sir Walter Raleigh* (1719) represents one of England's most famous royal favourites as a patriot brought down by the machinations of a corrupt Spaniard. Tobias Smollett's *The Regicide: or James the First of Scotland* (1749) demonstrates the complexities of royal favouritism and the danger of trusting ambitious men. Despite spanning thirty years of dramatic and political activity, the language associated with favouritism in these plays varies little. As with Hill's representation of Athelwold discussed in the previous chapter, the position of royal favourite is a privilege which ambition, love or poor judgement can lead even a patriotic man to abuse. Is favouritism depicted in these plays as unpatriotic, and thus absent from those qualities of Britishness demonstrated by the ancient Britons and purportedly integral to the character of modern

Britons? Two plays from 1731 provide a divided response to this question, which in some ways reflects political divisions of the period. The anonymous *The Fall of Mortimer* and James Ralph's *The Fall of the Earl of Essex* were premièred within three months of each other. Both plays respond to contemporary attacks on Walpole as the favourite of the Hanoverians. The idioms of patriotism and favouritism are employed in these plays in a reciprocal debate framing the political actions of Walpole and the Whig administration, a debate which was to dominate politics, public life and private conversation throughout the 1730s. In engaging with such topical issues these plays foreground the ways in which the London theatres, by representing the nation to itself through the lens of history, were active in the promotion, development and discrediting of Britain's mythologised self image.

## Favouritism and patriotism

By the early eighteenth century the favourite was a well-worn trope familiar in both literary and political circles. As I. A. A. Thompson has demonstrated, there exist an overwhelming diversity of attributes by which favourites could be categorised.[3] One common route to favouritism was the exploitation of a sexual, personal, familial or political relationship with the monarch and indeed, many of the favourites encountered in this chapter satisfy this categorisation. However, some favourites did not gain their position directly from the sovereign, 'ministers plenipotentiary ... whose position did not originate in the King's choice at all' can also be found amongst the favourites represented in the early eighteenth-century history plays.[4] But, whereas Thompson asserts that not all historical favourites were political, it is, the politically active favourite who dominates these plays. Despite assertions that the sixteenth century was the period in English political history which was dominated by the presence of the minister-favourite, it is this type of favourite who was, in the early eighteenth century, deemed a subject worthy of representation on the London stage.[5] Significantly, Blair Worden identifies only two types of favourite represented in the numerous plays discussed in his study. Worden describes the first type of favourite as the Machiavellian 'ruthless statesman', the second, as the over-reacher 'whose inevitable doom is as spectacular as his ascent'.[6] Despite the diversity in type of favourite outlined by Thompson, early eighteenth-century political and literary representations of favouritism are sharply focused on the minister-favourite. Although the plays depict the various types of relationship between favourite and sovereign, all of the favourites discussed in this chapter – Raleigh, Essex, Mortimer, Athol, and Gundamor – can be identified as 'ministers'. They are all active participants in the nation's politics, advising their monarchs on important issues of state. Thompson identifies the minister-favourite as 'a response to a crisis of government growth, and the attendant, increasing administrative complexity of the state'.[7] It is this 'crisis' and the attendant factionalism and patronage that eighteenth-century plays focusing on medieval and later English history respond to through various interpretations of the role of the minister-favourite. Can all of these 'ministers' be aligned with Worden's two-type description of dramatic favourites? Are they limited either to Machiavellian ruthlessness or the 'inevitable doom' of the over-reacher?

Certainly in terms of early eighteenth-century politics, representations of favouritism are more complex than the stage model proposed by Worden. The relevance of favouritism to politics during the period can be seen most clearly through oppositional responses to Walpole. During the print wars of the 1730s Walpole was attacked for, amongst other things, his alleged disregard of royal prerogative and his moves to concentrate power in an oligarchy of parliamentary placemen.[8] Accusations such as these formed the basis for numerous oppositional attacks levied against Walpole on the basis of these purported acts of favouritism. It should be remembered that just as favouritism was a recurrent literary trope, the political corruption associated with favouritism was by no means a theme new to politics in the eighteenth century and the 1730s were not the first period in which such rhetoric was utilised against a minister.[9] Opposition commentators adopted a method of attack already proven successful by their predecessors; they apportioned blame for unpopular or failed political decisions to the minister-favourite.[10] This is not to suggest that accusations of favouritism arose entirely from this political history of minister-favourites, but that the familiar language associated with favouritism provided the opposition with a powerful weapon that became increasingly difficult to contest. Walpole's position, however, was not limited merely to that of a minister-favourite, his role was made more complicated by the power he himself exercised as not only a favourite but also the maker of favourites. Walpole's securing of the favour of the Hanoverians was not a straightforward, linear process and his machinations go some way to demonstrate the value to the minister of monarchical support. At the beginning of his career Walpole enjoyed the support of George I and subsequently secured the backing of George II. This was itself a careful political manoeuvre. Between 1717 and 1720 George Lewis (later George II) set up a rival court in which

Walpole played a significant part. Having gained the trust of the future king, Walpole set about reconciling George with his father, thus securing his future position without surrendering his place in the affections of George I.[11] In addition Walpole also acted as 'patron' to his own band of followers, fellow and aspiring ministers who could themselves be termed, Walpole's favourites. Contemporary cartoons 'repeatedly focused on the bribery and blandishments that characterised election campaigns'.[12] In the anonymous *Ready Money the Prevailing Candidate, or; the Humours of an Election* (1727), folly presides whilst Justice is blindfolded and the throng of monied candidates mingles with the impoverished locals. The caption reflects on the sort of practices Walpole himself was accused of:

> [the foolish voter] Once paid, struts with the Gold newly
> put in his Britches,
> And dreams of vast Favours and mountains of Riches;
> But as soon as the day of Election is over,
> His woeful mistake he begins to discover;
> The Squire is a Member – the Rustick who chose him,
> Is now quite neglected – he no longer knows him.[13]

Although the system of patronage entrenched in eighteenth-century politics was not Walpole's invention, repeated accusations of his use of benefaction for his own political advancement are not unfounded. Mock-calls for his patronage are frequently made in the opposition poetry of the period.[14] In *A Familiar Epistle* (1735), Joseph Mitchell satirises Walpole the patron:

> "Then nought will do (You make Reply)
> "Without some certain Salary,
> "Some honest, snug, Life-lasting Place –
> Ay, now SIR, You have hit the Case;
> And if you'd please to do the Thing,
> *Paulo Majora* how I'd sing![15]

Walpole's patronage of the arts is here represented as thinly disguised payment for services rendered in the form of good publicity. It is through this sort of corruption, Mitchell's poem suggests, that Walpole secures his own political position. The favourites represented in plays from the period of Walpole's premiership are repeatedly seen paying for the services of others and securing followers with grand financial gestures. However, it is not just his purportedly corrupt use of patronage that identifies Walpole as more than merely a minister-favourite. By purchasing parliamentary placemen, Walpole himself selects favourites. The employment of placemen in order to strengthen his own political position suggests a shift of power away from the monarch, further than perhaps intended by the Revolution Settlement itself.

Contemporary representations of Walpole's combined role as both minister-favourite and, in turn, creator of favourites, clearly demonstrate the negative implications of favouritism. As the anonymous author of *The Norfolk Sting* (1732) asserts, 'the Absolute Reign of Favourites is always destructive to the People'.[16] Walpole is simultaneously purchased by the Hanoverian court whilst shoring up his own position in government by buying followers. Worthy men were hence refused access to politics because their views conflicted with Walpole's own self-interest and personal ambitions. In contrast to Walpole's rapid rise to power, *The Norfolk Sting* promotes steadily earned merit and honours which should be awarded only when:

> Regard be had to the Quality and Sufficiency of Persons, lest a Publick charge should fall into unworthy Hands: They should rise by Degrees, from little Offices to great: No incapable Person should be admitted by any means. The only way of coming to a Post should be Vertue, Capacity and Diligence, and should not be got without for love or Money.[17]

This overtly anti-Walpole pamphlet focuses on the dangers of favouritism within the administration. Walpole and his followers lack not only the morality necessary for positions of national importance but also the ability to perform such authoritative roles. But is favouritism necessarily restricted to opposition rhetoric such as *The Norfolk Sting*? Can favourites be represented favourably?

J. G. A. Pocock identifies Walpole as the first statesman to impress upon the opposition the belief that his policies *and* personality were undermining the moral structure of society.[18] Cultivating stability through compromise, peace abroad, economic prosperity and low land taxes, Walpole was seen as a threat to the ancient social structure of England and its moral code of chivalry or politeness. Such threats, the opposition contended, would ultimately destroy the nation, either by leaving Britain open to attack from her tyrannous Catholic neighbours or by promoting internal factionalism:

> For where unworthy Morals are advanc'd and insufficient Wretches prefer'd above able Persons; where those who have done no Public

> Services get the upper Hand of those that have; where Miscreants are
> honour'd, and Publick Thieves are respected like Patriots, there Men
> of the greatest Goodness and Merit, provided they have Spirit, will be
> apt to give into Sedition, sometimes to gratify their Revenge.[19]

As argued in the previous chapter, factionalism was seen as a corruption
of the parliamentary system and therefore a direct threat to British liberty. Here, the immorality of those subject to preferment destabilises the
system of government to the extent that patriots themselves threaten,
rather than protect, the nation's liberty. In Hubert-François Gravelot's
*The Devil Upon Two Sticks* (1741), Walpole is depicted with a group
of ministerial politicians trying to negotiate an area of infested mud-
land. Walpole is being carried – precariously balanced on two sticks.
His followers are already besmirched with 'mud'. As he attempts to
cross the mire unsullied the local villagers are being provided for with
drinks and money. The source of these bribes is Britannia whose wealth
is being stolen by a pickpocket.[20] In Gravelot's cartoon Walpole is an
immoral wretch of the sort who, according to *The Norfolk Sting*, is 'pre-
fer'd above able Persons'. Walpole's status as favourite suggests therefore
a tendency to negative interpretations of favouritism in parallel with
opposition representations of the minister himself. Morality is a key
issue for the history plays, and moral standing is invariably attributed
proportionately to demonstrations of patriotism. The plays demonstrate
not only the political implications of favouritism, but also its social
consequences. 'The ascent of favourites', Worden contends, is 'social
as well as political'.[21] Repeatedly the negative moral implications of
favouritism are compared with the altruistic qualities of patriotism. The
ideals of liberty and just kingship, so often undermined by the favourite,
enemy to 'true born gentry', make him or her the antithesis of the
patriot.[22]

Despite the obvious conflict between patriot rhetoric and the language of favouritism, which identifies the patriot as selfless and heroic
in contrast to the favourite who is self-interested and cowardly, in the
plays of the period the favourite is not necessarily subject to negative
representation. Although favouritism is associated with bribery, corruption and self-interest some plays do represent select historical favourites
positively. For example, in *The Tragedy of Sir Walter Raleigh*, Raleigh is
depicted as 'an English Martyr' whose presence on stage will 'Shame the
Last and Warn the Present Age'.[23] Given the negative connotations of
favouritism, how does George Sewell achieve this positive representation? Sewell overcomes his audience's notions of Raleigh, a favourite of

Elizabeth, condemned to execution for treason by her successor James I, by emphasising his hero's patriotism:

> Jealous of Virtue that was so Sublime,
> His Country Damn'd His Merit as a Crime.
> The Traytor's Doom did on the Patriot Wait:
> He Sav'd – and then He Perish'd by the State. (Prologue)

Raleigh, although a favourite, acts in the best interests of his country. He is no Machiavellian statesman or 'self-interested' over-reacher. Gerrard observes that, 'Ralegh's close friendship with Prince Henry in his final years in the Tower enabled the Patriots, capitalising on the identification between the two princes of Wales, to associate Frederick with Ralegh's dreams of imperial expansion'.[24] This somewhat obscure connection between Raleigh and Frederick Lewis does not in itself elide Raleigh's position as a minister-favourite. Indeed, despite this positive representation of Raleigh, Sewell's play does not unreservedly condone favouritism. Contrasted with Raleigh are the 'tribe of kissing Courtiers' (7). These favourites of the Spanish and English courts plot Raleigh's downfall out of jealousy for his position as royal favourite and an ambition to replace him. Sewell re-enforces Raleigh's patriotism by representing his enemies as distinctly unpatriotic. Gundamor feigns patriotism as a shield to guard himself from accusations of impropriety, 'I will at the last reluctantly submit / A private Injury to the public Good: / For that's the surest Mask for Statesmen's wrongs' (30). Not only is Gundamor unpatriotic but he is also Spanish and a favourite of the Spanish king. In terms of representation of the favourite, Gundamor is the obverse of Raleigh. As a Spaniard Gundamor is at a distinct disadvantage, he is unlikely to reach the levels of 'English' patriotism displayed by his 'national hero' rival. In Sewell's play favouritism and patriotism are not mutually exclusive terms. The favourite is not necessarily consumed by an unpatriotic self-interest. As a patriot Raleigh is a suitable favourite for his queen, his 'vertue, capacity and diligence' have been proven by past deeds. The language of patriotism and the language of favouritism are not therefore placed in automatic opposition. In *Raleigh* favouritism is condoned when bestowed upon a patriot; condemned 'where Miscreants are honour'd'. Gerrard notes that Sewell's play was instrumental in promoting Raleigh's image however, this text predates Walpole's rapid rise to power in the 1720s.[25] Walpole's image as minister-favourite and patron to political placemen is certainly inflected in the plays of the 1730s but this did not make favouritism a taboo subject for pro-Walpole drama. Instead, these later plays required their audiences to develop a more complex and sophisticated relationship with favouritism as a dramatic trope. The familiar rhetorical shorthand signified by the term 'favourite', which is both illustrated and invalidated in Sewell's *Raleigh*, took on additional, patriot resonances.

## The favourite and the sovereign

The representation of the relationship between monarch and favourite is significant for the rhetorical connections that were being forged between patriotism and favouritism. It seems reasonable to contend that the existence of a favourite who exerts political influence would necessarily reflect upon the patriotic reputation of his or her sovereign. Indeed, Eliza Haywood's *Frederick, Duke of Brunswick Lunenburg* appears to support this assertion. Haywood's *Frederick* is a patriotic 'conduct' play designed to promote Frederick Lewis, Prince of Wales as Britain's future patriot king. Her text adopts a highly moralistic tone against monarchs 'who careless sit and nod'.[26] However, Haywood's criticism of the monarch is not necessarily echoed in other plays of the period. On the contrary, in the relationship between favourite and sovereign, the monarch is rarely represented as culpable for the actions of his or her chosen minister. The sovereign who 'Rules by the will of Others' is repeatedly shielded from criticism. Even those plays most vociferously critical of the favourite are careful to protect the sovereign. The anonymous author of *The History of Mortimer* (1731) is quick to assure readers that, despite chastisements from pro-Walpole commentators to the contrary, in the condemned play *The Fall of Mortimer* (1731), 'Kingly authority is no where traduc'd'.[27] As contributions to a growing body of patriot literature, it might be thought necessary by writers, publishers, readers and theatre audiences, for these texts to curtail negative commentary on the monarch. It would be difficult for political commentary of any form to retain a sense of patriotic agenda whilst openly criticising the sovereign.

Despite their overt opposition agendas texts such as *The History of Mortimer* and *Frederick, Duke of Brunswick-Lunenburg* were firmly embedded in the myths of stability that shaped British identity during the first half of the eighteenth century. These texts resonate with nationalistic jingoism, supported by a belief in the innate patriotism of the national character. Thus, although the monarch was 'contracted' to the people, overt criticism of the Hanoverians is muted, even in opposition plays. Hence, Haywood's account of a monarch who delegates power to his favourite locates blame with the favourite rather than the king himself.

So despite overtly promoting Frederick Lewis as the 'patriot king' who will rid Britain and the Hanoverian court of minister-favourites and the corruption inextricably linked with political favouritism, Haywood's play does not dwell on the fault of the current monarch in capitulating and promoting the existing administrative system. What is important for Haywood, and her audience, is the patriotism of Frederick, not the questionable conduct of his predecessors. Other opposition texts negotiate the issue of sustaining their own patriot credentials by simply not questioning the patriotism of the monarch, which is invariably taken for granted, focusing instead on the conduct of the favourite. As a result even opposition texts appropriate political rhetoric that is reliant upon notions of national superiority, both in military and governmental terms, to bolster Britons' perceptions of themselves as the inhabitants of a uniquely stable and elite nation. Whatever the flaws of the current administration, the British system of government is represented in these texts as eminently superior to the shambolic and tyrannical administrations of Britain's European enemies; representatives of which are frequently implicated in the machinations of the favourite. In staging these plays the London theatres engage in a political dialogue encompassing theoretical as well as partisan concerns. Modes of government and ministerial conduct are two halves of an irresolvable debate in which patriot credentials could only be validated by resorting to unpatriotic means.

If Haywood's explicitly pro-Frederick and anti-Walpole stance results in a text which demonstrates zero-tolerance of favouritism, how is the representation of the relationship between sovereign and favourite influenced by the political agendas of other texts, both drama and political commentary? A short-lived battle of letters between Benjamin Hoadly, Bishop of Winchester and Bolingbroke presents us with two interpretations of the relationship between George II and Robert Walpole. In common with many of the plays under discussion, and despite the authors' diametrically opposed political affiliations, these letters demonstrate a reluctance to criticise openly the King's actions. Hoadly's pamphlet, *Observations on the Conduct of Great-Britain with Regard to the Negotiations and Other Transactions Abroad* (1729), is an example of hastily written Walpolean propaganda created with the intention of assuaging attacks by opposition commentators. An attempt to defend Walpole's policy of treaty making, the pamphlet was published between the signing of the Anglo-Spanish Peace (1728) and the Treaty of Vienna (1731).[28] Hoadly accuses opposition writers who 'endeavour to incense the nation against the Government' of a 'Dangerous and wicked abuse' of their 'Liberty'.[29] Hoadly's aim was to counter opposition claims that because of the restrictions placed upon them by the Anglo-Spanish Peace, British squadrons were forced to remain inactive and allow 'depredations committed by the Spaniards upon our Merchants in the West Indies'.[30] His pamphlet offers an examination of 'the most material parts of the Orders given to the Commanders of His Majesty's Squadron employed on the Coast of Spain',[31] which Hoadly claims vindicate the signing of the peace treaty and highlight the decisive response made by the British squadrons to subsequent Spanish hostilities. Hoadly extols the virtues of the government's policy of diplomacy by praising George II as a patriot unwilling to sacrifice the nation's peace in pursuit of personal glory:

> The highest Encomiums and Acknowledgements are due to his Majesty, whose Prudence and Fatherly Tenderness for his People have exalted him to resist the Temptations to which that Desire of Fame, inseparable from generous Minds, might have exposed him; and who, by his Endeavours for establishing a general Tranquillity, has shewn that he prefers the Glory of making his Subjects happy, to that Increase of Reputation which he might have had so fair a Prospect of gaining in the Field.[32]

Hoadly depicts George II not as an uncharismatic and passive monarch but as a patriot hero who forgoes the glory of battle, here termed a personal rather than public glory, for the sake of his people. The King, like all good patriots, is not self-serving. Hoadly's version of events places the prudence of these political treaties firmly at the feet of George II. Although Hoadly frequently refers to 'the government', no overt mention is made of Walpole. Such praise, however, is misplaced for, as most contemporary readers would have realised, it was Walpole's ardent pursuit of diplomacy and avoidance of conflict that prevented George II from leading a British army into battle – a state of affairs which continued until 1743.[33] Hoadly's overt praise of the king is therefore covert praise of Walpole's policy. This portrayal of the monarch as war-hungry but restrained is not unique to Hoadly and other writers of pro-Walpole literature. Political commentary repeatedly engages with the monarch as another element of the nation's mythology behind which the workings of government are, to some extent, concealed. Images of monarchical prudence and fatherly concern for the welfare of the nation arise from a rhetorical, semantic field which once again was being claimed by commentators from across the dominant political divides.

In his reply to the *Observations* in *The Craftsman* on Saturday 4 January 1729, Bolingbroke's criticism of Hoadly's lack of stylistic elegance foregrounds a more partisan attack on the authenticity of the Bishop's sources. Bolingbroke sees little to redeem the pamphlet; he accuses Hoadly of frequently misusing terminology and completely misunderstanding the military situation. However, he retains in his own reply a regard, albeit less reverential, for the King's conduct. In Bolingbroke's version, Walpole is charged with unpatriotic treaty-making and is represented as the self-interested minister-favourite. However, Hoadly's representation of George II as restrained by his own sense of patriotic duty is echoed in Bolingbroke's opposition response. Both writers recognise a need to depict the monarch as heroic and courageous, an intrinsic part of the mythology of British stability. Bolingbroke and Hoadly position the King, despite his distant lineage, within England's ancient monarchical heritage, whilst divesting him of the autonomous rule associated with that heritage. As in the ancient British history plays discussed in the previous chapter, these texts seek to establish a balance between the authority secured by analogising the nation's ancient heritage and the need to align that model with modern values and contemporary constitutional principals. George II becomes at once an embodiment of the heroic qualities of a war-hero such as Henry V and a modern statesman responsive to the diplomacy required of contemporary politicians. The King's patriotism is defined in accordance with the terms of the Revolution Settlement. The British monarch, no longer a claimant of divine right, retains his, or her, position in contract with the people. To expect the king to go against parliamentary policy would be in breech of the constitution. The monarch's actions, both in pro- and anti-Walpole texts, are de-politicised; he is a patriot figurehead, paternalistic but divest of the power of a true patriarch. The sovereign's role is primarily one of parliamentary support rather than political action. This de-politicisation of the British monarch transfers to the dramatic representations of the relationship between sovereign and favourite.

In Hoadly's account, Walpole's perceived immorality is displaced by the monarch's overwhelming probity. George II's 'prudence' and 'Fatherly tenderness' towards the nation, his patriotism, suggest that his favourite cannot be deemed unpatriotic. With a 'good' sovereign as his or her patron the favourite himself is necessarily a patriot. This representation of the relationship between sovereign and favourite can be seen in Sewell's *Raleigh*. Raleigh asserts in his own defence the noble reputation of his monarch. 'The good Eliza' (50–1), who smiled upon him, is contrasted with James I, who did not. Raleigh's moral worth, Sewell argues, is guaranteed by Elizabeth's own patriotism. His execution by command of James, the obverse of the Protestant patriot Queen, reinforces Raleigh's position as patriot favourite and emphasises doctrinal difference, rather than lack of moral worth, as the root cause of his downfall. In this way, religion can be seen as a significant part of the process of rewriting the trope of the favourite. As a Protestant the favourite can display patriotic qualities simply by being placed in contrast to Catholic others, thus merging the image of favourite with notions of Protestant patriotism, creating space for a positive rendering of the role of favourite.

Having established the morality of Walpole, Hoadly challenges the integrity of the opposition, 'their real View and Design, is, to foment the divisions between England and Foreign Powers, in Hopes to reap some private Advantage from the calamities into which they endeavour to plunge their country'.[34] Hoadly's rhetoric is echoed in Haywood's *Frederick, Duke of Brunswick Lunenburg*, despite the texts' divergent political agendas. Using Frederick, Duke of Lunenburg, the prince regent's political predecessor, as an exemplar of patriotic behaviour, Haywood offers Frederick Lewis a dramatic warning of the instabilities inherent in a state dependent upon political patronage.[35] Morality is a focal point in the representation of Frederick as a patriot and the contrasting representations of his predecessor's court of favourites. The play opens with the celebrations surrounding Frederick's election as Emperor. Before him, Wenceslaus lead a court of 'warring members, / Each to particular Interests attach'd'.[36] The play focuses on the attempts of Waldec and Ridolpho, envoys to the Archbishop of Mentz, to remove Frederick from power before he is crowned. Favourites of the old administration, Waldec and Ridolpho have themselves attempted to sway the election, 'Tho' half the Princes gave their Votes against him. / Like Fate his presence aw'd their best Endeavours, / And hush'd their vain Objections into Silence' (9). Their next and, eventually successful plot, is the murder of Frederick. Frederick is represented as a patriot king. He is devoid of self-interest, his past deeds and supreme merit 'secure our future Hopes, / Restores this Empire to her former Glory' (4). This laudable conduct is contrasted with Ridolpho's leadership by, 'Obligations,/On Obligations heap'd, ... he'll gladly / Embrace th' Occasion to repay past Favours, / And at the same Time make his future Fortune' (14).

Here Haywood creates an image of Frederick that draws an association between his monarchical policies and the development of empire and national economic growth. Ridolpho, in contrast, is defined, and his actions are governed, by personal interest and a desire for increasing his own rather than the nation's economic fortunes. In *Frederick* not only is the favourite unpatriotic, but any monarch who adopts favouritism as a mode of government is deemed to be failing his or her people. Haywood stops short of suggesting that the Hanoverian patronage of Walpole was unpatriotic. The power vacuum left by the death of Wenceslaus and the subsequent struggle for power by his favourites, over whom Wenceslaus had a precarious control, destabilise the Empire. However, her text comes very close to such a suggestion. Contrary to Hoadly's reading of the relationship between monarch and favourite, in *Frederick*, morality necessitates the rejection of political patronage. Favouritism is corrupt and potentially dangerous to the nation. Allowing those favoured undue, and inevitably self-interested, political sway leads to the extremes of unpatriotic conduct, immorality, murder and regicide. For Haywood, the political morality of a nation's government is dependent upon the sovereign's unequivocal rejection of favouritism.

William Havard's *King Charles the First* (1737), like Haywood's *Frederick*, is concerned with regicide as one of the consequences of, and threats posed by, favouritism to the stability of the nation. In Havard's play however the emphasis is less focused upon economic and commercial factors and more upon the irreconcilable effects of such dynastic interruption. Charles I 'by Nature virtuous, tho' misled by Slaves, / By Tools of Power, by Sycophants and knaves,' is only partially responsible for his own downfall.[37] Cromwell is ostensibly opposed to the monarch's use of favouritism, ''Tis not my favour, Bradshaw, but thy Worth / Brings thee to light; thou dost not owe me aught' (23). He publiclly criticises the King who, 'lets one Man / Ingross the Offices of Place and Pow'r, / Who with the purloin'd Money of the state / Buys Popularity' (33). However, Cromwell is represented by Havard as an employer of placemen and the audience witnesses his hypocrisy as he bribes soldiers in order to strengthen his own political position; 'let those Sums of Money I have order'd, / Be secretly dispers'd among the Soldiers; / It will remind them of their Promises: / Gold is Specifick for the Memory' (26). In private, he confesses to various abuses of power in creating favourites of his own, 'Such are the Tools with which the Wise must work / ... / He is my proper Instrument / To operate on those below my notice' (25). Harvard represents Charles as a reformed man. He is aware of his failings as a sovereign, is clearly repentant, and expresses his regret in patriotic terms, 'spare this luckless Land, / And save it from Misfortune's rugged Hand! / My ev'ry Wish is for its Joys Increase, / And my last Pray'r shall be my Peoples Peace' (35). His concern for his subjects rather than his own welfare is indicative of his patriotism. In contrast, Cromwell not only repeats Charles's past errors, but also increases them by purchasing the favour of multiple followers. Cromwell, unlike Charles, is conscious of the power he wields in his use of political patronage. Havard draws a distinction between the monarch who selects favourites and the minister who purchases followers. Royal favourites have the potential to assist the monarch in his or her patriotic duty. Conversely, the bribery and corruption associated with political placemen and the purchase of ministerial followers is devoid of justification in patriotic terms.

Havard represents Charles I as a man who understands and regrets his own failings. Does this vacillation between positive and negative representations of the role of the favourite suggest a pro-Whig reading of the play's political agenda? Despite rhetorical similarities with pro-Whig commentary, particularly in relation to rewriting the negative associations elicited by the trope of favouritism, certain events and episodes from Havard's text suggest a very different political agenda. Charles's reformation is represented as pivotal to the future of the Stuart dynasty. Before his execution the King requests an audience with his children. Charles addresses James with a message for the absent Prince of Wales:

> King: Bear him my Blessing, and this last Advice:
> ... his Promise, when once given,
> Let no Advantage break; nor any View
> Make him give up his Honesty to reach it;
> Let him maintain his pow'r but not increase it;
> The String Prerogative, when strain'd too high,
> Cracks, like the tortur'd Chord of Harmony,
> And spoils the Consort between King and Subject;
> Let him regard his People more than Minister,
> Whose Interest or Ambition may mislead him;
> These Rules observ'd may make him a good Prince,
> And happier than his Father – Wilt thou *James*
> Remember this?
> James: O doubt not, Royal Sir,
> Can what my Father says escape my Memory,
> And at a time when he shall speak no more. (58)

The implication is clear. Infected by his father's renewed patriotism, James (unlike his absent brother, the future Charles II) would 'remember' his last words, and given the opportunity, rule Britain as the rightful patriot king. Havard's play, premièred in 1737, thirty-six years after the death of James II, draws upon this image of the condemned monarch advising his sons, and extends the message beyond James's lifetime to the contemporary exiled Stuart dynasty. Havard depicts the English Civil War as a turning point in Stuart understanding of divine right, a promise of the potential glories of future Stuart rule. Charles's patronage of Buckingham, although immoral and unpatriotic, is insignificant in comparison to the levels of favouritism and preferment that, by the early eighteenth century, were seen by many to characterise Cromwell's commonwealth and subsequent British courts, 'Thus fell Charles! / A Monument of Shame to the present Age / A warning to the future' (62). Havard suggests that Charles's reign was more patriotic than the contemporary administration and that the reinstatement of the Stuart dynasty would recapture this patriotism and probity.

Havard is actively creating mythology through this play by reframing and revising contemporary interpretations of recent history. Charles I is represented as a patriot, or at least a reforming patriot, aware of his faults and responsive to his duty, he is re-defined in this way for a very particular political purpose. Havard's text is engaged in the promotion, not of the historical figure of Charles I himself, but of his modern representatives, the exiled Stuart dynasty. In this play the Stuart claim to the throne is re-enforced and deemed rightful, and the rewriting of Charles I reiterates the value of the Stuart lineage through moral qualities as well as dynastic rights. Charles's own favouritism is fragmented or reframed in order to detract from his own political faults and conventional interpretations of his self-interest. Dramatic representations of the relationship between monarch and favourite are subject to extensive qualification by patriot rhetoric. The inherent immorality of states in which the monarch delegates power to favourites is demonstrated in both *Frederick, Duke of Brunswick-Lunenburg* and *King Charles the First*. However, the political agendas of these two plays result in two very different interpretations of the relationship between monarch and favourite. Haywood focuses on the difficulty of converting an administration steeped in the corruption of patronage and favouritism. Her hero, Frederick, is clearly an enemy of favouritism and, by extension, the allegorised Prince of Wales. She appropriates the rhetoric of patriotism to stigmatise favouritism as the primary 'sin' to be avoided by the patriot king. Frederick has no favourites; his actions are patriotic and moral. His attempts to expel the self-interested ministers he inherits from his predecessor are thwarted by his naivety – something that Haywood wishes to arm Frederick Lewis against. Havard's representation of the monarch's moral position in relation to favouritism falls somewhere between the extremes demonstrated in Hoadly's *Observations* and Haywood's *Frederick*. In Havard's play monarchical favouritism is neither roundly condemned nor condoned. Here Charles's favouritism is excused, although not vindicated, on two counts. First, he only has one favourite. Second, he is seen to learn from his mistakes and reform his unpatriotic behaviour, using his paternal influence to guard future Stuart monarchs against the dangers of favouritism. Charles is represented as culpable for his actions, but in realising his errors and reforming, he validates the credentials of the Stuart dynasty as a patriotic alternative to the favouritism and corruption of the contemporary Whig/Hanoverian alliance. The connections between Havard's representation of Cromwell as a scheming minister, shoring-up his position and power with placemen and purchased followers, and contemporary criticisms of Walpole suggest that, like in Haywood's play, the presence of a minister-favourite points to inevitable doom.

Even after the resignation of Walpole in 1742, texts continued to attempt to represent the relationship between sovereign and favourite in a way which deflected criticism from the monarch. In Tobias Smollett's *The Regicide: or, James the First of Scotland* (1749), James's choice of the unpatriotic and rebellious Athol as his favourite is excused simply because the two men are related:

> I should have found in Athol
> A trusty Counsellor and steady Friend:
> And better would it suit thy rev'rend Age,
> Thy Station, quality, and kindred Blood,
> To hush ill-judging Clamour and cement
> Divided Factions to my Throne, again,
> Than thus embroil the state.[38]

James acted on Athol's 'false professions' (2), not out of gullibility or weakness but due to a belief in honour between kinsmen and an assumption that Athol's age, station and quality would dictate his actions. James's own patriotic code, abused by the machinations of a 'miscreant', led to misplaced trust and the king's untimely death.

Whatever the political agenda of the individual text, patriotism is key to the representation of favouritism. Patriot rhetoric is used to justify the relationship between favourite and sovereign. The sovereign's patriotism defends him or her from accusations of impropriety, or acts as protection against the formation of inappropriate relationships. That the sovereign who condones favouritism can be justified in his or her actions suggests that a carefully chosen favourite such as Raleigh can be of benefit to the nation. Even stridently oppositional texts such as *The Norfolk Sting* identify the possibility of such benefit, "'tis evident Favourites may be the Cause of as much Good as Evil in a Government; and are therefore not hurtful themselves'.[39] Examples of these 'good' favourites in the plays premièred during Walpole's term in office would seem to suggest support for Walpole and his policies, however, as an integral part of the nation's mythology 'the favourite' is a malleable term, deployed both as an object of abuse or criticism but also figured as an object of potential value to the monarch, and thus, the nation, not necessarily associated with a particular partisan agenda. In terms of national identity, the way in which individual favourites are interpreted depends less upon their actual actions and more upon their value in terms of sustaining and supporting national mythologies relating to the superiority of Britain. This comes primarily from the monarch themselves, because the existence of a 'bad' favourite suggests a reflection in the calibre of the monarch. But during the early eighteenth century the direct nature of this relationship is being reassigned and re-written in response to the inflection of the Revolution Settlement and the changing nature of the relationship between monarch and state. By making the monarch answerable (at least in conceptual terms) to the people, the choice of ministers, and hence the placing of potential favourites, becomes more dependent upon the quality of the British people and their chosen representatives than the monarch him or herself.

## Representations of Walpole in *The Fall of Mortimer* (1731) and *The Fall of the Earl of Essex* (1731)

Existing critical accounts of the 1731 versions of *The Fall of Mortimer* and *The Fall of the Earl of Essex* have led to a broad consensus among commentators such as Loftis, Goldgar and Bertelsen for the political contexts of these plays. Scholars suggest that the close premières of *The Fall of Mortimer* and *The Fall of the Earl of Essex* in 1731 were due to a shared political agenda. The themes of a sovereign misled, favouritism bestowed by a queen, the corruption of justice and the policy of treaty-making have all been identified as reflections on Walpole's ascendancy and his purported corruption in office.[40] However, despite the close parallels in terms of the allegorical subjects shared by these plays they respond to the political discourse of the early 1730s in very disparate ways.

Roger de Mortimer (1287–1330) and Robert Devereux, Earl of Essex (1566–1601) were political figures whose histories had been appropriated for dramatic representation many times prior to the 1731 versions.[41] Ralph's *Essex* is an adaptation of John Banks's *The Unhappy Favourite; or, The Earl of Essex* (1693), a play that was revived and adapted sporadically during the early eighteenth century.[42] The dramatic lineage of the 1731 version of *Mortimer* is less certain. Lance Bertelsen suggests a number of sources, including Ben Jonson's *Mortimer His Fall*, a fragment published posthumously in 1640 that, Bertelsen asserts, was used several times as anti-ministerial propaganda during the eighteenth century. *King Edward the Third* (1691) – attributed to, among others, William Mountfort and John Bancroft – is, Bertelsen contends, the most significant source.[43] The eponymous 'heroes' of these plays offer contrasting versions of minister-favourites. In accordance with the definitions of favourites proposed by Thompson and Worden, Mortimer is repeatedly represented as a Machiavellian statesman. Both historically and dramatically he is characterised as a ruthless, self-interested, minister-favourite. In Ralph's *The Fall of the Earl of Essex*, Essex is conspicuously not a self-interested favourite. His actions are neither intended to, and nor do they, result in monetary gain or even an increase in his standing at court. Essex may be defined as an over-reacher, but in Ralph's version Essex's representation does not demonstrate any of the negative qualities associated with this category of favourite. Although in acting against the Queen's orders, Essex exceeds his position, his action, far from resulting in self-advancement, is disastrous to his own preferment. The negotiation of a truce with Ireland is represented as Essex's duty and in the best interests of his country rather than pandering to the vanity of his Queen in order to advance his own career. Modern historical accounts of Essex continue to define him as a patriot whose aim to use his position as the Queen's favourite for the benefit of his country ultimately lead to his downfall:

> For Essex, royal favour was not an end in itself but merely a means to the greater goal of securing delegated authority from the queen, especially in matters of war and foreign policy. Ultimately, he believed that he must pursue certain policies for the benefit of the realm, regardless of whether the queen herself was actually prepared to endorse them.[44]

The 1731 representation of Mortimer closely adheres to both Thompson's and Worden's models for categorising the favourite. Mortimer is an enemy to the state and all true patriots should welcome his downfall. The 1731 representation of Essex, however, does not demonstrate the key characteristics of either Worden's literary favourites or Thompson's historical favourites. He is diametrically opposed to the Machiavellian Mortimer and does not demonstrate the true characteristics of an over-reacher. In the 1731 version, Essex becomes merely a titular favourite. Omitting any further reference to conduct associated with favouritism, Ralph relies on his audience's knowledge that Essex was indeed one of Elizabeth's many favourites to carry his political agenda.

Ralph's play, I contend, was not concerned with the deserved fall of an evil favourite but the unjust fall of a patriotic minister.

*The Fall of Mortimer* was performed sixteen times after its première at the Haymarket on 12 May 1731. During the sixteenth show, the performance was halted and the production was shut-down. The players were arrested for their part in what was widely reported as a flagrant attack on Walpole's government and his policies.[45] This response came at a time during which the government became particularly sensitive to slanderous attacks from the theatre, and audiences were alert to the potential for salacious political comment. The existing but sporadically enforced restrictions on contentious political drama were revived after the political uproar caused by John Gay's notorious *Beggar's Opera* (1728) and the subsequently banned *Polly* (1729). Although as Robert D. Hume has shown, prior to the imposition of the Stage Licensing Act of 1737 these restrictions had been applied somewhat arbitrarily, the obvious topicality of *The Fall of Mortimer* demanded comparatively decisive action from the authorities.[46] Critics have suggested that the suppression of *The Fall of Mortimer* was due largely to allusions to political events of 1731 and the years preceding. Opinion is divided as to the exact events alluded to; Worden argues that Walpole's use of placemen and mercenary parliaments was the chief target, whereas Bertelsen identifies Walpole's treaty-making as the key object of attack. There is textual evidence to demonstrate that both of these critically maligned aspects of Walpole's administration are criticised in the play.

Premièred three months earlier on 1 February 1731, Ralph's *The Fall of the Earl of Essex* did not receive the same public attention. One reason for this apparent inattention to the play may be, as Worden claims, the slight nature of Ralph's adaptation:

> A series of subtle touches conspires to adapt Banks's version to the political vocabulary of the 1730s and to hint at the resemblances between Walpole and Essex's rival in the play, Lord Burghley.[47]

But there is a problem with this assertion, demonstrated by the disparate audience and critical responses elicited by these two plays. If *The Fall of the Earl of Essex* was indeed an attack on Walpole and his administration, why was it seemingly ignored? Worden's suggestion that the parallels drawn between Walpole and Burleigh are very subtle would perhaps provide an adequate answer to this question; read as anti-Walpole comment this play is sleight in its attacks and allegorical references are rather opaque. However, this interpretation is far from convincing both in relation to the text itself and current critical analysis of drama during this period. If, as Hume argues, the production of politically subversive plays was considerably reduced post-1731, why did *The Fall of the Earl of Essex*, supposedly one of the last of such plays permitted performance, receive no critical or political commentary?[48] Hume asserts that 'the London theatre of the early 1730s was hardly a hotbed of partisan political activity', a contention which this book goes some way towards challenging.[49] It is true however, particularly in comparison to the theatrical activity of the preceding decades, that the 1730s was not a period of intense dramatic commentary on political affairs. Given this general trend away from the production of plays overtly critical of the Walpole administration, the lack of commentary on Ralph's *Essex* might seem to confirm Worden's suggestion that the play simply did not pose a threat. I wish to suggest an alternative. Was the failure of government supporters to attack *The Fall of the Earl of Essex* less as a result of the play's covert criticism and more due to the fact that, particularly in contrast to *The Fall of Mortimer*, Ralph's play is in fact pro-Walpole and pro the Whig administration?

Ralph's *Essex* depicts a favourite whose loyalty towards his monarch and country is unquestionable. The play does not adopt the language of favouritism as an attack on the patriotism of Essex or the political integrity of the monarch. Accused of treason, the Earl of Essex is unjustly executed, in part due to the jealousy of a woman scorned. The monarch, Elizabeth, realises her error in abandoning her favourite and Essex is eventually buried with honour. The treasonable act for which Essex is imprisoned is the negotiation of a truce with Ireland. Significantly it is the Commons, not Elizabeth, who demand his impeachment. Reflecting the signing of the treaties of Vienna and Seville, and Walpole's foreign policy of diplomacy and compromise, Essex 'the favourite' is culpable for unpopular political decisions and, based on his position as royal favourite, is attacked by his political opponents. Ralph represents Essex's treaty-making as a patriotic act. The treaty remains in force throughout the play and there is no indication of any negative outcome. Essex is portrayed as a shrewd commander and a true patriot, a worthy favourite. He is a loving husband who refuses the corrupt advances of the lascivious Lady Nottingham, and is equally resistant, despite the negative consequences of his rejection of her in terms of his own position at court, to the sexual advances of his Queen. It is through this relationship with Elizabeth that Ralph draws a further parallel between Essex and Walpole. Like Essex, Walpole enjoyed the favour of the Queen Caroline of Ansbach, consort of George II. Caroline supported Walpole's ambitions by promoting him to her husband, encouraging the King to engage his ministerial services. Furthermore, suggestions regarding the purportedly sexual nature of the relationship between Caroline and Walpole were widely circulated.[50] The powerful treaty-making Essex – minister-favourite of the Queen – is a more appropriate analogy for Walpole, than, as Worden suggests, the uncharismatic and ineffectual Burleigh.

In contrast, *The Fall of Mortimer* depicts Mortimer as a favourite who 'lord[s] it o'er us by the Queen's vile Favour'.[51] Isabella, the King's mother, is an unpatriotic figure. Mortimer is both her favourite and her lover, which places a double emphasis on her corrupt character. Women's sexual conduct is reflective of their patriotism, or lack of patriotism, and, unsurprisingly, sexual and political moralities were inextricably connected in the rhetoric of early eighteenth-century patriot drama. This suggests an important difference between *The Fall of the Earl of Essex* and *The Fall of Mortimer*. Unlike the unswerving fidelity demonstrated by Ralph's Essex, Mortimer's sexual appetite is scarcely satiable. Isabella and Mortimer are clearly engaged in a sexual relationship, but despite this Mortimer pursues the innocent Maria: 'I want, like the Heathen Monarchs, my Seraglio to refresh me after the business of the day' (23). In *The Fall of Mortimer* sex signifies power, corrupt and unpatriotic power, which is linked directly to the favourite. The 'patriot band', intent upon securing their monarch from Isabella's and Mortimer's combined influence, win the King's trust by their use of patriot rhetoric and make no attempt to gain, or exert, sexual power. Unlike Mortimer, they do not deal with Isabella, who, as guardian over her son in his minority, is the true site of power. In this play, patriotism is strictly confined to homosocial relationships; the presence of a woman as an active participant in politics merely emphasises the unnaturalness and lack of patriotism of the current administration. Here an idealised, gendered, relationship is set-up between monarch and subject which both draws upon and re-entrenches the myths of stability that dominate these texts.

In *The Fall of the Earl of Essex* attempts to exert sexual power remain unsatisfied. Lady Nottingham and Lord Burleigh are banished and the patriotic Essex does not succumb to Nottingham's enticements. The use of sexual power by the favourite produces two very different portrayals of favouritism in these texts. Both plays represent patterns of libidinous behaviour as unpatriotic. What is significant is the opposing position of the favourite in this paradigm. Mortimer exerts power through sex, whereas Essex rejects sexual advances, even from his sovereign patron. That these two plays offer very different representations of favouritism strengthens the possibility that they should not both be seen as direct attacks on Walpole.

In Ralph's *The Fall of the Earl of Essex*, it is clear that the audience should sympathise with Essex. However, this does not suggest that Elizabeth is represented as the antithesis of his patriotism. Given the prevalent attitude of nostalgia towards Elizabeth in the eighteenth century and her position as cornerstone to the national, Protestant mythology, it would have been imprudent, despite her role in the execution of Essex, to characterise Elizabeth negatively. Particularly amongst Protestant Britons it was impossible to incite resentment towards the Queen. In terms of her political value, Gerrard asserts that although the 'Elizabethan cult of the 1730s' was in part a response to popular pressure for war with Spain, both opposition and pro-government Whigs could appropriate Elizabeth.[52] England's Protestant queen was a valuable political and cultural icon, certainly not an image to challenge or attempt to rewrite. If it is accepted therefore that Essex can be interpreted as a positive analogy for Walpole, we have two possible versions for our reading of Elizabeth's role. Should we identify Elizabeth with George II – a cultural-political analogy – or with Caroline of Ansbach – a sexual–political analogy? Ralph struggles with this triangular correlation and the result is somewhat bland. He resorts to using Elizabeth's jealousy on discovering Essex's secret marriage to justify her anger and decision to execute him, an amalgamation of Essex's own history and that of the more infamous Raleigh. Michael Dobson and Nicola Watson have noted that this 'enduringly popular historical fiction ... carves out a secret susceptibly feminine Elizabeth from unpromising historical materials'.[53] Elizabeth, as an iconic figure signifying Britishness, holds an important place in the nation's mythology and it is this rendering of her image that undermines Ralph's re-appropriation of Essex's role, styled as a patriot favourite. This recourse to sentimentalising Elizabeth, is far from convincing in Ralph's allegorically confused version of the Essex history. Sewell's earlier representation of Raleigh resolves the problem of addressing Elizabeth's weaknesses much more effectively by placing Elizabeth on her deathbed. In Sewell's play, the Queen never appears on stage and both Raleigh's followers and his enemies report her physical weakness as the reason for her seeming lack of support for her favourite, an admission of the queen's fallibility, but one justified by the universality of human frailty.

A similar problem in the representation of the relationship between sovereign and favourite can be identified in *The Fall of Mortimer*. Here the monarch is the young Edward III whose determination and patriotism could be seen as a laudatory parallel with George II. Mortimer is not the king's own chosen favourite. His position in court is secured by Isabella's recommendation to her son. By the opening scene of Act II, Edward is beginning to realise the true intent of this seemingly allied pair.[54] He has a dream in which 'Mortimer led in my wicked Mother, / Who snatched the Crown from me, and gave it him' (14). The dream alerts Edward to Mortimer's true intention and the king is quick to remove favour from the minister. It is surely no coincidence that king, subject, and indeed audience, reach this conclusion concurrently. The fact that Mortimer is not the king's favourite, but the choice of an unnatural woman simply reiterates Edward's innocence. The resultant analogy between Queen Isabella on stage and Queen Caroline of the Hanoverian court alludes to contemporary court gossip regarding the inappropriate relationship between Walpole and George II's consort rather than the specific political events intimated by the Mortimer/Walpole analogy. Isabella's actions, particularly her open sexual relationship with Mortimer, do not accurately replicate Caroline of Ansbach's conduct. However, just as Caroline was censured for favouring Walpole and promoting his policies to her husband, Isabella bears the brunt of criticism for Mortimer's elevated position and ultimately Edward banishes his mother for her conduct, thus proving his own political, if not his familial, integrity.

As I have already suggested, the influence of a favourite on political affairs leads to a questioning of the patriotic reputation of the monarch. However, as with many of the texts discussed in this chapter, the *Mortimer* and *Essex* plays restrict censure of the sovereign. George II is not criticised by the representations of 'Walpole the favourite'. The 1731 versions of *Mortimer* and *Essex* negotiate the favourite/monarch relationship in three distinct ways. First, by exploiting the language associated with favouritism, both plays depict royal women whose susceptibility to the charms of the favourite, although not a vindication of that conduct, justifies submission to the 'will of others'. Second, in both plays the favourite is keenly aware that loss of his Queen's protection would lead, inevitably, to his own demise, 'While *she* protects, I cannot fail'.[55] In addition, the sovereign is distanced from the favourite in order to detract from his or her own culpability. Ralph's play depicts a female monarch, thus avoiding a direct analogy with George II, and in *Mortimer* the king is only a boy. Finally, the relationship between monarch and favourite is defended in Ralph's play by the representation of Essex as a patriotic favourite. Essex's patriotism outweighs his role as minister-favourite and justifies his position and the integrity of his monarch. The political agendas promoted by these texts are not only defined by the way in which they represent the sovereign/favourite relationship. In *Essex* and *Mortimer* a range of socio-political issues are debated in relation to favouritism. The relationship between government and church, bribery and treaty-making, are contemporary opposition concerns. How does the position of the favourite in relation to these themes affect representations of favouritism and contemporary politics in these plays?

In *The Fall of Mortimer* the role of religion is given particular attention. Religious policy divided the Whigs in the 1730s. The High-Church Bishop of London, Edmund Gibson, acted as Walpole's ecclesiastical advisor between 1723 and 1736. Gibson made his political objective the bolstering of the 'alliance between Church and State'.[56] Walpole and Gibson shared an understanding of the importance of securing party placemen to ensure the stability of their political position. As J. C. D. Clark has suggested, the coalition between the Whig political establishment and the bishops was a 'formidable combination'.[57] This burgeoning alliance was strengthened by the exclusion of clerics not willing to compromise their political beliefs. Such practices are openly criticised in *The Fall of Mortimer*. Like Walpole, Mortimer, the minister-favourite, in turn purchases his own followers. His patronage extends through all ranks of society, 'Not the sacred Gown, nor learned Robe, / Are unpolluted with his Servile Arts' (4). Directly mirroring Walpole's religious policy, in order to preserve and strengthen his position of power Mortimer bribes clerics, advancing those who accept his patronage. Echoing the opinions of Tories and opposition Whigs, Mountacute and his band of patriots condemn the interference of priests in political matters, 'thus luxury and Interest rule the Church' (4). The 'smooth-toung'd Prelates' (4) who succumb to Mortimer's bribery offer preferment to those priests who will promise allegiance to Mortimer and work towards securing a parliament of placemen. This episode is an overt reference to Gibson's activities, and opposition anxieties regarding a Church that was becoming increasingly embroiled in politics.

The purchasing of followers and bribery are themes common to both plays. *The Fall of the Earl of Essex* opens with Lady Nottingham's vow to exact revenge for Essex's rejection of her sexual advances. She bribes Lord Burleigh to assist her, promising him sexual gratification once her desire for reprisal is satisfied. Nottingham is a flagrantly libidinous woman who utilises her sexuality for financial and political gain. Any sense of natural femininity is distorted by Ralph, who depicts Nottingham's sexual urges as at least as powerful and dominant as her economic self-interest, certainly she has no desire to protect, preserve and nurture her country, she is a thoroughly unpatriotic woman.

Mortimer is repeatedly shown either accepting bribes or purchasing followers and, in the instance of Maria, even mistresses. Bribery is clear evidence of the prioritising of private interest over public welfare. The prominence of bribery and political placemen as the tools of the favourite clearly establishes Mortimer as unpatriotic. The rhetoric of patriotism makes clear the need to eradicate financial enticement from contemporary politics. For Parliament to consist of carefully selected members who will pose no challenge to the favourite's power is clearly unpatriotic and un-constitutional. According to the opposition, Walpole constructed just such a parliament. Conversely, Essex openly rejects these tools. Unlike Mortimer, his aim is not self-advancement but the prosperity of the nation. Such a minister, argued his supporters, can be seen in Walpole.[58]

Perhaps the most contentious political theme in these plays is that of treaty-making. *The Fall of Mortimer* is unreservedly anti-treaty. In order to secure peace with Scotland, Mortimer arranged the marriage of Princess Joan to Robert of Scotland. This marriage forms the basis for the tavern gossip that introduces the sub-plot at the beginning of Act I Scene ii. Initially, as Oldstile, Felt and Frame discuss these political events, opinion of Mortimer is divided. However, when Bumper reveals that Mortimer and Isabella have promised to supplement Joan's dowry ten times over, opinion turns against him. The 'Shameful Peace' of 1328 did indeed turn the country against Mortimer and awaken the people to the plight of their King. When the patriot soldier Bumper encourages the men to join Mountacute if the need should arise, they respond in the affirmative, claiming 'they are honest Men – they have the true *English* Spirit about them – Mortimer's Crew are of the Mongril Breed' (12). This drunken and bawdy scene is largely comic in its effect, but the anger and sense of betrayal felt by these men align the play not only with its historical period but also with the contemporary political situation. Walpole's policy of peaceful trade with Spain and France, intended to release Britain from costly European wars, was viewed by Tories and opposition Whigs as a threat to British liberty – a dishonourable, unpatriotic bargain. In *The Fall of Mortimer*, treaty-making amounts to bribery. Just as Mortimer is seen to use the public purse to purchase followers, he exploits the same funds to buy-off political aggressors, those who pose a threat to the nation's stability and, hence, his own private purse. Walpole, chief proponent of diplomacy, is accused of the same unpatriotic bargaining. His actions squander public and private money by allowing French and Spanish warships to take liberties with British merchants transporting goods from the colonies.

In *The Fall of the Earl of Essex* an apparently oppositional agenda is promoted in the relationship between treaty-making and treason. By negotiating peace with Ireland, Essex commits treason – ostensibly the offence for which he is executed. This seems at variance with my reading of the play as pro-Walpole drama. However, throughout the text, Elizabeth expresses her desire to acquit Essex. She recognises that his actions are in the best interests of the country. It is not until she learns of Essex's secret marriage that her passion and anger induce her to sign a warrant for his execution. In appealing for mercy, the Countess of Essex reminds Elizabeth of her own patriotic duty:

> 'Tis Great,
> 'Tis Godlike to forgive, but *Essex* sure
> Was never Guilty, never could offend
> So kind, so good a Queen; 'tis Malice all,
> 'Tis Calumny that taints his manly Deeds,
> And labours to subvert his Fame. (33)

The Countess's use of patriot rhetoric is successful; however, the reprieve comes too late. The Queen's responses are key to understanding the political agenda of the play. At no time should the audience consider Elizabeth's motives to be anything but patriotic. She is not portrayed as a weak monarch. Unlike the youthful Edward of *The Fall of Mortimer* or the misguided Charles or James of Havard's and Smollett's respective plays, Ralph's Elizabeth lacks even the 'pliability' commonly seen as the monarch's failing in relation to his or her choice of favourite. Her error in ordering the execution of Essex arises from her jealousy and is driven by the envy of the unmistakably unpatriotic Nottingham and Burleigh. Therefore, although Elizabeth is initially angered by Essex's treaty with Ireland, she subsequently endorses his actions as patriotic and not treasonable. Essex's death is portrayed as a great loss for both his monarch-patron and his country.

*The Fall of Mortimer* positions Walpole and his policies as unpatriotic. His deployment of parliamentary placemen, his use of bribery, even his purported sexual conduct are contrary to the best interests of the nation. Like Mortimer, Walpole should be overthrown by a 'band of patriots' for the well-being of the state. In *The Fall of the Earl of Essex* the rhetorical link between patriotism and favouritism shifts. The tropes are not connected by their opposing values, but by the representation of patriotic favouritism. Ralph employs the Essex history to parallel Walpole's career in order to create political panegyric.[59] The bribery and corruption practised by Nottingham and Burleigh are punished as are the more serious machinations of Mortimer and Isabella. Essex, however, does not participate in such un-patriotic activities. Essex falls not because of his own ambition but because of the malicious behaviour of those jealous of his position. In Ralph's play favouritism does not imply corruption.

Royal patronage of carefully selected favourites *can* therefore be in the best interests of the country. If Ralph's representation of Essex is read as an analogy for Walpole, the ensuing image of 'Walpole the favourite' becomes very favourable indeed. Walpole is aligned with an historical figure who, although not faultless (it should be remembered that in brokering the peace deal, Essex disobeys the Queen's orders), acts in the best interests of his country. Ralph repudiates accusations of bribery and corruption levied against Walpole by representing him as a stalwart patriot, an idealised favourite. Walpole should not be judged on the basis of malicious accusation – the nation should not repeat past mistakes and 'execute' another patriot minister. In denying himself the military glory associated with successful battle (the conventionally patriotic method of safeguarding English liberty) Essex prioritises England's economic prosperity.

Ralph's play mirrors Whig concerns for maintaining the commercial supremacy of Britain as opposed to the nation's military pre-eminence. By paralleling Walpole with Essex, Ralph depicts a patriotic minister subscribing to the Protestant ethic of placing the common good, in the form of the promotion of trade, above personal profit.[60] His patriotism is overtly commercial but nonetheless his actions *are* beneficial to the nation. Ralph's play, it seems, defends Walpole by manipulating the very rhetoric so often used against the minister. Ralph, like Havard and Sewell, is faced with the task of rewriting the mythologies surrounding his chosen favourite in order to convincingly declaim the patriotic value of these historical models for modern ministers. By rewriting the mythology of historical favourites, opposition representations of Walpole as minister-favourite can be rewritten to promote him as a patriot favourite, whose policies and actions are not driven by self-interest.[61] Walpole becomes a modern example of the commendable favourite whose very existence is repeatedly hinted at in the excuses made for sovereigns whose choice of favourite is not as prudent as the Hanoverians' favour of Walpole. The fluidity of these histories in terms of their relevance for partisan propaganda and commentary is never clearer than in dramatic representations of the relationship between monarch and favourite. Both figures are steeped in their own mythologies and it is these myths, rather than their histories, that must be rewritten and adapted in order to appropriate these icons for the purposes of multivalent political agendas.

## The fall of the favourite

In all of these history plays the conventional rhetorical link between favouritism and unpatriotic corruption is paramount. However, by manipulating patriot rhetoric, some texts offer an alternative version of the favourite. Whereas opposition texts represent the favourite exploiting his position for corrupt motives, Ralph's *Essex* shows the favourite rejecting the conventional role of ambitious minister. In these plays the representation of favouritism is influenced by the depiction of the favourite as either a patriot or a self-interested minister. If these alternative versions of favouritism relate directly to the political agenda of the text, why are the plays always concerned with 'the fall' of the favourite? Bertelsen's assertion that, 'Because negative political allusion sold papers (and theatre tickets) authors interested in turning a profit tended to attack rather than defend those in power' could be seen as one reason for the 'pleasure' historians demonstrate in retelling 'the Fall of Favourites'.[62] Does the term 'fall' suggest to prospective audiences that the play has scandalous potential? Is the use of 'fall' in the title of a play merely a marketing strategy?

Ralph's *The Fall of the Earl of Essex* certainly did not earn the same sordid and subversive reputation as *The Fall of Mortimer*. The notoriety gained by *The Fall of Mortimer* must in part be attributed to the public closure of the play and arrest of the players. Ralph's *Essex*, party to no such scandal, received little attention. The persistent focus on the 'fall' of the favourite is simply related to the lack of examples of successful favourites. In terms of English history, favourites have consistently 'fallen' either as a result of their own ambitious over-reaching, or due to the intervention of those jealous of their position. However, just as Essex's position is jeopardised by false accusations of self-interest prompted by his position as loyal favourite, Ralph's representation of Walpole as a patriotic favourite is destabilised by the incongruities of this manipulation of language. Working against the established rhetoric to create positive representations of favourites that would counter the opposition's appropriation of such language to defame Walpole was somewhat beyond Ralph's skills as a playwright.[63] Favouritism was too deeply associated with unpatriotic behaviour to permit either a convincing or a lasting representation of Walpole as a patriot favourite.

Despite Ralph's representation of Essex as a patriot favourite, Havard's representation of Charles I as a patriotic reformer and Sewell's representation of Raleigh as a patriot worthy of being favoured by his Queen, all of these plays continue to appropriate and represent the negative connotations of favouritism. The rise and fall of favourites cannot be rhetorically distanced from corruption, bribery and threats to national liberty. In contrast to Clark's observation that 'England's constitution was praised by comparison with other monarchies; was admirable because it was a *libertarian* monarchy', these texts share a concern for the perceived decline in England's 'ancient liberties' and the lack of value attributed to liberty by its supposed custodians, itself the cornerstone of national identity and the key to the eighteenth-century theatre's representation of the nation to itself.[64] In all of the plays discussed in this chapter the relationship between monarch and favourite is justified or condemned on the basis of patriotic rhetoric. These appropriations of English history reflect contemporary anxieties regarding the need to assert Britain's moral, political and military superiority. Although many of the texts attempt to support audience perceptions of the innate stability of Britain and the British government, fears for the permanence of the political system (particularly given the active role played by Walpole in securing and promoting the myth) are evident. In order to protect British supremacy, politicians should be patriots. The welfare of their country must be their primary concern, not their own political advancement, a somewhat idealistic ambition given the much maligned system of preferment that dominated eighteenth-century political circles. Resentment and revenge are corrupting influences that disrupt the patriotic code and threaten the liberties of all Britons. Favouritism, repeatedly responsible for breeding such discontent, works against public happiness and, ultimately, national stability. The representation of Walpole as a patriotic minister-favourite was never going to be a truly successful piece of party propaganda.

# 3
# Shakespeare, the National Scaffold

Foreign Foes could never make us bow
While to our selves w'are true, The World must own,
England can never be, but by her Self, Undone.

Theophilus Cibber, *King Henry VI* (1724)

Adaptations of Shakespeare can arguably be regarded as reconstructions of the plays suited to the contemporary stage. In her account of Restoration adaptations of Shakespeare, Jean Marsden argues that the original texts are altered to focus on themes of love, family and marriage, all subjects befitting the presence of women on stage.[1] But is this notion of the domestication of Shakespeare representative of later adaptations, particularly in relation to the rewriting of Shakespeare's history plays? Given Anne K. Mellor's suggestion that eighteenth-century theatre audience were perceived as masculine in opposition to the theatre itself, 'culturally gendered as "feminine", as both the object of the male spectacular gaze and the arena of vulgar spectacle or display', is there space for women in the adaptations to occupy anything but the role of object to the male subject?[2] It is clear from accounts of women's presence, both as writers and performers, in the London theatres of the eighteenth century that they continued to be key theatrical commodities. But again this suggests limited scope for women's roles to move beyond contemporary obsession with the effect of women's physical presence upon audiences. There is, in fact, a more complex dichotomy in which dramatic texts capitalise upon the potential for women's roles to have political resonance. This does not negate arguments relating to the actress as an objectified, or vilified, commodity but instead analyses the way in which eighteenth-century dramatists, managers and actresses utilised the sexual resonances associated with public display of the female body for the purposes of promoting partisan policies. Women in the adaptations of Shakespeare's history plays are given roles which conflate the domestic and the political, opening up the possibility for the representation of a feminine rendering of national identity, a gendered interpretation of Britishness.

This chapter examines adaptations of Shakespeare's history plays which premièred during the period which encompassed Walpole's rise to, and fall from, power between 1719 and 1745. Adaptations of Shakespeare were a staple of the eighteenth-century repertoire – the volume of plays adapted, even when limited to the comparatively less popular history plays, is striking. It is alongside this sense of the evident commercial value of Shakespeare and the significance of Shakespearean adaptation to the London stage that I wish to demonstrate the political value of the female body. In conjunction with Shakespeare's rise to the status of 'national poet' British actresses are given roles in which they validate contemporary political discourse relating to notions of nationhood. These 'Shakespearean heroines' are written into the nation's histories and become contributors to the myths of stability and superiority which dominated contemporary images of Britain.

Adaptations, particularly adaptations of history plays, are often read as direct respondents to specific political events.[3] In this sense, the process of adaptation is not simply confined to the updating of plays to suit the sensibilities and taste of the modern audience, but rather, it requires engagement with an imagined audience's communal political anxiety. Adaptations of Shakespeare during the late seventeenth and early eighteenth centuries can be seen as respondents to concerns relating to the volatility of contemporary politics, stemming from the expulsion and continued exile of the Stuart dynasty. In his analysis of eighteenth-century adaptations of Shakespeare, John Loftis asserts that, as all such plays depict faction and uprising, there is a clear relationship between the adaptation of Shakespeare and fears regarding Jacobite rebellion.[4] The implication here, that *all* adaptations of Shakespeare are anti-Jacobite, by association anti-Tory and can therefore be read as a form of government propaganda, is overly restrictive. What Loftis overlooks in this politically homogenous account of the adaptations is the potential for Shakespeare's plays to have cross-party appeal. Indeed, Michael Dobson has located the canonisation of Shakespeare during the eighteenth century as derived, in part, from the 'bewildering multiplicity of contingent appropriations' that took place during this early part of the century.[5] This 'multiplicity' is just that, a diverse appropriation of

Shakespeare for varied political purposes, resulting from contemporary anxiety over political discord, but not restricted to only those with an anti-Jacobite agenda. The dramatisation of tangible threats to the myths of national stability, in the form of real Jacobite incursions, is only one reason for the appropriation of Shakespearean history plays. In terms of both the repertoire of the London stage and the public conscious-ness, Shakespeare, as a 'product' with widespread appeal, became firmly embedded in the nation's self-image. Associated with the unique qual-ities of Britishness, his texts could just as successfully be adapted for the modern stage in the form of pro-Jacobite mythology relating to the veracity and strength of the threat posed by the Stuarts and their follow-ers. Thus the adaptations of Shakespeare serve to illustrate not the limits of a specific partisan concern but rather the density of political appro-priations of the myth of stability, itself a vital part of political rhetoric irrespective of political allegiance. Shakespeare, as a nascent icon for Britishness, was ideally placed for appropriation in order to propagate such myths. His image exuded stability and the notion that his texts were national artefacts with universal resonance could be manipulated to suit any political perspective.

Between 1719 and 1745, ten adaptations of Shakespeare's English his-tories and Roman plays were premièred on the London stage. Of these, two anonymous plays, *The History of King Henry the VIII and Anna Bullen* (1732) and *The History of King John* (1736) were performed but not pub-lished. The remaining eight plays were all published in the years in which they premièred: John Dennis, *The Invader of His Country* (1719) adapted from *Coriolanus*; Charles Molloy, *The Half Pay Officers* (1720) adapted from *Henry V* and *Twelfth Night*; Lewis Theobald, *The Tragedy of King Richard II* (1720) adapted from *Richard II*; *The Sequel to King Henry the Fourth* (attributed to Thomas Betterton)[6] adapted from *2Henry IV*; Aaron Hill, *King Henry the Fifth; or, The Conquest of France by the English* (1723) adapted from *Henry V*; Ambrose Philips, *Humfrey Duke of Gloucester; a Tragedy* (1723) adapted from *2Henry VI*; Theophilus Cibber, *The Historical Tragedy of King Henry VI* (1724) adapted from *2&3Henry VI*; and Colley Cibber, *Papal Tyranny in the Reign of King John* (1745) adapted from *King John*.[7] These adaptations document a multiplicity of political concerns, including but not limited to the perceived Jacobite threat. In addition, through the introduction of new female characters and by expanding existing female roles, the scope for action focused on women in the adaptations is increased. This development is not, as feminist critics have suggested, restricted to domestic affairs. In fact, domestic and political agendas frequently converge in these plays and the symbiotic nature of the relationship between domestic and public spheres repeatedly underpins women's roles in these texts.

In common with the plays discussed in previous chapters, all of the adaptations rely upon patriot rhetoric to establish nationalist credentials. They are, as Alexander Pettit has suggested, 'participants in a noisy debate about liberty, populism, kingship and the succession'.[8] As we have seen in the preceding chapter, patriotism was frequently used by commentators as a stick with which to beat their rivals. Political opponents were attacked for their lack of patriotism, which, as J. G. A. Pocock suggests, became the rhetoric 'that outsiders use to comment on insiders and how the latter keep them out'.[9] It is this representation of 'insiders' and 'outsiders' that forms the basis of the re-politicisation of Shakespeare's texts. The adaptations are not merely a response to the threat of Jacobite uprising or to the feminisation of the acting community, but rather a reaction to broader ideological concerns that subsume partisan or gendered differences. As a body of texts the adaptations of Shakespeare's history plays promote contemporary political discourse aimed at convincing Britons, and their opponents, of the nation's homogenous identity, integral to Britain's developing self-image of increasing global importance. Through revising Shakespearean histories, English patriot heroes are resurrected for the education of modern men and women. In this way the texts, as Shakespearean artefacts, the performers on stage, modern manifestations of these ancient heroes and heroines, and the audience, as intended modern emulators of these patriot visions, are engulfed in the national mythology that asserts Britain's superiority and stability. The adaptations of Shakespeare, from whatever partisan perspective they are written, adopt and promote this propagandistic, national self-congratulation, irrespective of the self-evident contemporary threats undermining such claims.

## Jacobite incursions and dramatic interventions

The often ambivalent interpretations of the threat posed to the Hanoverian regime by Jacobite incursions and the exiled Stuart dynasty demonstrated in the adaptations is in many ways a reflection of contemporary political attitudes. Nicholas Rogers has argued that 'despite the continuing unpopularity of the new regime, an English insurrection in favour of the Stuarts was never a serious possibility. Outside Catholic and non-juring circles, Jacobite militancy relapsed into nostalgia'.[10] However, as usual in eighteenth-century political circles, reality is not necessarily valuable currency and the gap between popular belief and shared experience is ripe for exploitation. Contrary to Rogers, other scholars suggest that Jacobite rhetoric was in fact a prominent part of political discourse during the period. In addition to the continued presence of Jacobite sympathies in political circles, fears regarding the threat of Jacobite insurrection at home and invasion from abroad can be discerned in pro-Hanoverian literature and government policy. Certainly, as Daniel Szechi contends, 'by the 1720s there would have been few plebeians or patricians disenchanted with the current order who could remember another discourse of opposition'.[11] However unlikely a serious Jacobite threat might have been in reality, both sides had a vested interest in exaggerating the extent of the threat. It is this culture of political posturing with which the adaptations of Shakespeare's history plays engage. Some texts demonstrate clear Jacobite sympathies, relying on historical acts of patriotism to validate Stuart claims but also borrowing the language of modern politics, with its obsession regarding stability – economic, cultural, dynastic and military – as a counter to opposition fears regarding a return to 'old ways'. The representation of faction and uprising in many of these texts is not unquestionable evidence of an anti-Jacobite agenda but rather demonstrates a concern shared by all parties for establishing constitutional permanence. Stability could only be guaranteed by taking heed of Britain's political legacy, and Britain's varied history provided polemicists with examples which could be used to support any party line.

Despite the apparent, and stridently proclaimed, stability secured by the Hanoverian succession and Walpole's Whig ministry, the period of Walpole's supremacy was in fact a time of political volatility and shifting alliances. Opposition to Walpole came from a variety of quarters; Tories, Jacobites and opposition Whigs all protested vociferously against his policies. However, domestic factionalism was not the only threat to political stability. During the first half of the eighteenth century Britain witnessed two failed Jacobite invasions in 1715 and 1745. Despite the fifteen-year Anglo-French alliance (1716–31), Protestant fears for the security of the realm were fuelled by the widely held (not entirely unfounded, but certainly exaggerated) belief that the Jacobites received support from the French monarchs, Louis XIV in 1715 and Louis XV in 1745. The French insistence that James II and his descendants were the rightful heirs to the British throne, and the raising of an invasion fleet in 1743 had, however, less to do with the Stuart claim than a 'worldwide struggle for commercial and imperial primacy between France and Britain'.[12]

The commercial community in particular saw the potential restoration of the Stuart dynasty as a direct threat, primarily due to fears that such a restoration would ultimately result in the imposition of French power and French interests upon British commerce. This anxiety is reflected in the accession of the Hanoverian dynasty itself. George I's claim to the British throne was secured by his Protestantism, the new monarch's religious doctrine took priority over the immediacy of the dynastic link. The early Hanoverians were not notably popular, they were a 'convenient and functional dynasty', but this made easy the task of representing the Hanoverians in terms of a binary opposition to the exiled Stuarts.[13] As representatives of British patriotism neither George I nor George II was particularly impressive; their continued close ties with Hanover were repeatedly brought to the public's attention as a means to suggest divided loyalties.[14]

But, despite the Hanoverians' fundamental lack of charisma, particularly in comparison with the more alluring Stuarts, national stability was clearly a more pressing concern for political commentators and the British people than the personal magnetism of the monarch. Although claims for the patriotism of George I and George II were largely unsupported by their actions, Howard Erskine-Hill argues that Bolingbroke's patriot rhetoric 'was not only an appeal to a large political public including committed Jacobites, but also a weapon nicely judged to turn in either direction'.[15] The political affiliations of Bolingbroke's idealised patriot king were essentially irrelevant. Jacobite, Whig or Tory mattered little, provided he was a patriot. To this end all sides were keen to promote their own patriotic worth whilst tarnishing the credentials of their opponents. For example, Walpole's policy of treaty-making was represented by pro-Walpole Whigs as a patriotic response to foreign threat, calculated in the best interests of the nation (hence Ralph's *Essex* (1731) depicts treaty-making as a patriot policy), whilst Tories and opposition Whigs criticised the minister for an unpatriotic Mortimer-like collaboration with 'the enemy' which would ultimately result in Walpole's, if not the nation's, downfall. In fact, Walpole's ardent pursuit of diplomacy was in part a response to the perceived Jacobite threat. Foreign powers intent on attacking British interests could easily engage Jacobite assistance both as part of an invasion force and for the invaluable support of British Jacobites at home. The British government was 'well aware of the implicit threat effective use of the Jacobite card posed to the established order, they were eminently blackmailable on the subject'.[16] Ironically, Walpole's policies were intended as a defence against the very opponents who criticised such unpatriotic bargaining.

Although the adaptations discussed in this chapter reflect the political volatility of the period, the plays are unified in their representation of Britain and the British people as superior to their European neighbours. Britain's supremacy over foreign powers is unquestioned so long as internal unity is maintained. As Cibber's prologue to his 1724 adaptation of *Henry VI* asserts, 'Foreign Foes could never make us bow, / While to our selves w'are true, The World must own, / England can never be, but by her Self, Undone'.[17] Patriotism is thus key to sustaining the nation's stability. These plays take part in a complex negotiation between the need to uphold and promote myths of stability, fostering notions of national supremacy whilst asserting partisan claims for patriotic superiority. Within this debate, the image of Shakespeare acquired significant cultural currency as the century progressed. Shakespeare's image, and the images projected in adaptations of his plays served as a scaffold to support notions of national stability. Shakespeare, as an icon, not only upheld such myths in the political arena but also shored-up interpretations of Britain as a nation of commerce. Of course, adopting an alternative inflection of the term 'scaffold', it is also possible to position the adaptations of Shakespeare not as celebrations of British supremacy but distillations of what modern Britain lacked in comparison with older versions of itself, an omen hinting at a nation 'hanging' in the balance.

Ambrose Philips's dedication of *Humfrey Duke of Gloucester* to William Pulteney suggests a pro-government appropriation of patriot rhetoric and Shakespearean history devoid of such ominous inflections:

> It is the Happiness of England, that, in the Age wherein You flourish, the nobles enjoy all their valuable Privileges; and yet, the Commons are neither Poor, nor Distrest: Whereby Liberty and Property become universal in Great Britain; the Government acquires a double Support; and every Representative of the People has yearly Opportunities to distinguish Himself as a Patriot![18]

Philips urges 'every representative of the people' to adopt a patriotic stance, to follow the example of his hero and protect Britain's liberty. This dedication was written whilst Pulteney acted as chair for the Committee of Inquiry into the Atterbury Affair (1722). Philips's play is clearly pro-Walpole. First performed in 1723, when Bishop Atterbury's arrest for treasonable correspondence with the Pretender and his subsequent exile were common fodder for the press, *Humfrey Duke of Gloucester* supports not only Walpole's government but also this public demonstration of what Katherine West Scheil describes as 'the need to maintain control of disruptive social influences'.[19] *Humfrey Duke of Gloucester* is, as Loftis suggests, a representation of public concern about the threat of Jacobite rebellion. His pro-Walpolean exaltation is overtly couched in the language of patriotism.[20] The evil Cardinal Beaufort, a version of Atterbury, although impeded by patriot Britons, identifies a constitutional weakness ripe for exploitation, 'the free, stubborn, Spirits of the *English*! / Tenacious of their ancient Rights and Customs, / They will not be Controll'd, but by their laws: / Nor, is the King without his Parliament, secure' (32). By controlling Parliament, Beaufort can control both King and country. Beaufort and the Queen's supporters are the 'other', the unpatriotic, the non-English, and it is the 'ancient virtues of liberty and self-mastery' that thwart Beaufort's plans and ultimately lead to his death. Beaufort is racked with guilt for the murder of his nephew and dies without absolution for his sins. Gloucester, leader of the 'Band of Patriots' (26), dies a hero's death, murdered by his enemy whilst fighting for an idealised future England:

> The happy Day,
> When *Rome*, no more, usurps Tyrannic Sway! –
> Or, That deny'd; may our Descendants see
> The Land throughout, from Superstition free:
> With Kings who fill an independent Throne,
> And know no Power Supreme beside their Own! (43)

This Protestant utopia is overtly Hanoverian and supports the government's stance against the Jacobite traitor Atterbury who threatens this ideal. However, the last lines of this vision suggest a need to curb Walpole's increasing power within the government. Philips desires 'Kings who fill an independent Throne, / And know no Power Supreme beside their Own'. Hanoverian rule and thus, by implication, the Whig government are preferable to the Tory or Jacobite alternative, but power must remain in the hands of an independent patriot and not become the province of a self-interested minister.

Lewis Theobald's *Richard II* (1720) also condemns insurrection; however in this play political uprising is staged against a Jacobite rather than a Whig hero. Richard II was forced to relinquish his throne by the usurper Henry Bolingbroke (later Henry IV). According to Jacobite commentators, his resignation, 'because exacted by force, had no validity'.[21] Richard II and James II were thus, in pro-Jacobite terms at least, similarly abused. Richard was one of many English kings who, 'Jacobites and Non-Jurors considered, proved the religious and political right of hereditary kings'.[22]

In Theobald's version, Richard's Englishness and his patriotism are compromised by the self-interest of his French queen. Isabella persuades Richard to vacate his throne, and abandon his hereditary right to 'this Thief, this Traytor Bolingbroke'.[23] Bolingbroke's actions are represented as unpatriotic. His usurpation of the throne is directed by the self-interested Northumberland who is described by Richard as that 'Ladder by whose steps / The mounting Bolingbroke ascends my Throne' (58). Theobald does not excuse unreservedly either Richard or Bolingbroke. The King admits his fondness for sycophants and admiring courtiers. Bolingbroke is a traitor, banished from England and seeking revenge on his monarch. However, despite these failings it is Northumberland who is represented as the real villain. Orchestrator of Bolingbroke's uprising, Northumberland is yet another example of a self-interested minister, 'Let me confirm the yet unsettled Crown / To Bolingbroke; and Fortune then is mine: / The Means will be to move King Richard hence, / And, by his Absence, cool the People's Love' (56). Northumberland's tactics for securing the stability of Bolingbroke's reign and hence his own position at court reflect what some critics have described as the inevitable 'marginalisation' of Jacobitism from mainstream British politics:

> Inevitably, as Hanoverian–Whig rule became 'normal', and hence developed ideological and emotional roots in the hearts, minds and pockets of Britain's population, Jacobitism was further and further marginalized.[24]

Written during the period which saw the very beginnings of Walpole's dramatic rise to power, Theobald's *Richard II* warns that the stability secured by the Whig/Hanoverian alliance is driven by the unpatriotic self-interest of the politicians concerned. The 'absence' of the exiled Stuarts leaves modern Britons with no alternative other than what, by 1720, seemed to be a dynastically secure and constitutionally appropriate monarchy, an assumption which itself seems to resonate the myth of British political stability. However, history, Theobald suggests, has shown such public acceptance of the status quo to be short lived, 'Tho' Vengeance may a while withhold her Hand, / A King's Blood, unatton'd must curse the Land' (61). In contrast to this 'home-grown' threat to British stability, Philips's *Humfrey Duke of Gloucester* focuses instead on the 'otherness' and lack of patriotism associated with Catholicism as the primary threat to British stability. For Philips the Hanoverians are the only viable option if national order is to be maintained. Both of these texts exploit stereotypes of French national characteristics as the obverse of British patriotism. However, this representation of the French as self-interested and repressive as opposed to the egalitarian British does not necessarily limit the political discourse of these texts to an exclusively pro-Hanoverian, anti-Jacobite agenda.

The heroic foci for the adaptations of Shakespeare's history plays are definitively English men and women – kings and queens – whose public displays of patriotism fulfilled the audience's 'hunger for a sentimental, highly coloured royalism that the early Hanoverians left unsatisfied'.[25] The staging of Jacobite sympathy offered audiences an alternative spectacle distanced from the reality of a drab functional monarchy – a spectacle which provided entertainment beyond the confines of party and sovereign allegiances. It could be suggested that this was the limit of the effect Jacobite sympathies had on the political agendas of the adaptations of Shakespeare's history plays. In creating a dramatic spectacle from the misfortunes of the Stuart dynasty rather than engaging with the realities of the contemporary Jacobite cause, these texts simply capitalise on a general dissatisfaction with the mediocre image of the Hanoverians rather than signalling a specific dynastic allegiance. However, this restrictive evaluation of the political and cultural weight of Jacobitism overlooks the direct influence Jacobitism had on notions of British identity. The Jacobites were more than simply an aesthetically attractive alternative to a 'drab and functional monarchy'.

## Homogenising a nation of difference

The significance of Protestantism as a crucial element of British identity is clear from many of the plays already discussed as well as contemporary commentary and modern scholarship on the subject of nationalism. However, it would be misleading to argue that all Britons were convinced either by the notion of Protestant supremacy or the importance of Protestantism to an idealised version of Britishness. Nicholas Rogers has observed that, 'Since the revival of their fortunes in 1710, the Whigs had persistently asserted that the Tory party was prey to Jacobite proclivities and that their own return to power was absolutely essential to secure the Protestant succession and Revolution settlement'.[26] However, Whig arguments against the Tories and Jacobites that emphasised the threat they posed to British Protestantism and the liberties secured by the Revolution Settlement were not unchallenged. As Szechi asserts, 'Jacobitism gave the opponents of the established order a common cause to rally around'.[27] Thus, the enduring image of British identity as, first and foremost, Protestant, is challenged by an alternative Jacobite version of British patriotism. However, the close relationship between Protestantism and Britishness poses a problem for texts in which Catholic monarchs are being heralded as the patriot ancestors of a redoubtably Protestant nation, a rhetorical conflict that proved difficult to resolve.

Many of the plays position the French, particularly French women, as the 'other' to British patriots. Despite the Anglo-French alliance which, as Jeremy Black observes, was crucial to the establishment and consolidation of the Hanoverian regime because throughout its duration, 'the French government refused to heed widespread pro-Jacobite sympathies with France', common perception of the French as enemies of the English, prevailed.[28] Aaron Hill's *Henry the Fifth*, Lewis Theobald's *Richard II*, Ambrose Philips's *Humfrey Duke of Gloucester*, and Theophilus Cibber's *Henry VI* all represent the French as the obverse to British patriotism. However, these plays do not necessarily all promote the Whig/Hanoverian administration. Some of these texts demonstrate Jacobite sympathies; others covertly promote an opposition agenda.

In Theophilus Cibber's *Henry VI* (1724) and Ambrose Philips's *Humfrey Duke of Gloucester* (1723), the unpatriotic Queen Margaret exerts divisive control over English politics. In both plays, the Queen uses her power against the King: 'Henry is beset with Priests and Sycophants; / And that imperious Margaret wrests the Sceptre, / From his weak Hand' (26). Cibber and Philips depict the French Margaret as a character who embodies unpatriotic iniquity. Both Cibber's and Philips's versions of Queen Margaret portray her adulterous relationship with the Duke of Suffolk. In these texts, sexual behaviour is a clear identifier of a woman's value and is closely linked to her patriotic worth. As Pittock observes, 'Jacobite disorder can be equated with immoral wantonness'.[29] Margaret is the 'political other'; her otherness comes from her unnaturalness. She denounces her femininity and participates in the political world as a self-proclaimed masculine woman. In *Humfrey Duke of Gloucester*, Margaret acts as the antithesis of the English heroine, Eleanor. She is driven by self-interest. Unlike Eleanor, who publicly sacrifices her own reputation for the sake of the peace of the nation, the Queen's actions are calculated to further her own political advancement. She has no concern for the well-being of king and country. Margaret's own vision of her future is vainglorious:

> Is Fortitude, and Wisdom,
> Given to Man Alone? – Prove me, in Council;
> Prove me, in the Field! – In Policy, let *Salisbury*,
> In War, let *York*, oppose me. – But, my Lords;
> Be sure you over-match this slighted Woman! –
> Urge me to all Extremes! – Friendship and Favour,
> I neither ask nor grant. – Success is Mine:
> If Courage claims Success! – Yet if We fail;
> Your Chronicles Shall witness to my Fame;
> Your Daughters boast, your Sons all emulate,
> A Woman's Glory; and the World avow,
> England, once, had a Queen deserv'd to reign. (81–2)

Margaret's words portend the conflict that is to come in *3Henry VI*, the historic events of regicide and civil disorder that Philips chooses not to portray, preferring instead to leave his audience with a vision of a political future governed by the rules of patriotism. Margaret's claim is of course denied historically and her imagined place in England's chronicles is supplanted by the more appropriately Protestant Queen of fortitude and wisdom, Elizabeth I. Cibber's Margaret embodies the battle-hungry self-interested woman hinted at by Philips at the end of *Humfrey, Duke of Gloucester*. In Cibber's text, Margaret again controls a weak-willed King. Although Cibber's adaptation varies little from Shakespeare's original *2&3Henry VI*, he emphasises Margaret's monstrous nature.[30] She taunts York with the body of Rutland, wiping his tears with his son's blood; she is the 'She Wolf of *France*' and the 'false *French* Woman'; her nationality and her failure to adopt the patriotic behaviour demanded of a Queen of England contrast with the politically less active but morally superior Lady Grey.

As I have already suggested, Isabella in Theobald's *Richard II* is depicted encouraging her husband to relinquish his throne in order to secure their domestic peace. In contrast to Isabella's Frenchness, emphasised throughout the text as the source of her weakness, Richard's nationality is elided. Born in Bordeaux in 1367, Richard did not come to England until 1371, after the death of his elder brother Edward. The legend that Richard was the son of a French canon was presumably disseminated as pro-Bolingbroke propaganda. Nevertheless, Richard's French connections are overlooked in Theobald's play. In Aaron Hill's *Henry the Fifth*, a more confrontational approach to the 'problem' of French influence on British royalty is taken. Capitalising upon popular nationalistic feeling during what Gerrard describes as 'a decade of mounting pressure for war against Spain – anti-Catholicism and anti-French sentiments', Hill's text is overtly Francophobic.[31] The Dauphin is not only treacherous but effeminate. His sexual overtures towards Harriet – who is disguised as a man – are a source of comedy. The French response to the threat posed by the English is deception and murder rather than military combat. In contrast, Catherine – the French princess who, despite her political allegiance, falls in love with Henry – is forthright and resolved in her patriotism. Initially Catherine refuses to comply with her father's commands to marry Henry. She sees such an alliance as 'treaty-making', an act of cowardice bound to result in compromising French authority and territorial control. However, Catherine's hatred of her nation's foreign aggressors does not lead her to resort to clandestine or immoral measures. She abhors her brother's treacherous plan to murder Henry. Catherine acts to prevent the plot, saving Henry's life. Her subsequent marriage to Henry is justified because she proves herself a patriot demonstrating both the moral integrity and heroic actions worthy of an English queen.

Although exceptions such as Catherine do exist, in general Frenchness is depicted in these plays as the antithesis of Britishness. The French are unpatriotic, self-interested and treacherous. The British are patriotic and heroic. Despite this clear delineation between Protestant Britain and the Catholic nations, on the whole the subject of religion, particularly the religious practice of the monarch, is overlooked. Some texts, such as Colley Cibber's *Papal Tyranny* are overtly anti-Catholic, and when direct reference is made to a character's Catholicism, it inevitably signals negative characteristics, such as in Philips's Cardinal Beaufort or the representations of Margaret. This would seem to lend credence to Szechi's assertion that as the century progressed, Hanoverian rule became normalised and thus Jacobitism was rejected. Certainly, repeated calls for the Stuarts to renounce their Catholicism suggest a belief that their religion and association with the perceived tyranny of the European Catholic dynasties would prevent a Stuart return to the British throne. British national identity, despite the diverse political agendas promoted in these texts, is represented as primarily Protestant. The Catholicism of England's historical heroes is repeatedly obscured by the need to distinguish 'this Land of Liberty' from her Catholic neighbours.[32] However, I do not wish to imply that the adaptations of Shakespeare's history plays merely revisit the obvious tension between Britain's Catholic past and Protestant future. Through representations of 'patriot women' these texts assert British superiority. Unlike the self-interested French women, Margaret and Isabella, these heroines demonstrate an unequivocally British patriotism. They are the representatives of Britain's self-perceived pre-eminence in Europe and as such become central to the nationalistic political agendas promoted by the plays and integral to the process of historical myth-making with which the adaptations engage.

## Patriot women, validating the myth

Marsden's assertion regarding the domestication of Restoration adaptations of Shakespeare – she describes the plays as feminised versions of the originals – cannot be directly applied to the adaptations discussed in this chapter, however developments made to women's roles in these plays should not be underestimated. Modern scholarly consensus holds that in the early eighteenth century actresses were seen merely as objects for the voyeuristic titillation of audiences.[33] This restrictive interpretation of the roles assigned to women is not supported by the adaptations of Shakespeare's history plays. The development of the roles for women undertaken during the process of adaptation neither domesticates the texts nor places emphasis on titillation, instead, the women in these texts are clearly defined according to their patriotic or unpatriotic conduct. Their function, we shall see, is repeatedly political in that they are either given open access to political processes and public spaces or their actions serve to exemplify a patriotic ideal of public behaviour. Feminist critics have suggested that the relative novelty of the actress during this period led to a profusion of women's roles and, more particularly, breeches roles that provided the added titillation of displaying an immoderate amount of leg.[34] I do not wish to contest the observation that 'conventionally attractive female bodies sell tickets'; this is clearly one motivation for the development of women's roles in Shakespearean adaptation during the eighteenth century.[35] This theory of titillation does not, however, account for the extensive presence of women engaging in public activities. Of the adaptations premièred and published between 1719 and 1745, only one, *The Sequel to King Henry the Fourth*, fails to enhance the roles available to women. Some playwrights chose to increase the speaking part of a female character (for example, Catherine and Harriet in Aaron Hill's *King Henry the Fifth*). Others increased the significance of a woman's actions. Two strong examples are the representations of Margaret; as I have already discussed, both Philips's and Cibber's texts emphasise Margaret's influence on the political action of the play alongside her libidinous character. In contrast, the asexual Volumnia in John Dennis's *The Invader of His Country* is shown to exert a powerful influence over her son, extending beyond that suggested in the original text. The implication of these revisions and additions is two-fold. First, as feminist critics have argued, the increase in women's prominence on stage confirms an actress to be an economic asset to a production.[36] Second, and more pertinent to my discussion, female characters are crucial to any attempt at politicisation undertaken during the process of adaptation.

The presence of politically-active women on stage challenges critical perceptions of early eighteenth-century literature which stress the 'lack of social and political recognition afforded to women', within the context of the eighteenth-century theatre however, this is not always the case.[37] Women's economic value within the theatre gives them, to some extent, access to public power within the confines of the spectacles they create in the space of the public theatre. Indeed, it is not just representations of women in the adaptations of Shakespeare's history plays in which politically active women can be found. Other plays of the period such as James Thomson's *Sophonisba* (1730) depict patriot heroines. In Thomson's play the heroine's actions are 'dominated by patriotic sentiment, intent to benefit her native land'.[38] *Sophonisba* demonstrates the potential for patriotic women outside the confines of Shakespearean adaptation. In direct contrast, Marsden has asserted that developments in women's theatrical employment are 'closely linked to the definition of women as inhabitants of the private or domestic sphere and their exclusion from the public world of politics and commerce.'[39] On stage, she suggests, women are precluded from participating in the male-dominated world of politics. Marsden's assessment of eighteenth-century dramatic representations of women echoes analyses of women's social position during the period. Linda Colley has argued that male anxiety about female aspirations towards political activity reached a crescendo during the eighteenth century. Throughout the period, British law assigned to women a negligible independent status:

> Stripped by marriage of a separate identity and autonomous property, a woman could not by definition be a citizen and could never look to possess political rights.... A female Briton could be punished for plotting against the state, but – in law – she could never play the part of an active patriot within it.[40]

Women had no active role in the political processes of the nation. Given this denial of women's political agency, is it surprising that dramatists created roles that depicted women participating in politics? As Rachel

Weil has argued, however, women's legal status bears little relation to the real opportunities available for women's legitimate political action or commentary.[41] Political events of the period work against the social restrictions placed upon women. For example, Pittock has argued for the significance of women's role in supporting the Jacobite cause, both domestically and politically: 'not only was there a romantic appeal to Jacobite outlawry; it also offered the opportunity for action in a wider public sphere, from the running and defence of estates which might be forfeit to the recruitment and even the leadership of troops, if not actual fighting itself'.[42] The effect of political events upon domestic arrangements forced women into public action. Pittock's image of Jacobite women rising to fill the void left by their menfolk is perhaps somewhat romanticised, however, his argument confirms Colley's assertion that men were anxious to prevent women's political activity. Were the fears of Protestant men regarding women's participation in politics connected with their fear of Jacobitism? Are representations of politically active women necessarily confined to unpatriotic women with Jacobite proclivities in pro-Hanoverian texts, or, patriot heroines in texts with Jacobite sympathies?

There are a number of ways in which the women of these plays move from the domestic spaces conventionally designated as female into the male-dominated public sphere of politics. One of the most frequently documented ways by which playwrights created politically active female characters was cross-dressing.[43] In Aaron Hill's *King Henry the Fifth* Harriet, Henry's rejected English lover, dresses as a man in order to gain access to the French camp at Harfleur and assist the Dauphin in his plot to murder Henry. Harriet's belief that Henry has toyed with her affections and tossed her aside in order to move on to bigger and better conquests, emphasising the slippage between domestic and political notions of romance, love and marriage, fuels her desire for revenge. Her presence creates a sexual tension that is full of ambiguity. Dressed as a young man she addresses the Dauphin and Princess Catherine. The French Prince welcomes Harriet enthusiastically:

> Come to my Arms, thou more than manly Spirit!
> Dress'd in a Woman's Softness! Why, Thou Charmer!
> Thou Angel of a Traitor! What a Treasure
> Of Honour and Reward does All *France* owe Thee![44]

This passage is reminiscent of the rhetoric of a courtship ritual, and the comedy of his unwitting double entendre should not be overlooked. The Dauphin's caricature carries a more serious implication however, by demonstrating a level of anti-French feeling that resonates throughout the play.

Harriet and Catherine provide examples of the way in which women's presence in the political space threatens masculine sexuality. Kristina Straub relates this threat directly to cross-dressing, 'The encroachments of the cross-dressed actress upon the territory of masculine sexuality are especially threatening since they seem to imply the inability of men to hold that territory'.[45] As a cross-dressed woman Harriet challenges the Dauphin's sexuality, his representation is not only Francophobic, but also homophobic. His emasculation undercuts his ability to defeat the English. Harriet's apparent masculinity gives her access to the political arena. She utilises this access to satisfy her desire for revenge. This 'borrowed' power is however rather transient and Harriet's plot is thwarted, notably, due to the intervention of another woman, the unashamedly feminine Catherine. Catherine's intercession enables Henry to recognise his would-be assassin as his ex-lover. But when Harriet is forced to discard her disguise, the threat she poses to Henry does not diminish, it merely shifts from the sexualised image of the breeches role to the equally potent image of martyred heroine. As a woman, Harriet has a more significant effect on the politics of the play than as a 'pretend man'. Joan Riviere has suggested that 'women who wish for masculinity may put on a mask of womanliness to avert anxiety and the retribution feared from men'.[46] This motif can be discerned in Harriet's actions. Dressed as a man, she is feared by Henry for the physical harm he believes she is capable of inflicting. As a woman, she 'guards herself from attack by wearing towards him the mask of womanly subservience, and under that screen, performing many of his masculine functions herself – for him'.[47] In this instance the 'masculine function' performed by Harriet is not sexual; instead, she fulfils a patriotic function. In a dual assault, Henry's patriotism is threatened by Harriet's presence and bolstered by her eventual self-sacrifice. In an intensely private yet publicly heroic episode Harriet kills herself in order to free Henry's heart:

> I have one new Discovery, yet, to make You, [feeling in her pocket]
> Containing the last Secret of my Soul;
> I did not think, so soon, to have disclos'd it:
> But since, without it, you can ne'er be happy,
> I send it, thus – directed to my Heart [draws a dagger, and stabs
>     herself]. (43–4)

Harriet's action mirrors and exceeds her monarch's patriotic virtue. Her presence diminishes Henry's altruism. His concerns for establishing his claim to the French crown are overshadowed by his desire for his ex-lover, 'O! Let me kiss away that mournful Sound'(43). Harriet's death restores Henry's ability to act selflessly, he is free to marry in the best interests of England. Harriet's real encroachment upon masculine territory is achieved not through cross-dressing, but in her representation as a patriotic woman.[48] It is significant that in this way Harriet becomes a tool for the promotion of ideal kingship. She forces Henry to abide by his own rules:

> Kings must have no Wishes for Themselves!
> We are our People's Properties! Our Cares
> Must rise above our Passions! The public Eye
> Shou'd mark no fault on Monarchs; Tis contagious! (42)

Like the honorary Briton Catherine, Harriet exemplifies the patriotic ideals expected of a just monarch. The representations of these two women influence the public arena by reflecting an idealised version of kingship, which, within the confines of the play, is emulated by their monarch/lover/husband. The subject of the play, England's conquest of France and Hill's own political allegiances do not support the notion that politically active women were derided by the pro-Hanoverians. This play is steeped in Protestant ideology yet, contrary to that ideology, women are not only active participants in politics, they also bring about positive results.

Of course, the patriotic actions carried out by these women could be construed as acts of filial obedience. As Marsden contends, women in the adaptations of Shakespeare are 'paragons of domestic virtue' who 'support England by supporting their fathers', in this way reasserting the 'hierarchical structure of the family and by extension the basis of patriarchal society'.[49] Family, however, is not the primary concern of women such as Catherine in Hill's *Henry the Fifth*. For the patriotic women of these histories, the welfare of the state is of greater significance than filial obedience or wifely duty. Catherine angrily objects when her father commands her to marry Henry in an attempt to secure peace between England and France: 'Let that Duty, which I owe my Country / Inspire me to confess, what fix'd Aversion / What rooted Hatred, Nature bids me bear / To Him of all Mankind, the most abhorid' (30). Notions of honour, pride and 'liberty' dominate Catherine's discourse throughout the play, she consistently demonstrates the attributes of Britishness despite her cultural otherness. Her primary 'duty' is to her country not her father. When she finally comes to admire Henry for his valour and patriotic virtue, she turns against her brother and not her country. Catherine sees her family's honour as inextricably linked with that of her country. Her brother's plot is treacherous; only a military victory secured by patriotic duty can lead to an honourable conclusion to Henry's invasion of France. Political manipulation through marriage or murder can only reinforce France's inferiority to England. To term her 'a paragon of domestic virtue' does not describe Catherine with any accuracy. Nor does it prove an adequate assessment of Philips's Lady Eleanor or Cibber's Lady Grey. All of these women privilege country over family. Eleanor endures public humiliation, preferring to be paraded through London as a witch rather than become 'the Cause of civil discord!' (15). Lady Grey initially refuses her King's offer of marriage to secure the welfare of her children, arguing that such a union would discredit his reputation, 'You mean Dishonour to yourself; / I am as much unworthy to be Queen / As I'm above serving an ill Design' (37). Her eventual marriage to Edward does not negate this sense of patriotic duty. As civil war erupts, the Queen once again takes up the role of royal protector, this time combined with the role of mother. Domestic and political roles here merge, and the role of 'mother' itself becomes politically active in its broader sense relating to the need to protect and nurture the nation. Lady Grey is both a mother acting to protect her son and also a subject safeguarding the future heir to England's throne.

Despite the bringing together of the domestic and public in Cibber's representation of Lady Grey, it could be argued that women who participate in the political worlds of these adaptations are necessarily stripped of their femininity and become represented either as manly-women or unpatriotic 'others'. Pittock's assessment of pro-Hanoverian representations of Jacobite women as 'the bold Amazon[s] of the North', created by the 'the sexual vigour, alien threat and role-altering qualities of an all too contemporary revolutionary movement' is, in part at least, supported by the adaptations.[50] On the whole such masculine women are French rather than Northern British but they are certainly represented as alien and threatening to their male patriot opponents. In her examination of popular representations of eighteenth-century actresses, Straub suggests that these women are positioned in an 'emergent role as the other to masculine sexuality, the commensurate image against which masculinity is defined'.[51] Straub's statement is relevant not only to contemporary accounts of actresses but also to the roles these women depicted on stage. Whether they are real or merely dramatic representations, women who gain access to the public stage are often endowed with traditionally masculine characteristics. However in the adaptations, politically active women are not confined to this image of masculinity; they cross the divide between feminine and masculine spheres, adjusting their image as required. There is a complex negotiation here between the extremes of gendered roles which results in a more realistic image of the modern British woman. Despite being prevented by law from political engagement she is active in influencing politics whether outside of the law, as in Pittock's examples of Amazonian Jacobite women, inside the law by exerting political influence from within the domestic sphere, or, in the case of actresses, writers and eminent social figures, by her direct engagement with the public sphere. However, for most women this type of active and sustained participation in politics was inconceivable and therefore these images of politically active patriot women become mythological in their representation as 'Amazonian' models. As versions of British identity these women are mere fantasies, the fulfilment of which would have been beyond the personal experience of the majority of women in the audience.

Constance in Colley Cibber's *Papal Tyranny* (1745) represents just such a woman who is able to move between the extremes of feminine and masculine conduct. She is power-hungry and participates vicariously in the battle:

> Hark!
> The wafting Winds, in audible Perception,
> Set all the Terrors of the Field before me!
> This Jar of Drums! The lofty Trumpets Ardour!
> The vaunting Echoes of the neighing Steed!
> This Clang of Armour! These sky-rending Shouts
> Of charging Squadrons speak the Battle raging![52]

Constance is inflamed by this imagined scene. Her gender prevents her from actively contributing to the exclusively masculine activity of battle and her image of the ensuing mêlée is somewhat romanticised, but her desire for and enjoyment of the conflict are not responses usually associated with femininity. In direct contrast, eight lines on Constance turns suddenly to thoughts of maternal care:

> Hear, Heav'n, my Pray'r! If thy dread Will decrees,
> Our House must fall, let not my riper Sins
> On hapless *Arthur's* Head be visited!
> O! spare, protect his youthful Innocence!
> That Life prolong'd may propagate his Virtues! (10)

She is fearful for the safety of her son, and although it may be argued that these fears are connected with her own desire for victory and fear of subjugation, her prayer for his survival *irrespective* of the outcome of battle presents an image opposed to her earlier demonstration of conventional masculinity. Here it is the safety of an individual, her own son, that consumes her thoughts, not the patriotic desire for victory. But, even in this more tender and conventionally feminine display of maternal fear, Constance's words are tinged with patriot rhetoric. Arthur's youth and innocence must be spared in order that he can grow into his promise of a man of virtue, a future patriot.

A further example of the way in which women achieve political agency through the manipulation of traditional gender roles can be identified in representations of asexual women. For example, in John Dennis's *The Invader of His Country* (1719), Volumnia, mother to Coriolanus, clearly has a sexual past. However, as an older woman, her sexuality is irrelevant within the confines of the play. Volumnia is neither feminine nor masculine. Her asexuality and the respect she commands from Coriolanus validate her political influence. In this text Volumnia's political agency is linked to the hierarchy between mother and son and the sexual inactivity of the matriarch. Volumnia is granted access to the public sphere not because she demonstrates masculine qualities or because she performs an act of self-sacrifice but because she is represented as genderless. Her power comes from her status as mother. This is not to suggest that such characterisation of gendered stereotypes was new to these adaptations. There are many earlier and contemporaneous examples of women who are both masculine and feminine.[53] However, in these plays, women who emulate both masculine and feminine characteristics gain privileged access to the public space, and become active participants in both the public and the domestic arenas.

I am concerned to pre-empt the criticism that these women essentially provide a sustained love interest for the text, audience and acting roles, thus sentimentalising the original plays. Although I have argued that women's presence in the public space in eighteenth-century adaptations of Shakespeare is not 'simply an extension of their domestic function' as dutiful daughters and wives, many of these women do gain access to these spaces as a direct result of their relationships with men.[54] To some extent therefore, these women can ultimately be represented as domestic patriots whose influence in politics is simply the result of their sexual and familial connections. This is further complicated by the repeatedly negative representations of the sexually voracious women in these plays. Women such as Margaret, explicit in her management of her sexuality in order to manipulate and sway the men around her, are clearly unpatriotic and hence, un-British. Women such as Harriet are more difficult to place. She, the audience is lead to assume, has been Henry's sexual partner. The difference here of course is the repeated assertion that their relationship is based upon love, not lust for political power, as in Margaret's case. Of course, in this context, Harriet's death is the inevitable conclusion for a woman in her unfortunate position, the only 'honourable' literary resolution for a woman in her predicament. So, in this context, women's roles in these plays, however politically active they might appear, simply reinforce an oppressive patriarchal system based upon inequality and double standards. Not all of these adaptations, however, follow this repressive pattern. Women are shown to be politically active, but their power is constrained by social hierarchy, not gender restrictions. Such a statement, although seemingly out of step with accounts of early eighteenth-century restriction of women's political activity, has much in common with modern scholarly analyses of the lives of Jacobite women during the period:

> Thrust out as it was from public action, Jacobitism was strong in the private sphere: passed on through marriage alliances and families, and by determined women who had to take responsibility for running property their menfolk had left to fight. More remarkable than this, perhaps, is the evidence for the direct involvement of women in the campaigns, and not always as camp-followers either.[55]

Women, Pittock suggests, were pivotal in sustaining the Jacobite cause. However threatening such women might have seemed to pro-Hanoverian observers, were women necessarily represented in pro-Hanoverian texts as either dutiful domestic goddesses or unpatriotic whores?

It is important to note that the women of the adaptations are not criticised for their political involvement. Despite repeated claims made in Hanoverian propaganda regarding 'the unnaturalness and threat of Jacobite women', the patriotic women of the adaptations are revered as equal to their male counterparts.[56] This lack of criticism is not confined to the texts themselves, but is also characteristic of contemporary critical comment. For example, in the anonymous poem 'To Mr Philips, on his *Humphrey Duke of Gloucester*, by a Gentleman of the House of Commons', Margaret's political involvement is not condemned. Rather she is pardoned as a victim of Beaufort's manipulation; 'When *France* and *Rome* mislead the reigning Queen, / Feign both would guess at him behind the Scene'.[57] If women's participation in politics is more than 'simply an extension of their domestic function' or a continuation of their representation as sexual objects then the line between these potential interpretations is exceedingly thin.[58]

The sentimental language employed by Blanche in *Papal Tyranny* seems to emphasise her place in the domestic sphere and highlight the limits of her active participation either in terms of politics or in relation to her own domestic future:

> Princes, born to Passions not their own,
> Are Slaves in Love, where happier Subjects reign:
> The Hearts of royal Maids, like publick Treasure,
> Are to the Exigents of State assign'd
> While private Comfort is referr'd to Virtue.
> Of this had I been train'd in Ignorance,
> Then yielding thus my Hand had dy'd these Cheeks
> With Shame; but conscious what I owe the Publick,
> With the same joyful Pride I seal this Peace. (16)

But this speech is not devoid of the codes of 'manly' patriotic conduct. Her words contrast the feminine response of shame at being forced to marry without love or affection with a masculine pride and the configuration of her 'duty' to her father as a public, political matter not a domestic one. Blanche's actions and her motives are comparable to those of Henry V in Hill's adaptation. She puts aside her personal romantic desires and privileges the needs of her country. She acts with a self-sacrifice characteristic of patriotic behaviour, but also essential to women's role as dutiful daughters and wives. Blanche conforms, sensitively yet rationally, to the strictures of patriot kingship. As J. C. D. Clark has suggested, the 'patriot king' was an ideal that appealed to Tories and Whigs alike by articulating 'the conveniently unspecific aspiration that a charismatic prince's accession would somehow bring about national regeneration or healing'.[59] These are Blanche's concerns, she sacrifices her domestic happiness in return for the nation's peace. Her actions are, nevertheless, ideologically unspecific, Whig and Jacobite doctrines of kingship were, Clark claims, generically similar.[60] However, the lack of partisan specificity attributable to Blanche's overtly patriotic actions does not imply the domestication of her political influence. Blanche represents a patriotic ideal, a version of kingship open to cross-gender representation.[61] Blanche's femininity does not limit the impact of her patriotism or restrict her influence upon the political action of the play.

In Theobald's *Richard II*, Lady Piercey's actions serve as a counter to Isabella's obsession with domestic healing. Piercey's role is developed as a love-interest for the heroic Yorkist Aumerle. Theobald's desire to 'heighten Aumerle's Character in making him dye for the Cause' places Piercey central to the action.[62] It is in part due to Aumerle's love for Piercey and his hatred of her father for commanding the cessation of their courtship that he devotes himself to Richard's cause, an act that ultimately leads to his execution. Piercey's function in the plot is therefore restricted to the domestic sphere of the play. Her influence, however, is not limited to this domestic space. Although her action is induced by her father's command, the cessation of her courtship with Aumerle has public as well as private significance:

> We must no more indulge the Theme of Love:
> Time's Severity hath interpos'd
> A strong Correction: Now Allegiance calls thee,
> A Subject's Duty, and a suff'ring Prince,
> Demand the Care of thy collected Soul;
> And must extinguish ev'ry lighter Thought. (13)

Piercey identifies Aumerle as Richard's and England's only hope. She does not see her action as one of rejection, merely as a temporary cessation until peace is restored. But what does this passage say about her political allegiance and her sense of duty to her father? Piercey is not represented as a dutiful daughter, but a dutiful subject. Her father, Northumberland, is Bolingbroke's ally. Piercey allies herself with Richard. She repeatedly demonstrates contempt for her father's commands, 'Hold, cruel Lord, reverse that needless Order. / I will not meanly linger, like a Slave, / To be, by Vassal Hands dragg'd from your Presence' (53). Lady Piercey prioritises her public duty over her domestic function. Unlike Isabella, she does not use her influence to protect her own domestic welfare. In placing herself firmly within the public sphere, Piercey risks losing her domestic peace. Her attempts to secure the re-establishment of Richard as rightful monarch privilege public over domestic welfare, a choice which Aumerle's execution and her own suicide prove a genuine sacrifice. Piercey inverts the usual trope of just kingship, the monarch's sacrifice for his/her people. Piercey and Aumerle, the subjects, sacrifice everything for their king. So, however thin the line between women's appropriate sexual activity and their domestic and political sexual transgressions, there is one clear statement which runs as a discernable thread through all of the adaptations and that is the duty of women, as British citizens, to adopt, promote and sustain patriotism. Whether public or private, activist or apolitical, all British women should fulfil their duty as patriots.

Playwrights use female characters to carry their political agendas. In terms of contemporary politics, Hill's *Henry the Fifth*, despite an overt endorsement of Francophobia, tentatively supports Walpole's foreign policy of treaty-making.[63] Historically, Henry secured English control of Normandy and gained recognition as heir to the French throne by his marriage to Charles VI's daughter, Catherine de Valois. In Hill's adaptation, Catherine's initial reluctance to marry in order to secure peace and her eventual acquiescence, influenced by Henry's demonstrations of his patriotic virtue sit uncomfortably with the closing images of heroic England overcoming the barbarous French. This tension remains unresolved and disrupts the political consistency of the play. Catherine's version of patriotism, the play suggests, does not allow for the element of compromise required for effective government. Walpole's treaty-making may not be conventionally heroic, however, his policy of 'compromise' is patriotic and, like the death of Harriet, a necessary evil.

The analogous representations of Margaret in Cibber's *Henry VI* and Philips's *Humfrey Duke of Gloucester* contribute to divergent political agendas. Philips's play is, as I argued at the beginning of this chapter, pro-government and openly in support of Walpole's response to the Atterbury affair. Bertrand Goldgar notes that the play immediately became the centre of controversy in the political press. It was seen as an attempt by Philips to gain preferment from Pulteney and Walpole – a political faux pas as the relationship between the two ministers was, by 1723, becoming increasingly antagonistic.[64] Margaret, the unpatriotic other, manipulates the immoral Cardinal Beaufort, thus clearly declaring the political allegiance of the text. The tone of *Henry VI* is less obsequious. Cibber's version of Margaret is used to criticise weak kingship and advocate the interminable duty of the monarch to his or her people.

Colley Cibber's professed motive for writing *Papal Tyranny* was 'to inspirit *King John* with a Resentment that justly might become an English Monarch, and to paint the intoxicated Tyranny of Rome in its proper Colours'.[65] Constance's fear of political subjugation by the French reflects this aim. The première of *Papal Tyranny* on 15 February 1745, five months before the Jacobite uprising, suggests the topicality of Cibber's intention and Constance's fears. However, the play was written eighteen years earlier in 1727 and is therefore chronologically closer to the attempted invasion of 1715 than the 1745. Although Cibber had plentiful opportunities in which to alter his text during this period, there is no evidence to suggest that he made any extensive revisions.[66] The apparent topicality of *Papal Tyranny* is therefore a complex issue. The play's relevance to the political situation in February 1745 was perhaps little more than a happy coincidence for Cibber – a coincidence which finally saw his play performed.

Constance's maternal fears and her imagined participation in the battle are experiences which a significant proportion of the contemporary audience, reflecting on the past invasion and the implications of the Young Pretender's assembling army on the continent, could well relate to. Constance shares the fears experienced by Protestant Britons, fears that Clark identifies as common amongst dissenters and High Churchmen alike, and which remained prominent for the two decades between the writing of Cibber's adaptation and its first performance.[67] Representations of patriot women are not therefore confined to plays with a specifically anti-Hanoverian agenda. Patriotic and unpatriotic women gain access to the public sphere in pro-Hanoverian plays as well as in plays with Jacobite sympathies. As Pittock suggests in relation to his work on the Jacobite Amazon women, 'there were also women active on the other side'.[68]

These representations of patriotic and unpatriotic women are integral not only to the political plots of the plays but also to the political agendas of the texts. Women's behaviour has direct implications for the political stability of the nation, whether the England of the plays or contemporary Britain. In these plays women's responsibility to their country is clearly outlined in terms of patriotic duty and although some women's patriotism will be determined by their domestic role as mother/daughter/sister, for others, their patriotism will be judged in terms of dynamic participation in the political arena. Despite actively influencing the political situations re-enacted on stage and engaging with the political agendas of the texts, the language, desires and the expectations of these women are evidence of their continued involvement in the private sphere. By participating in politics these women are not excluded from domestic cares. However, this continued emphasis on conventionally feminine concerns does not limit their actions to a domestic imitation of their male counterparts. Conversely, the ideological power behind these representations of patriotic women is strengthened by their ability to influence both arenas. Are patriotic women therefore representative of a mythology in and of themselves, re-enforced by the visual fictions woven by the women on stage through which these imagined historical heroines become idealised versions of Britishness?

## Shakespearean patriot heroines as idealised Britons

The female characters in Shakespearean adaptations are given a didactic purpose, either as role models or representations of unpatriotic individuals. This moralistic function, I suggest, has both a domestic and a public purpose. Weil contends that the boundary between public and private spheres was not fixed and immovable but shifting and malleable. Exclusion from or inclusion in the public sphere was 'a matter of perspective'.[69] In the adaptations, women's domestic relationships with kings, princes and courtiers, and, in some cases, their own social status, grant them political agency. This is not to suggest that women are represented as the facilitators of men's political function. Their political role is not simply an extension of their domestic status. By utilising the shifting boundaries between the domestic and the public, dramatists created female characters whose participation in public political activity is legitimate if not always patriotic and, to some extent, this participation is legitimated by women's presence on the public stage, the actress delivering the role becomes a politically active female icon, requiring emulation by and adoration from her audience.

Women in these adaptations are portrayed as cross-party patriots and idealised versions of Britishness that can be appropriated for Whig, opposition Whig, Tory or Jacobite propaganda. It is important to note that the gap between Tory, Whig and Jacobite policy was not always clear. Jacobite, Tory and Whig versions of kingship were not entirely disparate and, according to Erskine-Hill, 'It is as hard to distinguish Jacobite from Tory rhetoric as it is to tell a Jacobite from a Tory'. He goes on to argue that the most potent staples of Jacobite rhetoric, such as nationalism, integrity and independence were shared by Tory commentators.[70] Similarly, links between Tory, Whig and opposition-Whig agendas lead to much shared rhetoric. Although, as Bruce Lenman argues, modern scholars have over-emphasised the universality of 'an enduring triumphalist British identity based on imperial trade, imperial swagger, and Protestantism', some elements of British identity were, nonetheless, idealised by all parties.[71] However, this myth is exactly the image that political commentators were struggling to impose, either because they wanted to emphasise the extent to which this status was under treat from the current administration or the success of the current administration in generating and sustaining this claimed stability. Such characteristics and shared desires are promoted by and reflected in the representations of patriotic women, in texts which have a dual cultural potency as adaptations of British history and versions of the nation's history viewed through the lens of Britain's incipient Bard.

The potency of the adaptations, in terms of their intersection with debates relating to national identity, thus relates to the position of Shakespeare in the cultural heritage of the nation. The concept of 'updating' Shakespeare to comment on contemporary political events was a recurrent concern of eighteenth-century literary theory.[72] As the century progressed, Shakespeare came to represent 'English Liberty' and a resistance to neo-classical rules and decorum.[73] The works of Shakespeare were therefore relevant to modern Britons not only because playwrights adapted these texts to comment on current political crises but also due to a developing image of Shakespeare as both literary and political exemplar. The growing political currency of Shakespeare as national icon is illustrated by the public row that broke out, during the late 1730s, over the erection of Shakespeare's statue at Westminster Abbey. By 1735 the opposition had already enshrined Shakespeare in William Kent's Temple of British Worthies.[74] When the 'establishment' unveiled their own monument in 1741 the 'empty scroll' caused considerable consternation in the London press. As Dobson points out, the scroll could be seen as indicative of 'Shakespeare's availability for multiple appropriation', a position which is echoed in the multiplicity of political appropriations of Shakespeare's history plays.

By the end of the eighteenth century Shakespeare was represented as an idealised Briton. His plays were viewed as educational texts, well suited to encourage appropriate British behaviour. Commentators such as Elizabeth Montagu, whose *An Essay on the Writings and Genius of Shakespeare* (1769) devotes a whole chapter to 'the historical drama', made claims for Shakespeare as 'moral philosopher'. Montagu suggests that the history plays are 'excellently calculated to correct'.[75] History is representative of the manners of the times and the characters of the most illustrious persons concerned in a series of important events. In terms of eighteenth-century literary theory, the history play provides an ideal vehicle for political comment and more importantly political, not just moral, correction. Such ideas were neither unique nor indeed new to Montagu. She was neither the first woman to write about Shakespeare's value as moral educator nor the first commentator to identify history as a way of bringing, 'the Transactions of past Ages to the present view and of exploring Vice (be it found in what Character or Regime so ever) and rewarding Virtue'.[76] Adaptations of history are not devoid of political agendas and versions of British history were integral to party ideology during the period. As I argued in relation to plays representing ancient

British history, all sides sought to derive authority for their positions by claiming historical precedents. The adaptations of Shakespeare's histories are clearly susceptible to re-politicisation and their political agendas enjoy a dual validation. As part of England's cultural heritage, the original texts lend credibility to the revised versions and uphold the integrity of any political agenda proposed.

The validation of these plays as both national histories and derived from the national 'poet' immerses them in idealism and fantasy; a fantasy that extends to representations of women. The fact that many of the women in these adaptations are not represented as merely domestic patriots but are allowed an active participation in the political sphere suggests a potentially dynamic image for the 'ideal Briton' in terms of its female manifestation. The plays offered their audiences images of the ideal British citizen, male *or* female, as active protectors of the nation, thus giving these adaptations a wider cultural significance beyond simply reaffirming existing distinctions between gendered roles or resurrecting old plays updated to modern sensibilities and taste. Resurrecting or rewriting Shakespeare was not only attractive in that it could secure, for the theatre managers, cheap economic returns in terms of box office profits. These plays also gave playwrights, actors, actresses and audiences the opportunity to participate in the formation and revision of national identity with reference, positive or negative, to England's varied history. As Benedict Anderson has observed, print-capitalism was a key element in the creation of what he describes as 'imagined communities' of nationality. The rapid growth in numbers of readers and the corresponding growth of print-capitalism allowed consumers to think about their own identities and to relate themselves to others in new ways.[77] The history plays, and here I am purposefully extending the assertion to include not just the adaptations of Shakespeare but all of the plays discussed in this book, participated in this exploration of national identity. Like readers, theatre audiences were given the opportunity to relate to representations of Britons, figures of fantasy endowed, whether positively or negatively, with mythological status. Adaptations, particularly adaptations of Shakespeare's history plays, are significant contributions to the debate surrounding national identity. The plays provoked audiences into thinking about themselves in relation to the characters on-stage, not by presenting something new, but by reconfiguring well-known historical circumstances, and well-known texts, to suit current political events. In addition of course, the incipient image of Shakespeare as the father of English drama gave credence to a national identity inspired by his plays.[78]

Read as participants in a cultural debate concerning national identity, these adaptations depict a British nation made distinct from its European neighbours by a perceived historical and literary superiority. Contemporary military failures are insignificant when compared with this illustrious past. Lenman observes that:

> Defeated by Spain, thrashed by France, and humiliated by the very Protestant Scottish Episcopalian Jacobites the British monarchy staggered out of wars which had highlighted the violent clashes of interest within the devolved, multi-national Atlantic, and global web of interests it ruled or had ruled or hardly ruled at all.[79]

Such facts, as Lenman outlines them, which emphasised the precarious control Britain had over its widespread colonial interests, not to mention Jacobite and party conflicts carried out much closer to home, are obscured by the insistence, present in all of the adaptations, on British superiority. This perceived pre-eminence arises from a long line of predominantly English patriots whose very histories are being rewritten and re-politicised in the plays themselves. The adaptations impose upon these historical figures the political and social morality of a modern patriot. These 'ideal Britons' form part of a cultural and political heritage central to the formation of a British national identity based upon myths, both historical and contemporary, which validated claims of national superiority. Ambitious modern politicians and seemingly politically inactive monarchs who do not have the pedigrees of these men and women threaten this ancient heritage. It is therefore necessary for the cultural debate about national identity to transcend the usual divisions between masculine and feminine, public and private, and embrace politically active women as key proponents of 'a national ideology of liberty and truth'.[80] Whichever side of the party divide(s) these texts occupy, frequent calls for liberty, freedom and images of heroic historic victory make a clear and homogenous demand. In order to secure an illustrious British future, modern Britons must emulate the glories of England's past.

# 4
# Britain, Empire and Julius Caesar

When awful Rome became the savage spoil
Of wild Ambition, and of factious Broil;
When by the Ruin Tyrant Nero rose,
Lucan found Cause for Triumph from her Woes:
He pardon'd all the Civil Sword had done,
And bless'd the War, which fix'd That Nero's Throne.
Lewis Theobald, prologue to The Fall of Saguntum (1727)

When Empires are at Stake, nothing is Just,
Or Great, but what implicitly maintains 'em.
Colley Cibber, Cæsar in Ægypt (1725)

In the opening chapters of this book I located my discussion of notions of British national identity in texts which re-appropriate the histories of the British Isles. With the exception of Haywood's venture into European history and the adaptations of Shakespeare's Roman histories, all of the plays encountered have focused on historical events of direct and geographically localised importance to the British nation. Both this and the subsequent chapter move away from plays concerned with English or British histories and look at the ways in which playwrights appropriated foreign histories to comment on contemporary British politics. In particular, these plays participate in a shift in notions of Britishness which became necessary to accommodate the nation's developing sense of itself as a colonial power. One group of plays which sustained a notable presence on the early eighteenth-century stage and engaged overtly with issues of colonialism and empire are those that appropriated the histories of ancient Rome. Rome has conventionally served as a mirror for Britons and British history and, indeed, the eighteenth century was no exception.[1] Throughout the eighteenth century historians, politicians and playwrights continued to appropriate the histories of ancient Rome as commentary on contemporary British politics. My focus is not to establish these plays as domestic allegory, using Rome as provenance for contemporary political actions. This appropriation of Rome and the Roman heritage as self-validation has already been well documented by scholars, particularly in relation to significant political shifts such as the Glorious Revolution. What the plays discussed in this chapter show us is the appropriation of Rome to address a specific social, political and economic enterprise. Rather than simply authorising a partisan agenda, these texts participate in a pro-colonial discourse which takes ancient Rome as a model for British colonial endeavour. The plays engage with an image of Britishness which reflects the nation's increasing concern with colonialism, power overseas and the prospect of Empire. They grapple with a linguistic conflict which discloses ideological fears and uncertainties. The representation of Britain as a nation of liberty, the citizens of which enjoy an inherent freedom, sits uncomfortably alongside concepts of imperialism. The Britain of colonial conquest, engaging in the aggressive subjugation of others synonymous with expansion is not easily reconciled with libertarian codes of conduct. However, for the imperial nation, securing and maintaining Empire, as the quotes from Theobald and Cibber at the opening of this chapter assert, are the primary goals. What these quotes and the plays they are taken from reveal to modern readers, and yet attempted to suppress in contemporary audiences, are the fears that imperial power necessarily compromises liberty, encourages tyranny and positions the just treatment of citizens as of secondary importance. This chapter will negotiate the transition from domestic to colonial concerns by moving from the national myths of liberty and patriotism, the foci of the English history plays, to an imperial fantasy which, despite its seeming incompatibility with those cornerstones of the national identity, is justified by the self-same national myths. Notions of Britain as a nation of free patriots are appropriated by pro-colonialist commentators to proclaim British supremacy and authority on a global scale.

Despite my suggestion that the manipulation of ancient Roman history for the purposes of partisan political discourse during the early-modern period has been well documented it is necessary to consider briefly the predominant political appropriations of Rome and Roman history and the influence of some enduringly popular manipulations of ancient Rome as a context for the Roman plays we shall be considering.[2]

By the eighteenth century the Roman Republic had long been identified as a gauge by which England and Britain could be judged. Partisan discourse was frequently imbued with classical references and overtones which legitimised its claimed authority.[3] Perhaps one of the most infamous examples from this period is *Cato's Letters*, published in *The London Journal* during the early 1720s. Gordon and Trenchard's Cato was a vehicle for their comment upon the interrelated problems of opinion, faction and ministerial corruption. They insisted that, at that particular political moment in which their 'Cato' was writing:

> What was needed was a new understanding of the principles of human nature and new histories of Rome and England to teach citizen to distrust all ministers, as a matter of principle, even those who held office in a country which was governed by 'a wise and beneficent prince, a generous and publick-spirited Parliament and an able and disinterested Ministry'.[4]

This updated version of 'Catonic liberty' presented its readers with a political model that idealised the Roman Republic and identified parallels between the present British constitution and its ancient Roman predecessor. The enduring success of *Cato's Letters* further indicates the popularity of, and interest in, literary interpretations of Rome as a model for British emulation. It was an interest that engaged audiences as well as readers, from the Restoration until the 1750s, during which period the London theatres presented a variety of politicised perspectives on the Roman Republic and Empire and, like much post-1688 imaginative literature, juxtaposed the political justification of the Glorious Revolution with the idealised manifestoes of the Roman Republic.[5]

So if, as modern scholars have suggested, the Roman Republic was adopted as justification for the Glorious Revolution and became the model to which all parties, indeed all factions aspired, is this reflected in the history plays performed on the early eighteenth-century London stage? During the period 1719 to 1745 nine plays that took ancient Rome as their subject premièred in the London theatres. John Dennis, *The Invader of His Country* (1719), William Philips, *Belisarius* (1724), Colley Cibber, *Cæsar in Ægypt* (1724), Philip Frowde, *The Fall of Saguntum* (1727), Samuel Madden, *Themistocles, The Lover of His Country* (1729), James Thomson, *Sophonisba* (1730), William Bond, *The Tuscan Treaty* (1733), William Duncombe, *Junius Brutus* (1734), and William Havard, *Regulus* (1744). In addition, Shakespeare's *Julius Cæsar* was staged throughout the period, five new operas based on Roman history were produced and a popular song, Purcell's *Let Cæsar and Urania Live* (1737), was performed repeatedly. However, only one of the plays discussed in this chapter focuses on the Roman Republic, the remainder are all set in post-first triumvirate – imperial – Rome. This is an important distinction because although the Roman Republic was obviously a colonial power, eighteenth-century commentators often ascribed a more expansionist outlook to the Roman Empire from the rule of Julius Caesar onwards. For the purposes of this discussion therefore, Imperial Rome seems a fitting description. The implications of this shift in focus away from 'the virtuous Republic' to the Rome of insatiable military expansion are, I suggest, significant to representations of Britain's own national identity during a period of political and social conflict regarding colonial endeavour and imperial ambition.

British imperialism during the eighteenth century has been characterised by historians as a distinctly commercial imperative. Colonial expansion was desired by merchants for the purpose of personal economic profit, but this expansionist outlook frequently conflicted with Walpole's markedly Eurocentric and seemingly Hanoverian focused foreign policy.[6] Certainly what Kathleen Wilson identifies as the resentment felt by British merchants towards Walpole's failure to address a growing trade imbalance between Britain and her European rivals – an imbalance caused by the comparatively 'aggrandizing imperial politics of France and Spain' – is addressed in the Roman history plays.[7] These plays are involved in what could be described as an aggrandizement of British imperialism through a comparison of British and Roman colonial growth and aspiration. Whereas a number of scholars have suggested that despite the classical ideals of liberty and virtue remaining dominant concepts in eighteenth-century political debate, only Roman-republican models were held in any esteem, these plays suggest that Imperial Rome had a number of specific political lessons to impart to a developing colonial power. The assumption that eighteenth-century commentators unanimously rejected Imperial Rome as a political model on the basis of Julius Caesar's expansionist policies and his subsequent depiction as 'the chief architect of the world's hatred for Rome' is not upheld by these plays.[8] Assertions such as these have effectively obscured those texts that resist this purportedly unanimous denouncement of Roman imperialism. Indeed, the plays I shall discuss here define both 'Imperial Rome' and Julius Caesar in a much more favourable light. These persistent anomalies undermine such a polarised view of early eighteenth-century representations of ancient Rome. Howard D. Weinbrot has convincingly argued that eighteenth-century attitudes to Augustus Caesar have been over-simplified in modern literary and historical analyses of the period. I would argue that critical assessment of eighteenth-century perceptions of Julius Caesar is similarly flawed in that scholars have ignored a persistent strain of pro-Caesar literary, historical and political texts. Critics have identified Julius Caesar as the representative of the obverse of eighteenth-century pro-Roman values, asserting that, to eighteenth-century Britons, Julius Caesar's notoriety for his part in the demise of the Republic meant that he was representative of all that was wrong with Ancient Rome. This view, we shall now see, is belied by a number of plays from the period.

## Julius Caesar rewritten

The profusion of publications promoting the Roman Republic and Senate as political exemplars would excuse many readers of early eighteenth-century accounts of ancient Roman history from considering the description of Julius Caesar as a hero somewhat oxymoronic.[9] There are however some prominent exceptions to these pro-Republic, anti-Caesar discourses of which Colley Cibber's *Cæsar in Ægypt* and Handel's *Giulio Cesare* are two examples. Handel's opera and Cibber's play focus on the events following Caesar's defeat of Pompey at Pharsalia, the action commencing with Pompey's arrival in Egypt requesting asylum from Ptolemy, his supposed ally. *Giulio Cesare* premièred on 20 February 1724 and was enormously successful. Cibber's production at Drury Lane on 9 December the same year was less auspicious, despite presumably capitalising on Handel's earlier success.[10] In *Giulio Cesare* Caesar is depicted as a man of action but his moral perspective is just, denouncing Tolomeo's barbarity and mourning the demise of the patriot Pompey.[11] Cibber's play takes this enlightened morality of the conventionally tyrannous Caesar further by depicting him as a hero. His tyranny is, according to Cibber, misunderstood:

> Men one Day, may change their Thoughts of Cæsar
> The Time may come when his destructive Arms
> Shall well repay this Ravage of the World,
> And force them by Obedience to be happy.[12]

The emphasis here on the potential for Caesar's imperial project to result in a benign dictatorship has been overlooked by critics who have insisted that Cibber's text merely reiterates the predominant anti-Caesar stance of contemporary political commentators.[13] Such interpretations are not convincing. Cibber's text, from the outset, challenges contemporary depictions of Julius Caesar as an ambitious, ruthless tyrant. Why is the representation of Julius Caesar in Cibber's play so seemingly out of step with those of his contemporaries? One way of reconciling these apparently discordant versions of Caesar is to juxtapose contemporary attitudes to colonialism with the words of Cibber's Caesar. Caesar's insistence that his militaristic policy, his ravage of the World, will 'repay' not only Romans but those peoples and colonies subject to Roman incursions has clear resonance in relation to contemporary British colonial interest. Early eighteenth-century pro-colonial rhetoric was formed on similar assumptions, that the colonies were commercially viable, that the resultant increase in trade possibilities and therefore national power made expansion a strategic imperative and that Britain had the right to exercise her power over such trading posts.[14]

Cibber's Caesar therefore, can be seen to exemplify this pro-colonial vision, a position in keeping with Cibber's own pro-Hanoverian politics. If Britain's 'destructive arms', through the supposed mutual benefits of colonialism, will 'repay the ravaged world', surely Julius Caesar is an appropriate model for British colonial aspiration. If we accept the assertion that, in endorsing colonialism eighteenth-century British writers imagined 'their colonial and trading empires as peaceful and mutually beneficial consumer communities', it is clear that representations of Julius Caesar as an unpatriotic tyrant destructively obsessed by expansion, would be counter-productive in a pro-colonial text.[15] Cibber rewrites Caesar as an imperial hero, imbibed in Republican values but responding to the military, economic and political benefits of colonial expansion.

Another example of a pro-Caesar text is John Sheffield, Earl of Mulgrave's adaptation of Shakespeare's *Julius Cæsar*. Mulgrave divided the original play into two parts which were posthumously published as *The Tragedy of Julius Cæsar* (1723) and *The Tragedy of Marcus Brutus* (1723). Again, critical accounts of these plays have either overlooked Mulgrave's positive rendering of Caesar or simply depoliticised his text. Commentary focuses on Mulgrave's structural alterations, the rather awkward adherence to Aristotelian poetics, and not the thematic alterations which allow for a more positive interpretation of Caesar's moral and political standing.[16] A counter to the somewhat reductive interpretations of Mulgrave's adaptation is the broader perspective taken by Michael Dobson, who sees the text as part of 'the whole batch of topical revisions of Shakespeare which appeared in the wake of the Jacobite rebellion of 1715, designed to counter the 'Whig view of the play' which positions

Brutus as a 'freedom-loving patriot' whose suicide is an act of defiance rather than apology.[17] As part of this broader debate and appropriation, Mulgrave's adaptation squarely positions itself as a counter-political reading of Shakespeare's original text. Mulgrave's version bemoans the assassination of Caesar. The senatorial chorus at the end of Act III in *Marcus Brutus* warns of the consequences of such 'unnatural' actions:

> We little thought when Cæsar bled
> That a worse Cæsar wou'd succeed . . .
> . . . Hark to all Rome's united Voice!
> Better that we a while had born
> Ev'n all those Ills which most displease,
> Than sought a Cure far worse than the Disease. (407–8)

These adaptations are clearly political, particularly when considered in relation to Mulgrave's own political affiliations. Although disgraced for his capitulation and self-interest in 1688, Mulgrave's political allegiances are demonstrably Jacobite, and his Caesar and Brutus clearly oppose Whig interpretations of the text. Of course, I have already suggested that Cibber's pro-Caesar text has a Whiggish pro-colonial agenda, and again here we can see the malleability of drama and history for partisan purposes. Cibber's Caesar echoes Mulgrave's chorus in the prophetic statement; 'Is there a Crime / Beneath the Roof of Heav'n that Stains the Soul / Of Man, with more infernal Hue than Damn'd Assassination' (27). In Mulgrave's play the assassination of Caesar is a clear parallel for the ill-fortune that had beset the Stuart dynasty in more recent times. For Cibber assassination is also rejected although it is not the deposing of the Emperor that is important but rather the act of misguided 'regicide' – misguided because the true purpose of Caesar's actions, his imperial vision, will never be realised. Caesar will, as the audience knows, die at the hands of his favourite, but his motivation was not avarice, his heroism has been overlooked, his actions misjudged. With the exception of this brief allusion to his untimely demise, ironically and purposefully spoken by Brutus, Caesar's assassination is not dwelt upon in Cibber's text, perhaps a direct consequence of an allegoric conflict which he found too awkward to resolve. This pro-Hanoverian representation of Julius Caesar celebrates the Emperor's colonial success offering Caesar as a model for the Whig ministry and British colonial aspirations. Despite their antithetical political agendas all of these texts represent Julius Caesar as a hero, not the traditionally maligned villain, destroyer of the glorious Roman Republic. The dual focus on Rome as both a pro- and anti-imperialist model, identified by Norman Vance and others, is echoed in these bi-partisan representations of an heroic Julius Caesar. Caesar, like Rome, can be appropriated for any political agenda. It is clear however that in order to appropriate Roman history for a pro-colonial agenda, conventional representations of Caesar must be transformed in order to successfully impart a positive rendering of colonial ambition. Pro-colonial, anti-Caesar commentaries are open to self-contradiction.

The Pro-Caesar dramatists were not an isolated group. Ayres identifies the Whig writers John Dennis and Aaron Hill as commentators who, through their narrative histories, demonstrate an admiration for Julius Caesar 'precisely for understanding that this once-admirable institution [the Republic] had become an empty shell', an awareness which both Cibber's and Mulgrave's Caesar demonstrate and act upon.[18] Another example of a pro-Caesar commentator is the narrative historian Laurence Echard. Echard's *The Roman History: from the Beginning of the City, to the Prefect Settlement of the Empire by Augustus Cæsar* (1695) had reached its sixth edition by 1707 and continued to be reprinted into the 1720s.[19] Although, as Weinbrot notes, Echard's 'pro-Augustan royalism' became increasingly unpopular, his depiction of Julius Caesar as a hero retained authority during the periods in which it may be assumed both Mulgrave and later Cibber were writing their dramatic accounts of Roman history.[20] Echard writes of Caesar:

A person of the greatest Soul, the most magnanimous Spirit, and of the most wonderful Accomplishments and Abilities that Rome, or perhaps the World, ever saw; whether we consider him in his Care and Vigilance, in his Valour and Conduct, or in his knowledge and learning; all which noble Qualities made him belov'd and reverenc'd by the People, honour'd and ador'd by his Friends, and esteem'd and admir'd even by his Enemies. And setting aside his Ambition, which was the Fault of the Times, as well as his Temper, he was never much justly tax'd with any great Vice, but that of Women.[21]

This analysis of Julius Caesar as a caring, vigilant and honourable leader contrasts starkly with what scholars have depicted as the normative description of Caesar; a tyrant and a villain. But Echard was not the only commentator to describe Caesar in such a positive light. The immensely popular, *Histoire d'Angleterre*, written by French historian Paul de Rapin-Thoyras and translated into English by Nicholas Tindal between 1724 and 1731 is another example of an influential narrative which redirects normative interpretations of Caesar.[22] Rapin's 'profess'd design was the

Information of Foreigners, to let them see by what Steps and Degrees England has grown up to that Height of Power and Grandeur it is in at present'.[23] Indeed such pro-English, pro-Whig, rhetoric, whether intended by Rapin, as O'Brien suggests, or imposed by Tindal's editorial hand, ensured that 'During the first half of the eighteenth century, Rapin's history played a role in the political education of the nation'.[24] Rapin's account of the Roman invasion of Britain, although lacking the overt approbation of Julius Caesar demonstrated in Echard's text, is hesitant to represent Caesar as an ambitious self-server, 'Some have accus'd him, but how truly is uncertain, of aiming in this Enterprize at nothing but his own private Interest, and enriching himself with the Spoils of the Island'.[25] Rapin goes on to describe Caesar's military manoeuvres during the invasion in some detail. He questions the dominance of Rome over Britain, using accounts from Lucan, Dion, Horace and Tibullus to substantiate his assertion that the:

> Reputation *Cæsar* aquir'd by these two Expeditions was not near so great as it is represented to be in his *Commentaries* – But be this as it will, certain it is the Advantages that accrued from them to the Commonwealth were inconsiderable; which no doubt was the reason of *Tacitus* saying, *Cæsar* had rather shewn the *Romans* the way to *Britain*, than put them in Possession of it.[26]

In this way Rapin both defends Caesar against accusations of self-interest and positions Britain as a colony that was not only non-compliant, but, through the nation's lack of contribution to the commonwealth, does not adhere to contemporary understanding of the mutual benefits of the coloniser/colony relationship. This could be read as anti-colonial comment, as a challenge to the normative economic justification of colonial ambition on the basis of potential material gains. I would argue however that Rapin's text is negotiating a rhetorical tightrope created by Britain's dual role as ex-colony and burgeoning colonial power. In effect, Rapin removes the indignity of Britain's past as a Roman colony by suggesting that Britain was never beholden to Rome and that Rome did not benefit from Britain.[27] What Rapin's account of Julius Caesar does suggest is a softening in representations of Caesar himself but without challenging established notions of the British national character which juxtapose the constructed Roman Imperial machine with the natural vigour of the insurgent Britons. Rapin's adjustment of conventional representations of Caesar's avaricious colonialism and his depiction of Britain's non-compliance with Rome effectively rewrites British history in order to facilitate images of Britain's own potential for colonial prowess. In relation to the nation's nascent colonial role, Britain's own imperial progress is given validation by the suggestion that the nation resisted Rome and remained an untamed non-compliant colony. This linguistic massaging suits Rapin's intended project – the glorification of 'England' – but, to what extent do other commentators, those less concerned with effusive and profitable nationalism, adopt and adapt Rapin's reconfiguration of Caesar and Roman Britain in order to suit pro-colonial discourse?

Aaron Hill's *An Enquiry into the Merit of Assassination* (1738) is an example of another pro-Caesar Whig narrative. In a letter to Bolingbroke, Hill criticises contemporary accounts of Caesar, and recommends his own 'impartial' account:

> The mistakes of his modern accusers, men of inflexible, unarguing prejudice: who, having accustom'd themselves to think Cæsar a tyrant, sacrifice reason and facts to opinion; and condemn the great martyr of popular liberty, as one, who was for trampling on the rights of his country. The injustice of this lazy concession in writers, and the original cause … shewn in as obvious a light as, at this distance of time, I was able to throw on the subject – I wish may have had strength enough to travel so far, as to the honour of your Lordship's notice, in a late enquiry into the merit of Assassination, with a view to the character of Cæsar, and his designs on the Roman republic.[28]

Hill was aware that his account of Caesar 'the great martyr of popular liberty' and the demise of the Roman republic, in direct opposition to already popular representations of Roman history such as Addison's *Cato* (1713), would require impressive support. This anxiety is evident in the many letters Hill wrote on the subject, all of which pre-empt criticism and resistance to his representation of Caesar. Writing to his brother, Hill comments, 'I shew Caesar in a light which, though unexceptionally just, will appear so very new, as to provoke, I hope, the curiosity and attention of the public'[29]. Of course the claimed novelty of his representation of Caesar has to be questioned. In 1737 Hill is contributing to an already established debate, not generating a new discourse. For whatever reasons, responses to his rewriting of Caesar are generally positive. Bolingbroke's reply upon reading the tract suggests at least sensitivity to Hill's feelings:

> If the treatise has not entirely convinc'd me, that Cæsar was a Patriot, it has convinc'd me, at least, in spite of all ancient and modern

prejudices, that he was so, as much as Pompey; and that liberty would have been as safe in his hands as in the others.[30]

Hill's tract represents Caesar not as a villain, tyrant and destroyer of the republic but as a man whose intentions were genuinely pro-Republic. Caesar, whose plan was to save Rome from itself, was merely misunderstood.[31] Hill rejects Addison's earlier representation of Caesar as a tyrant who 'ravaged more than half the globe, and sees / Mankind grown thin by his destructive sword'.[32] Addison's text was the source of much material which Hill sought to refute, particularly in relation to Caesar's imperial project. Certainly Addison's negative depiction of Caesar's military expansion does have obvious and damaging connotations for the representation of British colonialism, 'While Cato lives, Caesar will blush to see / Mankind enslaved, and be ashamed of empire'.[33] If the colonial expansion of Rome is shameful, the implications for Britain as a developing colonial power are clear. Hill and Cibber both attempt to reconfigure Addison's version of history in order to suit their own pro-colonial agendas. Cibber blatantly uses Cato as evidence for Caesar's status as an Imperial hero:

> Cato woul'd term it but a specious Bribe
> For power: That Pompey's Blood was, in regard
> To Rome, reveng'd, to court her Senate's Favour:
> That Cleopatra's beauty, not her Cause,
> Regain'd her Crown: Yet Cato has his Merits:
> And Men one Day may change their Thoughts of Cæsar. (30)

Cibber's Caesar pre-empts Cato's criticism. But Cato, despite such error in judgement, has some virtues and likewise, the actions of Caesar may one day be properly understood. However, as Bolingbroke's response to Hill suggests, for Caesar to become accepted as a 'hero', rather than a tyrant, more evidence was necessary than simply the suggestion that commentators have erred in their judgement of him. As we have seen with regard to Rapin's *Histoire* the place of Rome in terms of constructions of national self-hood during the eighteenth century is complex. Rome occupies the space of both other and model for the British national identity. It is this conflict which prompts Rapin to emphasise Britain's non-compliance in the coloniser/colony relationship.

Ambrose Philips's *The Briton* engages in a similar agenda, the Romans here are characterised by their effete manipulation of language and operate in opposition to masculine renderings of the British-self. The

Britons in Philips's play are manlier, more heroic than the almost foppish Roman invaders. Caesar in particular occupies a space that traverses both spheres, as we have already seen he can be variously interpreted to suit partisan inflection. Representing Caesar as a convincing imperialist hero is problematised by his oft cited role as destroyer of the idealism of the Republic, the difficulty which Aaron Hill identifies and anticipates in his letters. In order to generate a convincing case for Caesar and Imperial Rome as models for British colonialism, Caesar had to be transformed into more than just an imperialist hero.

Bolingbroke identifies this very shortcoming in Hill's account of Caesar. Hill's tract falls short of recasting Caesar as that model of political probity – a patriot. This is exactly what the pro-Caesar plays attempt to create. The rhetoric of patriotism is employed in order to shift perspectives of Caesar and re-interpret his actions as the acts of a patriot, not just an imperial aggressor. This benefits both the project of manipulating Caesar as a hero but also promoting Imperial Rome as a colonial model for Britain. Caesar and Rome are recast as a fantasy for British colonial emulation but it is not simply a case of retelling the histories; the plays have to re-appropriate Roman history and this re-appropriation occurs through the manipulation of patriot rhetoric. The plays reposition Julius Caesar as a patriot hero and importantly depict his imperial project, his actions as a colonial leader as justified, not a rejection of Republicanism but an attempt to force Rome to return to Republican virtues, 'Cato's Lectures shall give laws to Caesar' (36). Rome's colonial expansion has to be authorised and represented as morally justified if Britain's own colonial prospects are to be encouraged and developed. Caesar had to be transformed into a patriot equal in merit to any of the English, Welsh, Scottish and Irish national heroes who litter the stage in the British histories.

## Caesar and the patriot fantasy

By representing Caesar's military expansion as an heroic achievement the plays of Cibber and Mulgrave, although challenging conventional perceptions of Caesar during the period, do not make unprecedented statements.[34] Caesar's foreign campaigns, fought under the Republican government, were seen by most commentators as proof of his military excellence.[35] His involvement in the civil war however was not so easily justified and as a result transforming Caesar from war hero into a convincing patriot was a distinct challenge. First and foremost the notion that Caesar was a patriot conflicts with a significant number of contemporary representations of Rome's first Emperor. In Addison's *Cato*

(1713), Caesar threatens the liberty of Rome and the Roman Empire. In Rowe's translations of Lucan's *Pharsalia* (1718), 'Caesar is the incarnation of ruthless ambition operating to the destruction of the res publica, Cato is the most glorious of the republican heroes'.[36] In these accounts and others like them, Caesar is a tyrant – the antithesis of a patriot.

The challenge such entrenched representations of Caesar posed to alternative accounts is again evident in the letters of Aaron Hill. Writing about plans for his own Roman play, Hill comments that, 'the reputation of Mr Addison's Cato upon our stage, has made it an indispensable necessity, that whoever, in the same place, would see justice done to an opposite character, must proceed with a great deal of caution and delicacy'.[37] Hill took his own advice by publishing *An Enquiry into the Merits of Assassination* which he intended to act as a precursor to his play *Cæsar* an adaptation of Voltaire's *La Mort de César* (1731).[38] It is this fervent detachment from negative representations of Caesar and the subsequent re-negotiation of Caesar's character and moral credentials that makes these texts particularly significant to a study of the patriot drama of the period and raises the simple but pertinent question – why is it so important to recast Caesar as a patriot?

I would suggest that for some texts this shift in the representation of Caesar reflects a concern for rendering British colonial identity in a positive light. This purpose for the rewriting of Caesar's character can be usefully discussed and perhaps most obviously evidenced in relation to Cibber's play. In *Cæsar in Ægypt* Caesar's participation in the civil war is shown to be an act of patriotism, not the result of his oft criticised unfettered ambition. Cibber challenges Caesar's reputation for tyranny and he is repositioned as the avenger of tyrants, 'Tremble, ye Tyrants for your impious Power! / The Gods are just and send their Caesar's arms, / T'avenge the Injured, on the guilty Head' (19). Cibber's methods here might well be viewed as somewhat clumsy; this is not the only time his audiences had to endure a bombardment of opaque refutations of Caesar's 'unfounded' reputation. His representation of Caesar as a patriot is a flight of fancy repeatedly contradicted by Caesar's search for power, 'While Earth contains a *Roman*, that presumes / With Means coercive to reduce my Power, / All thoughts of Peace are but inglorious Dreams' (39). But Cibber's dramatic licence operates to support and substantiate broader notions of imperial benevolence. If, as contemporary pro-colonial commentators asserted, Britain's own colonial project was not simply designed to benefit the few, but the whole nation, economically, socially and politically, Cibber and pro-colonial writers like him had to create examples of Imperial leaders who function as patriots. What pro-colonial writers needed to support their cause were colonial exemplars who could feed and support notions of a beneficent British colonialism. Cibber's Caesar is created as just such an exemplar, to promote an image of morally circumspect Imperial self-hood. His failure, which is merely hinted at in Cibber's text, is not through lack of vision or a destructive self-interest but the short-sightedness and greed of others. Texts such as Cibber's play provide a model for Britain to both emulate and surpass.

It could of course be argued that the fact that patriotism was a popular dramatic as well as political trope suggests that Cibber and Mulgrave were simply opportunist in their appropriation of patriot rhetoric rather than responsive to a specific topical issue. Plays with a political agenda, whether acknowledged or denied, were popular crowd pullers and there is an obvious motivation for any playwright to utilise politically resonant rhetoric. Fashion and commercial incentive can clearly not be overlooked in any discussion of publicly performed dramatic texts. However, I would assert that all of the Roman plays discussed here employ patriot rhetoric for specific and identifiable political purposes and not simply to cash-in on politically rapacious and alert audiences. As I have already discussed, Mulgrave's texts re-appropriate Caesar for a specifically Jacobite agenda. His plays act as a reaffirmation of his political allegiances and in this sense Mulgrave's treatment of Caesar as patriot is evidence of a deeply personal political dialogue. In contrast, Cibber's play, in common with the other texts I shall discuss, engages with broader, more public political discourses relating to colonialism and the compatibility of colonial politics and patriot rhetoric. The association in Cibber's text between a patriot Caesar and patriot colonialism is suggestive and its parallel repetition and development in other contemporary texts lends compelling evidence to the argument that these plays offer more than simply a depoliticised manipulation of populist rhetoric.

So how do the pro-Caesar plays go about re-appropriating Caesar and reinterpreting him as a patriot? As I have already indicated the central conflict here is between the conventional interpretation of Caesar as an avaricious power hungry tyrant and the rhetoric of patriotism which denies self-interest and personal ambition. Here the sceptical audience could view a re-interpreted Caesar's claimed patriotism as further evidence of his attempts at amassing 'power and self-promotion'.[39] The self-proclamation of patriotism could be negatively perceived as political spin of the sort employed by numerous politicians keen to establish their credentials as worthy representatives. It is exactly these images of power and advancement that had to be obscured from a representation of Julius Caesar as a patriot because these are the accusations so frequently levied against Caesar as evidence of his tyranny and abuse of power. Echard's attempts at reconfiguring Caesar culminate in his somewhat casual dismissal of Caesar's oft-chastised ambition as simply 'the fault of the times'. Other commentators went further and were keen to re-invoke this image of Caesar's destructive ambition identifying it as political, rather than personal, ambition for the nation not for personal glory. Cibber does just this and his methods, if not more convincing than Echard's contextualised acceptance of Caesar's ambition, are certainly more complex and more politically resonant.

*Cæsar in Ægypt* juxtaposes two politically volatile states, Egypt and Rome. By decree of the Roman Senate and the old king, Egypt was to be ruled conjointly by Cleopatra and Ptolemy. However, the Queen, 'the people's Idol' (2), is powerless in her brother's court. She is perceived by her subjects to have political sway, but this perception is merely a contrivance of Ptolemy to safeguard his own position. Ptolemy allows Cleopatra a degree of outward freedom for fear that the people would revolt should they become aware that the young King and his counsellors control Egypt, 'The Force of Ægypt wou'd not curb their Rage, / Nor Ptolemy were safe upon his throne' (2).

The Roman republic is also suffering internal conflict, albeit of a more public nature, and again this internal wrangling provides the people of the Empire with an opportunity to exercise their own power. Ptolemy and his counsel see in the civil war between Caesar and Pompey the possibility for extricating Egypt from Rome's control:

> The Storm of civil War, now rais'd by Cæsar,
> Withdraws their insolence from foreign Realms,
> To waste their Valour on their proper Subjects!
> Their distant Care of us, is but their Pride,
> And Wantoness of Power; intestine Jars
> May humble them to Justice, and reduce
> Their Empire to its old Italian Bounds. (3)

Although Ptolemy's fears for his own safety under similar circumstances are later justified, his analysis of Egypt's power not only underestimates Rome's hold over its dominions but also contrasts with Julius Caesar's justification for the war with Pompey and his envisaged conclusion to the conflict. Upon hearing of Pompey's assassination Caesar is moved to tears, 'With what transporting Joy, the harrass'd World, / Had, in one peaceful, public Chariot seen / Pompey, and Cæsar, o'er their Jars triumphant!' (28). Caesar's intention was not to overcome Pompey but to persuade his enemy to join with him against those responsible for the decay of the Republic. Caesar identifies Pompey as a good man whose ambition coupled with that of the Tribunes turned him against Caesar and by association the values of the Republic. Civil war, according to Caesar, was the only option:

> Had Rome her ancient Virtue, with her Power,
> Cæsar had trembled at her Civil Wars:
> But Luxury, Corruption, Vice and Fraud
> Have draind' her down, ev'n to the Lees of Rome.
> Her Honours, now by publick Price are bought;
> Her Magistrates, by Blows, not Votes, elected:
> Thus is the Carcass of her Freedom torn
> By Beasts of Prey, each scrambling for his Share.
> Where Men are Wolves, what Wretch wou'd be the Lamb?
> Where Laws are violated, Arms are Virtue. (33)

This justification of his actions denies all accusations of personal ambition. Caesar is a patriot, protector of republican ideals, acting in response to violations of Roman law. Therefore, when Achoreus questions Caesar on his 'famed' ambition Caesar replies, 'Where it opposes Virtue, charge me freely! / Be bold, If I am justify'd to one / Good Man, the Millions I offend are Railers. / Virtue, like the Sun, shines not for Applause' (32). Caesar's ambition is for Rome, accusations of self-interest are merely 'Wherewith thy Enemies asperse thy Fame' (32).

Mulgrave's representation of Julius Caesar demonstrates a similar focus on the patriotism and public benefit of Caesar's actions. Mulgrave transforms Casca's report of Caesar refusing the crown from Shakespeare's original descriptive passage to a substantial dramatic scene. In giving Caesar a voice, Mulgrave questions conventional representations of the Emperor as an ambitious tyrant, ''tis the Tyranny, not Name, ye fear; / And that my Soul abhors, as much as you. / Witness, ye Gods, I have no other Aim / Than to advance your Good, and my own Honour' (223). But it is not only Caesar's words which shift his representation, his presence dominating the stage is suggestively heroic, a physical manifestation of the adroit nature of his words. By removing Caesar's collapse, Mulgrave reverses the negative impact of the original reported account. In Shakespeare's text Casca claims, 'the rabblement hooted, and clapped their chopped hands, and threw up their sweaty night-caps, and uttered such a deal of stinking breath because Cæsar refused the crown, that it had, almost, choked Cæsar, for he swooned, and fell down at it'.[40] In Mulgrave's version, Caesar's commitment to Republican ideals remains untarnished. His refusal of the crown is staunch and his physical strength uncompromised. Instead of swooning at the 'stench' of the crowd, Mulgrave's Caesar challenges and refutes their judgment of him:

> How have I us'd my Pow'r, that you should fear it?
> Then, to be more secure, here take my Life;
> I freely offer it to every Roman.
> Let out that Blood, you think boils with Ambition,
> I'd rather lose it, than out-live my Fame;
> Nor would accept of Pow'r, unless to please. (225)

It would be inaccurate to suggest that Mulgrave's *Julius Cæsar* represents Caesar as entirely faultless. Such an assertion would over-simplify the text and elide Mulgrave's intimate portrayal of Caesar's personal struggle with ambition, a complicating factor which Cibber's and Mulgrave's texts share in common. However, these alterations do clarify and quantify Caesar's position. Whatever his faults, Mulgrave's Caesar is clearly a patriot. In a statement about the role of kings, comparable to that of Henry in Aaron Hill's *Henry the Fifth*, Caesar declares his intentions towards the people of Rome, 'I'll guard them from themselves, their own worst Foes; / And will have Pow'r to do whate'er I please; / Yet bear my Thunder in a gentle Hand. / Like Jove, I'll sit above; but 'tis to show / My Love and Care of all the World below' (225–6). Caesar accepts the power of a dictator in order to safeguard his people from the vice and corruption that have polluted the ideals upon which the glorious Republic was founded. When, after the assassination, Antony finds a scroll on Caesar's body, he reads the contents to the assembled citizens:

> Behold this Scroll, the very hand of Cæsar!
> In it he notes this firm and settled Purpose,
> First to subdue the Parthians, our worst Foes,
> And then restore Rome to her ancient Freedom.
> "I'll keep the Pow'r, saith he, of Rome's Dictator,
> "Till I have vanquish'd all her Enemies:
> "Then, O ye Gods! May she be free for ever,
> "Tho' at th' expence of all our dearest Blood!
> That precious Blood is here indeed let out,
> But where's the Liberty we purchase by it?
> Slaves as we are the Murderers and Villains. (324–5)

Caesar's intentions were honourable; his ambition was for Rome, not himself. Mulgrave's version of the reading of Caesar's will departs from

Shakespeare in that, rather than granting the citizens of Rome money and land (II.2.2. p. 112), the will reveals his patriotic intention to restore to them their liberty. Mulgrave's adaptation shifts the emphasis away from bribery and economic incentive onto a morally emblazoned restoration of rights and freedoms which by implication is, as Caesar, forever lost.

In *Cæsar in Ægypt* Julius Caesar is again depicted refusing a crown. Cibber uses the trope to highlight contrasting attitudes to arbitrary rule. In advising Ptolemy to refuse assistance to Egypt's ally Pompey, Photinus rejects obligation and gratitude as guiding principles for a monarch. In contrast Achoreus urges Ptolemy, 'To guard your Crown, Sir, is our eldest Duty: But what are Crowns that are not worn with Honour?' (5). Ptolemy, settling for the self-serving advice of Photinus, rejects Pompey's plea for help and offers his own crown to Caesar. Caesar's response reinforces the moral position of Achoreus and further undermines the role of monarch, 'What Heirs from Heirs receive, blind Fortune gives, / Where Birth prefers the Infant to the Man! / While heritable Crowns entail not Virtue, / The Boast were greater to bestow, than wear them' (25). Cibber emphasises in his Caesar a Republican attitude towards monarchy, 'Crowns are the Trophies of Tyrannick Sway. / Romans may conquer, but disdain to wear 'em' (25) in order to valorise the British constitution as determined by the Revolution Settlement. Cibber's Caesar engages with Court Whig rhetoric, celebrating modern Britain's parliamentary monarchy and safeguarded Protestant future. His aims and ideas are represented as approbation of the constitutional order presaged by the Glorious Revolution.[41] Cibber's text contrasts the Egyptian arbitrary monarchy, a monarchy of faction, disorder and tyranny, with the ideals of republican Rome in order to highlight the superiority of the British, Whig government, the supposed antithesis to Ptolemy and his followers. But here, Republican values are projected onto Imperial Rome. Cibber's Caesar, unlike Mulgrave's, is not merely a misunderstood retrograde, one of only a few Romans to uphold true Republican standards; he is instead an Imperial patriot, intent on re-immersing the Empire in the ideals of the Republic. Throughout the play however, it is not the mode of government that forms the focus but the personal credentials of the opposing leaders. As such, Julius Caesar is represented as a patriot who engages with and evokes Republican rhetoric yet occupies the space of a dictator – balancing the liberty of citizens against the economic wealth and growth of the nation. This conflict between modern notions of democratic government and demonstrations of ancient Roman imperial dictatorship is, I suggest, a recurrent impasse which problematises attempts to dramatise colonial and imperial politics within a framework of patriot rhetoric.

One way of analysing the significance of these attempts to rewrite Caesar as a patriot with regard to notions of British colonial identity is to consider the role of favouritism in the plays. Favouritism is, as we have already seen, a recurrent theme in patriot drama of the period, where favourites are repeatedly positioned as the enemies of the patriot and his or her nation. Favourites and the consequences of favouritism are, unsurprisingly, important motifs in these pro-Caesar plays. Caesar's own favouritism was the subject of many contemporary commentaries and often cited, along with ambition, as his fatal flaw. Unlike the English history plays however, favouritism is used by Cibber and Mulgrave both to impugn the villains *and* to justify the actions of the patriots. When Caesar's enemies are accused of favouritism, it is a sign of their weak leadership and lack of patriotism. When Caesar's favourites turn against him, Caesar is merely too trusting, placing a disproportionate emphasis on military honour, itself often employed as evidence of patriotic credentials, indicative of the measure of a man's character.

In Cibber's *Cæsar in Ægypt* Ptolemy's counsellors demonstrate the danger favouritism represents to the nation. Having received Pompey's letter requesting support, Ptolemy turns to his advisors. The King directs his request for counsel as challenge, an opportunity for obsequiousness, and in response his counsellors vie for his approbation. Achoreus, the first to speak, responds as usual with the voice of reason and his position is predictably and summarily rejected. From then on, each counsellor's response 'improves' upon the sycophancy of the previous one until finally Photinus asserts:

> What Laws of Nations, Justice, or of Honour,
> What Contracts, Leagues, or Treaties bind us down,
> To prop this falling Pompey with our Bones,
> To be by Cæsar crush'd and trampled into Ashes? (7)

Ptolemy's own ambition is awakened by Photinus. Photinus toys with the King's desire to retain absolute power over Egypt; failure to act against Pompey would, he argues, allow Caesar to 'veil his vengeance, in an Act of Justice ... T' invest her [Cleopatra] solely with the sov'raign Power' (13). In serving Ptolemy's ambition and greed Photinus secures his position as royal favourite and in accordance the remaining counsellors are commanded to 'obey / The Orders of Photinus' (8).

As ever, such transfer of sovereign power has far-reaching consequences and the eighteenth-century audience, well-versed in the various
dramatic histories of absentee monarchs, would immediately recognise
Ptolemy's mistake and eagerly await his inevitable downfall, guaranteed
not only by history but by dramatic convention. In this instance it is
not entirely clear what motivation Photinus has beyond merely out-
doing his fellow counsellors. He does not demonstrate Machiavellian
ambition, he has no plan to augment his own power and his advice is
not tailored to assist his own promotion beyond that of becoming 'chief'
counsellor. Nor is he a patriot manoeuvring his monarch for the good of
his country. Photinus's advice is simply bad, stemming, initially at least,
merely from the desire to win a contest of rhetoric. When, in accordance
with his advice Ptolemy presents Caesar with Pompey's head on a stick,
the outraged and grief stricken 'Tyrant' grants Ptolemy a reprieve for his
'youth and inexperience' and declares he will 'turn the Eye of Vengeance /
On elder Criminals, thy Flatterers' (29). In response to Caesar's threat
Photinus exerts his influence over Ptolemy with renewed vigour and
motivation. When Ptolemy commands his followers to act like 'men'
and give themselves up to Caesar in order to save their King and country,
Photinus's response is a model of patriotic resolve, 'Our Sovereign's Will,
not Cæsar, shall condemn us' (47). By massaging the King's ego in this
way Photinus paves the way for his own survival, or so he thinks. Despite
Ptolemy's initial insightful caution, 'What vaunting Project brooding in
thy Brain, / To save thy self, wou'd plunge thy Prince in Ruin?' (49), he
is quickly swayed by Photinus, who invokes an image of the victorious
Cleopatra aided by Caesar, 'Wanton, and toying with the Fate of Ægypt'
(49). Photinus presses all the right buttons, 'To give your Vengeance
Choice, on whom to fall! / Whether on us, whose Arms wou'd set you
free, / Or on this wasteful Tyrant, that enslaves you' (49). He incites
revenge in the King and presents him with the means, the catacombs
beneath the city in which Egyptian troops are hidden ready to pounce on
Caesar. As a favourite, Photinus is forced to exercise his influence not for
self-aggrandizement but for self-preservation. Of course this second and
more urgent reason for Photinus to sway Ptolemy is fruitless. Photinus is
killed fighting against the united forces of Caesar and Pompey. Not only
is Photinus an ineffectual favourite, he is also a poor soldier.

In Cibber's play it is not the favourite who is at fault but the ambitious and vainglorious monarch. Adopting the familiar pro-Walpole
defence that when the favourite is carefully chosen, favouritism is not
in itself unpatriotic – *Cæsar in Ægypt* hints at the potential for patriotic favouritism. Cleopatra firmly places blame with her brother, not

his favourites, 'I thought thy Youth misguided by thy Creatures, / That they alone had wrought thee, to the Tyrant; / But find thy Nature to their Hands, had form'd thee' (74). It is Ptolemy's tyrannous nature, his greed and unrestrained ambition that have led him to endanger the safety of Egypt and his people. It is ironic therefore that Ptolemy's death is depicted as an involuntary act of regicide. In their desperate attempts to escape Caesar's forces, the Egyptians clamber aboard the King's barque. Ptolemy is killed by his own followers, the over-laden vessel, 'Sunk floundring down, and perish'd in the Deep' (75).

In contrast, Mulgrave's play depicts favouritism as Caesar's 'fatal flaw'. It is a flaw that Caesar himself is aware of:

> I confess my Weakness, I am frail
> Like other Men, and partial for a Friend;
> Yet that's a fault Heav'n easily forgives.
> Be thou, my best lov'd Brutus, Chief of Praetors:
> And, Cassius may accept the second Place,
> Not only in the State, but my Affection. (277)

For Cassius, second place is intolerable. Mulgrave depicts Brutus hovering between the extremes of supporting his patron or following Cassius in turning against Caesar, 'What, kill the best, and bravest of Mankind, / Only for Jealousy? Of being Slaves./Oh dismal Sound! Who can dread that too much? / The fear of Slavery is Fortitude.' (249). When Brutus finally resolves to reject Caesar's patronage, he justifies this rejection on the grounds of his abhorrence of favouritism, 'Frowns had not frightened me, nor shall his Favours / With all their Syren Voice entice me to him' (278–9). Brutus justifies his treachery by accepting that the slavery of Roman citizens will be the undoubted result of Caesar's rule. Brutus turns Caesar's favouritism against him, portraying Caesar as the purchaser of allies whereas, in fact, by 'purchasing' Brutus Caesar has offended Cassius, the more likely subject for opportunistic acquisition.

Favouritism is a key concern of many of the Roman histories, not only those texts which focus on Julius Caesar. In Philip Frowde's *The Fall of Saguntum* (1727), a play set during time of the roman Republic, the high priest Eurydamas and his co-conspirator Lycormas attempt to curry favour with Hannibal in order to secure their own safety when the inevitable Carthaginian victory occurs. It is significant that their attempts to secure the favour of Hannibal are based on the sacrifice of Fabius and Curtius, the Roman heroes, protectors of Saguntum. In William Philip's *Belesarius* (1724), a play concerned with a history which for many confirmed the demise of the Roman Empire, the tragic hero is Justinian's favourite.[42] As the play opens the Emperor decrees that Belesarius shall marry his sister Valeria, 'Pow'r and Honour will attend the Gift'.[43] Justinian divests himself of imperial power, choosing to follow academic pursuits whilst Belesarius acts in his absence. This relegation of power is a familiar theme and the consequences of such absenteeism are as serious in the Roman histories as in the English histories we have already considered. Ambition, favouritism, and factionalism epitomise the failings of Rome. But in the plays of Cibber and Mulgrave these failings are not shared by Caesar. His ambition and his favouritism are excused and explained. The factionalism he engaged in was a necessary evil participated in and perpetuated only with an eye to the greater good of the Empire. For the imperial leader, recourse to older forms of government, less egalitarian and seemingly less patriotic leadership are essential for sustaining the stability of the Empire. Without his favourites, his personal and imperial ambition and his dictatorial leadership, Caesar's Empire would self-destruct and the demise of the Roman Empire can be attributed to the short-sightedness of those citizens who turned against him before his project could be completed.

The representations of Julius Caesar in the texts of Cibber and Mulgrave are akin to that of Echard's *Roman History*, 'A person of the greatest Soul, the most magnanimous Spirit, and of the most wonderful Accomplishments and Abilities that Rome, or perhaps the World, ever saw'.[44] Whereas the patriots of the English histories are conventionally opposed to the favouritism of their monarchs, in the Roman histories favouritism is accepted as an integral part of the Roman Imperial model. Simultaneously condoned and condemned, favouritism reveals one of the complexities of establishing Caesar as a patriot imperialist. In all of these texts Caesar is not a violent war-hungry villain but the protector of Rome, who, had he not been so brutally prevented, would have restored the ancient rights and liberties of that once great Empire. Caesar, rewritten as a patriot, might well serve as a benchmark by which British colonial leaders should be measured, but in order to establish Caesar and Imperial Rome as convincing exemplars, patriot rhetoric itself has to be utilised somewhat selectively by these pro-colonial playwrights. Patriot colonialism, particularly based on a Roman model, is, as we shall see, fraught with tautological instabilities.

## Rewriting patriotism: a model for British colonialism?

Despite having established the ways in which Caesar was rewritten as a patriot leader, misunderstood by his people, misrepresented by his enemies and falsely criticised by successive commentators, there remain many conflicts which threaten any fantasy of patriot colonialism founded on a Roman model. First is the subordinate place of Britain in relation to Rome. It was impossible to effectively obscure the role of Rome as enemy to the 'Ancient Britons' and by extension the British liberty so frequently cited as originating from these resistant forefathers and mothers. Second, the obvious weaknesses in Roman history – Rome's often delayed and slight response to threats to its colonies from other, sometimes lesser, powers outside the Empire and of course the blatantly pertinent fact of the eventual disintegration of the Roman Empire. How can these problems, which clearly resist the interpretation of Rome as colonial model, be reconciled? How can Rome and Julius Caesar act as models for British colonialism given these inherent insufficiencies?

Bridget Orr's account of an earlier dramatic engagement with Rome may be of some use in addressing these questions. Writing about representations of the Roman Republic and Empire on the English stage between 1660 and 1714, Orr suggests, 'the ideological emergence of the first Empire is legible in the often ambivalent fashion in which English playwrights identified their nation's ancient accession to civil society, true religion and domestic propriety'.[45] What Orr defines as an interest in England's 'own heroic age' is, she claims, demonstrated in dramatic representations of Britain's conflict with the Roman Empire. In texts such as George Powell's *Bonduca; or the British Heroine* (1695), Britain as a colony benefits directly from her coloniser in that the Britons are civilised by contact with the superior culture, their skill in combat is strengthened and their sense of national identity coalesces in the face of a militarily aggressive and superior other. However, later plays, such as the British histories discussed in this book, are not concerned with exploring Britain's heritage as a Roman colony and the impact of the Roman occupation in terms of civilising and shaping Britain.

The plays that discuss Roman history during the early eighteenth century focus on the parallels between the ancient Roman Empire and modern British colonial expansion. In order to draw on this analogy, Britain's place in the coloniser/colonised relationship has to be redressed. Rome and Britain are reconfigured to occupy the same imperial space. Despite the evident shortcomings of Rome at the time of Julius Caesar, depicted not only by dramatists but also by historians and politicians as removed from the ideals of the Republic, Imperial Rome could still offer Britons an obvious model, albeit not an entirely flawless one, for their own colonial interest. However, this model and the notions of patriot colonialism on which it is constructed are part of a colonial fantasy which the plays, historical accounts and commentaries I have discussed, all subscribe to. With reference to national self-awareness Karen O'Brien has argued that in order to construct a sense of unifying identity concrete political ideas about the nation's past and future are necessary, 'the journey, however, from political ideas to modes of awareness is an imaginative one, entailing, in the case of narrative history, a process of literary implementation'.[46] O'Brien's assertion can be usefully applied to the Roman plays and histories discussed here. In order to determine through a figuration of Imperial Rome, what colonial Britain 'should be', a degree of literary implementation is required. Both narrative histories and dramatised histories are instrumental in the transformation of Rome and particularly Julius Caesar as models for British colonialism. Readers and audiences alike are asked to subscribe to fantasy. To some extent this is achieved by a shift in focus away from viewing the Roman conquest of Britain from the position of a 'colonised nation' to that of a colonial power, a shift suggested in part at least by Rapin's account of the Roman invasion of Britain as more beneficial to the colony than the coloniser, emphasising Britain's resistance to Rome rather than Rome's success in colonising Britain.

Cibber's *Cæsar in Ægypt* draws upon the image of Britain as a beneficent but recalcitrant colony by contrasting British resistance with Egyptian acceptance and thus authorising Roman control of Egypt, or British control of other lands, through the complicity of the colonised peoples. The Egyptians are represented as willing participants in the subjugation of their country. Upon his arrival Caesar is greeted with adulation, 'From Ear to Ear, a joyous Murmur flies, / Bursting, anon to Shouts! Lo! Cæsar comes' (19). As the play closes Caesar explains his military actions to the widowed Cornelia:

> The Laws they [Scipo, Cato, and Pompey's Sons] fight for,
> Cæsar will maintain;
> Nor are they safer in their Hands than his!
> When I look round the World and see
> What Miseries attend Abuse of Power,
> I judge my Conquests by the Gods assign'd,
> To give their Laws new Force, and mend Mankind!
> If then Ambition prompts me to excel
> The greatest Patriot fam'd for ruling well,
> Let foul-tongu'd Envy burst her swelling Heart,
> My conscious Virtue shall perform its Part.
> Cæsar his Period to the Gods shall trust,
> Nor can, 'til Gods forsake him, think his Arms unjust. (77)

Here Cibber's Caesar stages a justification of the *pax Romana* which had the potential to resound as offensive to an eighteenth-century British ear and had its roots in 'an ethic of war which was opposed to the ethic of trade'.[47] Of course in the context of Whig politics and Walpole's policies in particular there is a clear conflict between Roman militarism and the contemporary self-image of the beneficent merchant nation. However, Cibber's construction of Caesar as the protector of Republican values, not their assailant, has clear political resonance for the contemporary audience in relation to colonial ambition and the fantasy which authorises colonial expansion. Cibber creates a Caesar who upholds the ideals of the Republic, but has realised that, as an institution, it was destructing from within. Cibber's text therefore presents us with an analogy between Britain and Rome which is simultaneously critical and deferential.[48] Caesar is portrayed as the rightful commander of the Roman Empire, subduing Egypt into submission with the aim of ruling as the Republicans had intended.

So whereas critics such as Weinbrot have argued that literary texts during this period were forced to engage with an ongoing political dialogue which rejected Roman military expansion in favour of British commercial expansion, I would suggest that these plays accept military expansion as a means to achieve economic and political stability.[49] In *Cæsar in Ægypt*, and the tragedies of *Julius Cæsar* and *Marcus Brutus*, Caesar's expansionism is depicted, not as immoral or barbaric but as patriotic and honourable. The Roman intervention in Egypt served to exact vengeance for the murder of Pompey and, more importantly, to secure the rule of Egypt as both the Senate and the old Egyptian King had decreed. Thus Caesar's actions are justified by both patriarchal and constitutional law. Although this text appears to deny Ayres's analysis that analogies with Rome became less deferential, in fact, Cibber positions those responsible for the degeneration of the Republic in opposition to Caesar. As with Mulgrave's adaptations, Cibber's play suggests that in Caesar the Roman world loses not only a patriot hero, but ultimately the hero who, had it not been for his assassination, could have restored Rome to its former glories.

It is important to note that not all Roman plays of the period positioned ancient Rome as a model for British colonialism. The history upon which Philip Frowde's *The Fall of Saguntum* is based suggests the potential for an anti-Roman model of empire. Saguntum was seemingly abandoned to its fate by the Romans when Hannibal laid siege to the city for eight months. The inhabitants, not to fall into the enemy's hands, destroyed themselves in the conflagration of their houses. The response from Rome was purely ambassadorial and it was not until Hannibal turned his military threat directly to Italy that the Romans began to act against him and the second Punic war began. Clearly, in choosing to abandon rather than protect their territory, this version of their history suggests that the Romans are not model colonialists. However, it is intriguing that Frowde chooses to criticise Roman colonialism through Republican rather than Imperial history. The dictator Fabius, whose prudent measures in the face of this mighty enemy were labelled cowardice by the Roman counsel, is the hero of Frowde's play. His role, however, is somewhat different to that ascribed to him in history. Frowde's Fabius is a young Roman in love with the governor's daughter Timandra. Fabius and his fellow Roman Curtius are represented as the epitome of Roman nobility and heroism. Fabius curses, 'th' eternal Infamy of guilty Rome' and Curtius declares, 'We must not live to see the City taken; / But, bravely dying in Saguntum's Cause, / May our Blood expiate our Country's Shame'.[50] Throughout the play Fabius, Curtius and Theron (the chief priest of Hercules) are the only morally upright characters to voice criticism of 'Rome's Offence' (17) in failing to support Saguntum. Eurydamas and his confederate Lycormas, spread lies and insinuations about the Romans in order to secure Carthaginian favour. The message to Britain is clear. Rome, despite the glorious virtue of individuals, forsakes her colony and in doing so neglects the implicit duty of a colonising nation to protect its dominions:

> We did e'er to our own Honours fail;
> If e'er unhappy Counsels did prevail
> To let a brave Confed'rate miss our Aid,
> Be That ill-fated Period thrown in Shade!
> Or, to ease the memorable Blame,
> Lets mend by Glory what we can't disclaim! (Prologue)

To 'mend by glory', certainly in terms of military victory is, it could be argued, exactly what the Romans did after the fall of Saguntum. Frowde's play therefore can be seen to offer the Roman Empire as an example, not only of the failure of colonial duty, but also the importance of reasserting imperial authority and, by doing so, saving face. The analogy between the Roman loss of Saguntum and Britain's loss of St. Lucia to the French in 1723 could not have been missed by a contemporary audience.[51] Britain, the new colonial power, should make amends for past indiscretions by asserting the nation's true glory, 'Our British Arms this gen'rous Pride avow, / To guard Allies, – and Empires to bestow' (Prologue).

In William Philips's *Belisarius* the hero is depicted, like Cibber's and Mulgrave's Caesars, as a Roman hero greatly wronged by his countrymen. For Belisarius, however, it is the actions of his Emperor that promote the jealousy and factionalism which bring about his tragic demise. Belisarius is compared favourably with both Julius Caesar and Fabius:

> Not the first Cæsar as in his Resolves
> More firm or flew more swift to execute.
> Not Fabius was more wise, more circumspect.
> Never was Man more lavish of his Blood
> In Glory's hot Pursuit; the Conquest gain'd
> Joyful he gives the Soldier their just Fame,
> He shares the Fame, but yields them all the Spoil. (3)

Belisarius's virtues eclipse those of the Roman military heroes who have gone before him. Roman imperialism is again applauded.[52] The tragic end to Belisarius's life is not as the result of his expansionist outlook. Belisarius's military prowess harks back to the heroes of the Republic. It is the envy of his fellow Romans, the absenteeism of Justinian, the failings of Imperial Rome that secure his fate. When Belisarius returns victorious 'adorn'd with Conquest' his friend Proclus declares:

> He were no Friend to Honour, Justice, Truth,
> No Friend to Cæsar, or the Roman Name,
> If Joy dilated not his Breast this Day.
> Again the Roman Name is great in Arms,
> To Heav'n ascends, with former Splendor shines,
> And Rome again obeys her rightful Lord. (5)

His words, ironically spoken to the very people who do *not* feel such joy at the success of Belisarius, are in stark contrast to the preceding and subsequent vitriolic discussions between Hermogenes and his brother Macro, 'Already I have spy'd the Path which leads / To gratifie Ambition and Revenge' (5). Hermogenes and Macro typify the unpatriotic behaviour identified by eighteenth-century commentators as the catalyst for the downfall of the Roman Republic. Self-serving ambition was not only the scourge of the Republic but also the affliction of Imperial Rome. Belisarius, like the Caesars of Cibber's and Mulgrave's plays, is a model patriot, a hero despised for his success and his emulation of republican political ideals.

So although there is no resounding and unanimous approbation, many of these plays identify from the histories of Imperial Rome an appropriate model for British colonialism. But it is a model which lacks stability, shored-up by individuals who, at moments of crisis, act with a profound patriotism. One clear reason for the textual instabilities and contradictions in these plays is the simple fact that Rome failed and the Empire fell. Obviously the disintegration of the Roman Empire was impossible to obscure and this fact inevitably raises pertinent queries regarding the suitability of Rome as a model for British colonial endeavour. Indeed, the fact of Rome's disintegration is not elided in these plays, as might be expected, but rather, in selecting individuals who were great leaders, the plays demonstrate Rome's failings in not reaching the great heights promised by these individuals. It is therefore Rome's potential that is dramatised through these representations of virtuous men (and this is a distinctly masculine model of patriot colonialism) who lead the nation, albeit momentarily, in the right direction.

We have already discussed the identification of ambition and factionalism, 'the faults of the times' as instrumental to Rome's failure and these notions are key to the representation of Rome as an imperial exemplar – British politics, so the argument goes, is devoid of such faults and therefore British colonialism will succeed. But it is not only factionalism and ambition that are blamed for the demise of the Roman Empire and as such there are other ways of validating British colonialism on a Roman model. Religion is a significant factor with important resonance for an audience of contemporary Britons. Roman paganism, and for some writers Roman Christianity, disturb the pro-colonial narratives of these texts. Religious unorthodoxy, according to modern doctrine, coupled with the predominance of ambitious self-interest, prevents Rome from being represented as the pre-eminent colonial model. But it is religion and religious difference which allow these texts to promote British colonialism and the British imperial future as capable of surpassing the Roman model. This key difference between ancient Rome and modern Britain lends further support to the fantasy of patriot colonialism. Protestant Britain will succeed where heathen Rome failed.

## Protestant Britain: validating colonial fantasy

The notion that Britain's Protestantism guarantees a moral and political superiority is nothing new and is repeatedly reflected in the various

Whig, and many of the opposition, versions of Britishness we have already encountered. Similarly the concept that Protestantism authorises British colonialism is not a claim unique to early eighteenth-century drama. But what is interesting here is the way in which these plays promote and rely on the fantasy that Britain has the authority to colonise because it is a Protestant nation. What can be seen in these plays is a deepening of this fantasy of Imperial authority which moves towards notions of divine appointment. Britain's power over her colonies is re-inscribed as a 'divine right' a term no longer applicable as part of the political heterodoxy of the nation itself but not incompatible with advocacy of the freedom and liberty associated with the Revolution Settlement and Britain's self image when applied to colonial encounters. Britain can justifiably exercise divine right outside the confines of the nation, on citizens other than her own, simply because Protestantism signifies superiority.

The pro-Rome and pro-Caesar plays manipulate the disparity between authorised Roman and British religions in two distinct ways. In emphasising the infidel beliefs of Rome's enemies, Rome and Britain are brought closer together as powers acting in opposition to the heathenism of their imperial opponents and their own colonies. Cibber elides Caesar's non-Protestant credentials by highlighting the paganism of the Egyptians. Cibber's Romans evoke their gods very infrequently, no prayers are offered by Caesar or his followers. Caesar is made more acceptable to a Protestant audience by not pursuing images of Roman religious beliefs and practices. Conversely the Egyptians criticise both their religious leaders and their gods, yet repeatedly demand favours for a myriad of different political and personal reasons. The prayers of the Egyptians are juxtaposed with outcomes directly opposed to the desires of the supplicant. For example, when Ptolemy invokes the 'Pharian' gods to 'Incline this Day propitious to our Vows!' (51), the lack of divine intervention during the subsequent action of the play reminds the audience of the Egyptian counsel's earlier disrespect for the 'holy function' (6) of Achorus. In addition, the irony of his somewhat pre-emptive thanksgiving, 'Gods! I thank you! / This Hour has well repaid the Wrongs of Empire' (70), followed shortly by the news that 'Pharos is in Flames' (72), is not lost. Caesar merely mentions the gods in relation to his own fate, 'Cæsar his Period to the Gods shall trust, / Nor can, till Gods forsake him, think his Arms unjust' (77). In order to retain a sense of Caesar's appropriateness as a British colonial model Cibber elides the fact that Caesar is clearly not Protestant. Similarly Mulgrave strips *Julius Cæsar* of references to Caesar's paganism. Mulgrave eradicates the soothsayer and omens from Shakespeare's text but retains the more palatable and theatrically spectacular ghost of Caesar in *Marcus Brutus*. But this sleight-of-hand convergence of British and Roman religious practice does little to respond to the central problem generated by literary interpretations of Rome as an imperial exemplar – the demise of the Empire itself. Caesar as an individual can be made more palatable as a model if his real religious practices are obscured but Rome as a nation cannot be so easily re-written. Indeed, for a pro-colonial text, emphasising Roman heathenism as a contrast to British Protestantism is a much more fruitful direction.

In Frowde's *The Fall of Saguntum* it is significant that the villains, Eurydamas and Lycormas are pagan caricatures. Their doctrine is practiced whimsically and with only a view to furthering their ambition and self interest. In contrast their Chief Priest, Theron, is paternalistic, using his status in order to scold the crowds for their naïve acceptance of the libel spread by Eurydamas against Fabius. Unlike his subordinates Theron's engagement with pagan ritual exists in his name and title only. As the play draws to a close, Theron has a vision of a new Saguntum arising phoenix-like from the ashes of the city. To some extent Theron can be seen as a device designed purely for the purpose of reporting this vision. His place in the action of the rest of the play is insignificant, serving only to establish his moral circumspection. Theron's morality follows a notably Anglican, Protestant, 'good works' model and his authority is derived more from these familiar morals than from his hierarchical position as chief of the Pagan priests. He is essentially a Christian dressed in pagan clothes. According to Theron, the new Saguntians shall maintain their pagan faith until the time comes for them to be freed from political and religious tyranny:

> When as circling Years have roll'd their Round,
> O'er various Realms shall Tyranny abound;
> A mighty Nation then shall Heav'n ordain
> To curb th' Oppressor, and to break his Chain;
> A gen'rous People, that delight to save
> Pleased from the Tyrant to set free the Slave,
> Polite as Romans, and as Romans brave.
> Hail, glorious Warriors! Wellcome to our Shore;
> With Joy I hear your future Engines roar;
> With these combin'd shall mighty Deeds be done,
> I see Iberia's Empire soon o'er run (72).

It is clear from Theron's use of patriot rhetoric that the generous, liberty loving, Roman-like, glorious warriors are future Britons. This vision of Britain as a colonising yet liberating power suggests a moral role for colonial expansion. Protestantism is the key to this moralised version of colonialism. Britain as a Protestant nation is free from the tyranny imposed by her Roman Catholic neighbours. According to Theron's vision, Britons will free Saguntum from the Catholic tyranny of Spain; the British Empire will expand as an act of liberation achieved by the conversion of infidels.

Theron's vision conforms to what O'Brien describes as the imagined, 'peaceful and mutually beneficial consumer communities' of the British Empire, the introduction of Protestantism to the 'heathen' world being one of the benefits to the colonised society.[53] What else makes Imperial Britain better than her European counterparts, better than her Roman predecessor, but Protestantism? Conceptualising British colonial expansion in terms of civilising, liberating and educating was of course enduringly popular.[54] In terms of the nation's expansionist endeavours commercial gain is repeatedly obscured by the emphasis placed upon moral enterprise or religious conversion of the 'other'. The pro-Caesar plays adopt these very concepts in order to vindicate Julius Caesar's expansionist actions. Given Britain's colonial losses to the French during the 1720s and the growing threat perceived to be posed by Spain, not only to British colonies but also to British trade links, the representation of Britain as the successor to the glorious Roman Empire was also clearly attractive – if not to everyone, at least to a large proportion of an increasingly commercial-minded population of colonial investors.[55]

According to these texts therefore, the Roman Empire failed because of the ambitious self-interest of its citizens and, perhaps more importantly, the Empire's lack of religious purpose. Rome, even when converted to Christianity, was not the 'Heav'n ordained' nation many commentators chose to envisage Britain as. These plays are not underscored by the 'cultural and political anxieties' that Gerrard identifies in James Thomson's *Liberty* (1734–36) they are instead absorbed by the fantasy of colonial expansion. Cibber, Frowde, and Philips ignore 'the gloomy possibility that Britain may and perhaps must go the same way as Rome'.[56] Protestant and free, Britain will be, these texts suggest, more successful. Colonial endeavour is valorised in these Roman histories as the province of a libertarian Protestant nation.

There is however one play which questions the moral validity of colonial expansion on a number of counts. We have already seen the criticism levied at Rome for abandoning her colonies in Frowde's play. The same text makes a further anti-colonial statement in the form of Candace, the

Amazonian Queen. Candace remarks: 'How poor a thing is Empire! And how vain, / To pride ourselves upon its short-liv'd Glories! / The mightiest Monarchs of the peopled Earth / Are still the Subjects to Capricious Fortune' (24). Candace's role here is problematic. Her presence in the history is purely fanciful and her words and actions throughout are those of a sentimental heroine, not the matriarchal warrior who, as an Amazon we might expect her to represent. Her words here are clearly levied against both the Carthaginians and the Romans but are they supposed to act as a warning to modern Britons? Frowde's purpose is unclear; the Queen's observations regarding the transitory nature of Empire certainly qualifies and undermines Theron's hopeful vision of Saguntum's future and Britain's beneficent colonialism. Here the demise of Empire is seen as inevitable and as a consequence the effort of colonialism is futile. Religion, patriotism and authority are all subject to the ebb and flow of fortune and Britain's claim to govern its colonies by the authority of its Protestant superiority is mere rhetoric. Candace's words question the true motivation for empire-building and challenge the notion of patriot colonialism. But her voice is a lonely one in these Roman plays and for now our focus will rest on the fantasy that effectively obscures less egalitarian colonial ambitions.

Despite the fact that the commercial gain of the colonising nation has ostensibly no place in these plays commerce continues to underscore the imperial fantasy these texts depict. Although the financial benefits of colonialism are obscured from direct representation, the commercial interests of the colonising nation are conspicuous – consider for example the contrast between Caesar's subjugation of opulent Egypt versus Rome's strategic abandonment of Saguntum. Again these texts can be seen to be negotiating a difficult rhetorical path in that the moral and commercial interests of their audiences need to be reconciled. The obfuscation of commercial gain suggests that even for middle-class merchant audiences the dominance of morality over economics is an essential element of the fantasy surrounding colonialism. Caesar's expansionist policies are rewritten as the protection of Republican ideals from the corruption and disorder of the Republic itself. Belisarius' patriotic efforts in protecting the Roman Empire are thwarted, and ultimately the Empire disintegrates, due to the economic self-interest and jealousy of his political rivals. Commerce, particularly the commercial gains of the coloniser, needs to be eclipsed by a moralised conceptualisation of the colonial model. Moral superiority is key and all of the Roman plays assert Britain's dominance in moral terms, either as a reflection of Imperial Rome or as an improvement upon the Roman example.

What guarantees this conceptualisation of the colonial model in all of the dramatic texts and histories discussed in this chapter are Protestantism and patriotism, so fundamental to British identity in the early eighteenth century. The colonial fantasy relies on these cornerstones of British notions of moral, political and religious superiority and to some extent the histories of ancient Rome have to be rewritten, with these concepts at the fore, in order for Rome to act as a suitable model for British colonialism. In the pro-colonial plays Julius Caesar is reinvented as an imperial patriot. His credentials as an imperial hero and expansionist aggressor are not enough to establish a pro-colonial account of Imperial Rome with resonance for contemporary British colonial interests and ambitions. As a patriot Caesar achieves the moral credentials essential to the construction of Rome as a pro-colonial model for Britain's own imperialism. As a patriot colonialist, this alternative version of Caesar becomes another myth reflecting Britain's own notions of the nation's right to and enjoyment of liberty, as well as religious, political and moral superiority. These pro-colonial texts build upon the mythologised image of Britain, discussed in earlier chapters, utilising the same rhetoric in order to feed contemporary fantasies regarding the egalitarian nature of British colonial endeavour and the legitimacy of British imperialism. It is here that Caesar's reputation for ambition and tyranny can be seen to support rather than undermine Britain's imperial self-image. Caesar's role as patriot protector of the Roman Empire justifies his recourse to tyranny.

The rhetorical conflict between notions of British liberty and freedom and the subjugating role of colonial Britain is smoothed over in these plays in that Caesar and Imperial Rome authorise British colonialism by establishing a moral framework for acceptable tyranny. Commercial gain, either in national or personal terms, is not the endgame for either Caesar's or Britain's 'tyranny' over their territories; both share an image of stability, securing the nation at its core as well as at its furthest extremes. The plays justify British expansion by distancing the coloniser from the colonised in moral terms, obscuring the motivation of commercial profits and suggesting the divinely ordained right of Britain over the 'other'. Alongside this, notions of mutual beneficence further obscure the commercial imperative that drove colonial ambition during the period and add to the sense of moral incentive on the part of the coloniser. Each of these elements combine to create a powerful rhetorical fantasy which was clearly attractive, and endured in various manifestations, throughout Britain's Imperial history.

What these plays also reveal is the instability inherent in this type of pro-colonial discourse which attempts to simultaneously assert the moral superiority of the coloniser and notions of mutual beneficence. However compelling, the fantasy of patriot colonialism, as we shall see, does not withstand close inspection. There are frequent rhetorical conflicts in these texts, tyranny juxtaposed with liberty, ambition combined with patriotism, enslavement converging with freedom. These contradictions stem from the attempts of the playwrights to dramatise an image of colonial stability from an Empire that simply did not endure. Like the British histories already discussed, the Roman plays rely on myth – the rewriting of history – in order to project an image of British stability. All of these plays rely on iconic figures (Shakespeare, Alfred, Raleigh, Elizabeth, Caesar *et al.*) to carry valid and useful allegorical comparisons that would otherwise lack positive political resonance. The only rejoinder to this conflict is further recourse to fantasy in the form of the easily deconstructed contention that British Protestantism will assure colonial success and the longevity of empire far in excess of that achieved by the ancient Roman model.

# 5
# Turks, Christians and Imperial Fantasy

> Are we turned Turks, and to ourselves do that
> Which Heaven hath forbid the Ottomites?
>
> William Shakespeare, *Othello* (1604)

> I also hope that none civil think that I am an Advocate for the Saracens, Arabs, or Moors (the Reader may call them as he pleases) when I bestow on them the honourable Epithet of *Warlike* ... since in Eighty Years Time or, less, that Martial Nation erected an Empire of incomparably larger Extent than the Romans were ever able to do in eight hundred.
>
> John Morgan, preface to *Mahometism Explained* (1725)

The observation that the eighteenth-century theatre was a place of 'interculturalism' is an assertion which is perhaps not well demonstrated by the plays discussed in this book thus far. With the exception of the various identities that formed Britain itself and representations of Britain's Catholic neighbours, these history plays do not travel beyond culturally familiar territory. Where foreign soil is represented it is exploited in order to showcase Britain's self-image of Protestant superiority. However, three Turkish history plays from the 1720s and 1730s illustrate interculturalism in a way that is particularly pertinent to my discussion of theatrical engagement with imperial fantasy.[1]

The Ottoman Empire had long held the fascination of British theatre audiences and by the beginning of the eighteenth century the Turk was well established in the repertoire of stock characters in the London playhouses.[2] The stage Turk was popularised in the sixteenth and early seventeenth centuries, as Othello's disbelieving outburst reveals, in the form of a distorted demon, an object of fear and disgust. By the late seventeenth century a gradual softening in representations of the Turk had occurred. No longer perceived as a demon, the Turk acted as a reminder for the audience of their own religious, political and moral superiorities.[3] Continuing this development, the early eighteenth century witnessed a growing tolerance in attitudes towards the Near East, with Islam and Islamic culture having significant influence upon literature, art and fashion.[4] As the Islamic world moved closer to the West in logistical, political and cultural terms, the growing popularity and volume of print accounts of 'real' experiences of Muslim life demanded a reassessment of these vilifications of the Turk on the basis of cruelty and lasciviousness.[5] There remained, however, a conflict between cultural shifts in imaginative interpretations of the Turk and the desire within the establishment, in both political and religious spheres, for sustaining national fear and mistrust of the Islamic East. As a result, literary, historical, political and social commentaries on the Turk were engaging in fluctuating and often self-contradictory discourses, manifest in John Morgan's attempt to distance himself from the epithet of 'Saracen advocate' in the epigraph above. Mita Choudhury's notion of 'interculturalism' suggests a two-way process of cultural exchange which is certainly evident in early eighteenth-century accounts of Turkish culture. Nevertheless, dramatic representations of the Turk during this period move beyond this notion of mutual exchange by engaging the multifaceted nature of images of the East, a pliability exploited to serve numerous political, doctrinal and pecuniary causes.

In the 1730s two new plays based on the history of Scanderbeg were performed on the London stage.[6] William Havard's *Scanderbeg* premièred at Goodman's Fields in 1733 and George Lillo's *The Christian Hero* premièred at Drury Lane in 1735. In addition a third, unperformed text offered another dramatisation of the same history; written some time in the 1720s, Thomas Whincop's *Scanderbeg; or, Love and Liberty* was published posthumously in 1747.[7] This concentrated dramatic interest in Islamic history suggests a social and political topicality, and the choice of the re-converting Christian hero Scanderbeg implies an anti-Islamic agenda.[8] However, this small cluster of Scanderbeg plays represents more than a simple continuation of the recurrent theme of the subjugation of Islam by Christian moral supremacy. Like many plays from the seventeenth and eighteenth centuries that share the subject and setting of the Scanderbeg plays, issues of empire and colonial politics are woven into the texts. In dramatising Ottoman history the plays examine a geographically local yet threatening colonial power. Juxtaposed against the backdrop of Britain's own colonial ambitions, the Scanderbeg plays re-appropriate the Turk for his imperial rather than lascivious credentials.

The 1730s were a decade in which notions of British colonial expansion were politically and socially significant. It is a decade in which the imagined future of the British Empire shifts, in terms of its geographic focus, moving east, towards India, and in relation to the perceived function of empire, the domain of merchant economics rather than expansionist politics.[9] By representing in microcosm the downfall of the Ottoman Empire at the hands of a Christian rebel, the three Scanderbeg plays participate in the ongoing construction of Britain's national and increasingly colonial identity. In addition, these texts have their own partisan agendas, which influence the representation of colonialism and frequently problematise issues of empire. The multifaceted figure of the Turk further compounds the variety of interpretations of Britain's colonial role. Unlike the English histories discussed in previous chapters, in which the French and Spanish are consistently referenced as the antithesis of Britishness, in these plays unpatriotic behaviour is not indiscriminately associated with the religious 'other'. Sixteenth- and seventeenth-century religious polemic linked Turk, Pope and Antichrist, but this connection is not unquestionably accepted in the Turkish history plays of the 1730s where the allegorical purpose of the Turk is multivalent.[10]

This chapter examines the Scanderbeg plays in the light of all of these issues: popular taste for 'la Turquie', interculturalism (in trade terms and in relation to the unique possibilities for cultural exchange presented by the theatre) and the delicate balance between the nation's imperial fantasy and the realities of colonialism. The position of these plays, as ostensibly anti-Islamic texts, is considered in relation to contemporary accounts which created 'a picture of Islam as at once splendidly luxurious, admirable in its severity, sombre in its cruelty and sensuality and terrible in its strength'.[11] The three versions of the Scanderbeg history discussed here engage with and manipulate the dominant interpretations of Ottoman culture evident in contemporary commentary. But more than simply re-establishing familiar stereotypes associated with the Turk, this chapter argues that not only do these texts have political resonance but that they can also be read as contributions to debates concerning the maintenance of empire and the impact of colonial expansion on the nation's identity and governance.[12] Britain's relationship with the Ottoman Empire during this period was primarily focused on commercial exchange and this chapter examines the plays in light of this social and political context. Ottoman culture and merchandise were frequently equated with luxury, imbibed with both the negative and positive associations of the term and thus, similarly multifaceted in their signification. These plays can be read as attempts to negotiate the difficult relationship between commerce, luxury and Empire by positioning the Ottoman Empire as a model, exemplar or warning, for British colonial endeavour; a modern, commercial alternative to the ancient empires of Greece and Rome.

Despite what the eponymous heroes of these plays might suggest, as voices in the debate about the growth of the British Empire these texts are far removed from the deprecating representations of Turkish culture that dominated older accounts of the Ottoman Empire. However, we must be careful not to over-simplify the reception of, and interpretation of, the Turk by eighteenth-century audiences, commentators and readers. Although the beginning of the eighteenth century can be identified as a point of closure for the demonization of Islam, so prominent in early modern drama, the erosion of Christian prejudice against Islam was, as we shall see, a process requiring more than the expansion of profitable trade relations to reach any definite conclusion.

## Rewriting the demon Turk

Viewed from the perspective of a small colonial power, the Ottoman Empire could be seen by Britons as the obverse of their own nation yet, at the same time, a conspicuous manifestation of British colonial ambitions and potential. The Ottoman Empire was used by commentators as a direct reflection of Britain's own colonial endeavour but was also constructed as an inverse image, a way of demonstrating Britain's innate superiority to this religious and political 'other'.[13] Furthermore, by the 1730s the simultaneous benefits and costs of colonial power were manifest to any observer of Ottoman culture. This once terrifying Islamic empire was beginning to deconstruct. Once described by Richard Knolles as 'the scourge of God and present terror of the world',[14] the Ottoman Empire was on the verge of stagnation, subject to internal conflicts and an erosion of its power and influence in the region.[15] Like the Romans, the Ottomans proved that political instability at the heart of an empire would herald its demise. In contrast to early seventeenth-century writers who described the Turk as a threatening and potent adversary, commentators of the early eighteenth century were faced with the need to revise this inherited anti-Islamic polemic and consider instead the implications of the downfall of this once great empire for British colonialism. Of course, as recent scholarship has shown, the Ottoman Empire was not, at this stage, in serious decline and Western European powers saw no opportunity during this period for a military challenge to Ottoman control.[16] Thus, the relationship, or connections perceived between the Ottoman Empire and Britain were complicated by speculation regarding both the status and future of the Ottoman territories and Britain's own future as a colonial power.

Despite notions of Ottoman disintegration, Linda Colley's image of the Ottoman Empire as an awe-inspiringly 'vast, alarming bloc' sits comfortably alongside eighteenth-century reiterations regarding the magnitude and significance of these Muslim adversaries.[17] Irrespective of any sense commentators may have had of the political instability of the Ottoman Empire, Britons continued to perceive the Turks as a danger to their own nation's political security and economic prosperity.[18] During the first half of the eighteenth century the activities of the corsairs based in the ports of the Barbary States of Morocco, Algiers and Tunis became synonymous with the increasingly frequent capture and enslavement of European traders. Anti-Islamic propaganda disseminated via sermons and royal proclamations, designed to raise ransom money to free British captives, ensured that for many Britons, 'North African Islamic society stood for tyranny, brutality, poverty and loss of freedom, the reverse and minatory image of Britain's own balanced constitution, commercial prosperity, and individual liberty'.[19]

Discordant accounts of the present political state of the Ottoman Empire were amplified by the place occupied by the Turk in the public imagination, the subject of propaganda and anti-Islamic sentiment for many generations, but also an enticing image of exoticism. By the beginning of the eighteenth century the reality sat somewhere between seventeenth-century rhetoric that had over-emphasised the threat posed by the Turk to Europeans, representing the Ottoman Empire as an immeasurable threat, and contemporary notions of a disintegrating and dysfunctional Empire.[20] Nonetheless, imaginative interpretations of Turkish culture and Ottoman imperialism continued to oscillate between these two extremes, the Turk remained in the popular consciousness as a figure of ambiguity and contradiction.[21]

Trade relations between Britain and Turkey further augmented this broad spectrum of interpretations of the Turk and Islamic culture. The Ottoman Empire was a crucial source of trade for the supply of Britain's own Mediterranean empire.[22] In historical terms this was a brief moment in which intensive trade took place between Britain and Turkey, a period of vigorous but un-sustained exchange. So the image of the Turk here undergoes yet another revision, becoming symbolic of a valuable trade link and of significance to Britain's own economy. This reso-nance, along with older conventions of the Turk as tyrannical other and more contemporary notions of Ottoman Imperial failure, are com-bined in the representation of the Turk and the Ottoman Empire in the Turkish history plays. These texts speculate about Britain's colo-nial endeavour and imperial future by engaging with, and in some cases rejecting, an imperial fantasy modelled upon the Ottoman Empire, which itself had proved a valuable dramatic spectacle due to popu-lar associations with fantastical exoticism. Surprisingly, given the clear evidence of public fascination with the near East, and unfortunately for the managers and actors involved in the productions of Havard's and Lillo's plays at Goodman's Fields and Drury Lane, this combi-nation of exoticism and colonial star-gazing was a speculation that returned little in the way of hard profit, a matter I shall return to shortly.

Knowledge of Ottoman culture amongst the general populace was thus based upon a combination of fact and fantasy, neither of which could be disentangled from the other. Of course, fantasy was not limited to the Turk, but extended beyond Ottoman territory, encapsulating those aspects of British life that came into contact with such otherness and exoticism. One fantasy which had particular public appeal was that of the Levant merchants, 'famous for their wealth' and their position of power in the City, to such an extent that 'the term "Turkey merchant" was often applied to wealthy businessmen, even when their connection with the Levant was slight'.[23] The 'Turkey merchant' was therefore, from one perspective, an object of reverence, but of course not all accounts of trade during the early eighteenth century reflected such approbation, 'for many in eighteenth-century Britain commercial enterprise, far from providing an avowed and unqualified imperative, was at once the source of a new culture and the cause of imminent collapse'.[24] Just as representa-tions of the Turk and Ottoman culture were riddled with contradictions and open to conflicting interpretations, trade itself was subject to var-ied, and often fantastical, representation. Economic growth was, for some commentators, not a sign of 'national greatness, but degener-ate luxuriance'.[25] So, at a time when Britain's trade with the Ottoman Empire was at its peak, the Turk could be employed to represent a fan-tasy of economic exchange (symbolic of luxury) and the worst evils of modern consumer culture (excessiveness and unnecessary consumption) whilst simultaneously posing a threat to British liberty, both literally, as a prospective captor, and figuratively, as a symbol of the encroachment of a new, economically driven and politically influential lobby. If we are to envisage the Ottoman Empire as a model for Britain's own colonial progress then it must be viewed with one eye firmly fixed upon British trade interests. Issues of governance, religion and culture, explored by the various factual and fictional accounts of the Ottoman Empire, contribute to the fantasy of otherness that surrounded eighteenth-century interpretations of the Turk but, as equal in significance as this mark of difference between the two powers was what the Ottomans and the British shared in common; an economic fantasy based upon trade, growth, power and commercial prosperity.

Curiously, however, the utility of Empire was not at the top of the government's agenda during the early decades of the eighteenth century. Exploitation of the colonies in trade terms was a merchant- rather than government-led agenda. There was a lack of government action during the early eighteenth century, even in terms of utilising the colonies as a discreet source of taxation revenue. As a result, the mythology surrounding Britain's claimed power overseas, in economic terms at least, is undercut by this lack of control exerted by the government over its Empire.[26] This is not to say that government took no interest in income from the colonies, but rather that matters closer to home were seen to be more pressing:

> What was different about the 1730s and 1740s was not the enlightened and liberal imperialism of Walpole and Pelham, but the domestic distractions which ministers of George II faced, the limited public and political consensus which they were able to call on in the implementation of policies, and the limitations of the administrative process.[27]

With domestic politics essentially preventing a coherent colonial policy – as Langford notes, 'even to speak of colonial policy before the Seven Years War is somewhat misleading' – where the economic utility of Empire *was* recognised it was difficult for government to establish a sustainable agenda.[28] Indeed, the primary impetus for colonial activity, from the government's perspective, came as a reaction to European politics. Empire was a matter of political posturing within a European context rather than broader interest in commercial benefit. But from a commercial perspective Empire and the economic benefits of colonialism could not be overlooked. The increasing significance of the merchant-class to early eighteenth-century politics and domestic experience, allowed for the assimilation of merchant-values into the nation's self-image, 'commerce's increasing ideological sway as the century progressed could thus be easily grafted on to the pre-existing mythology of the country as the "sceptr'd isle", a state providentially defined by its natural geography'.[29] Where merchant ideology is entwined with the authorised national fantasy of Protestant Britain as the 'elect' land, notions of liberty and patriotism become synonymous with economic growth; personal and public prosperity become integral to articulations of British national identity. Given the significance of trade with the Ottoman Empire, both in terms of supplying Britain's Mediterranean Empire and in relation to the provision of luxury goods for the domestic market, it is easy to see a specifically commercial rendering of British identity which rewrites existing versions of British supremacy derived from the country's difference to Catholic imperial neighbours, drawing instead upon trade and ideological connections with Ottoman culture.

The Ottoman Empire thus becomes a model in which speculative versions of British colonial policy can be played out, a colonial fantasy against which British colonial ambition could be measured. The Turkish history plays can therefore be situated within this framework as texts that attempt to negotiate the problems of promoting a colonial model based upon exoticism and otherness without dispensing with the imagined identity of Britain as the land of liberty. This very negotiation, I would suggest, contributed to the financial disappointment experienced by Henry Giffard and Charles Fleetwood in their productions of Havard's and Lillo's Scanderbeg plays. Neither play was particularly successful, in part perhaps because social interests overtook Havard's and Lillo's agendas, subsuming popular taste for the East. The 1733–34 season became embroiled in preparations relating to the impending marriage of the Princess Royal to the Prince of Orange, resulting in a degree of patriotic fervour amongst dramatists, alongside which, analogies between Britain and the Ottoman Empire would not sit comfortably. The Ottoman Empire as model for British colonial policy was an allegory that, for all but the most ardent of merchants in the London audiences of 1733 and 1735, stretched imaginations too far.

The vagaries of the taste of London audiences aside, as commentators began to recognise that their predecessors had underestimated the internal difficulties plaguing the Ottoman Empire, approbation of Ottoman policy became less seditious and so the disintegration of the Ottoman Empire, ironically, gave commentators greater opportunities to expound the Empire's virtues for British emulation. In *A Full and Just Account of the present of the Ottoman Empire* (1709), Aaron Hill identifies within the floundering empire a colonial policy worthy of envy, albeit an envy focused on the impressive size of the Ottoman dominions.[30] Hill makes repeated reference to the political, religious and social divisions that he claims are the cause of the current decline and likely fall of the Ottoman Empire:

> A conspicuous Probability of the approaching Downfal of the Turkish Empire, which has grown by gradual Acquisitions, to a most amazing Bulk, and Constitution, but at present seems so weaken'd by the Natural Corruption and Infirmities of Age, that Terrible Convulsions shake its Frame as if 'twere hastning onwards, towards a Sudden Period.[31]

According to Hill's account, the Ottomans 'built the most absolute Empire, and Arbitrary Monarchy, that has ever flouris'd since the Worlds Original.'[32] It is not however the securing of this empire and the related atrocities that interest Hill. He is quick to remind his reader that Britons are quite capable of emulating the immorality associated with Ottoman colonial policy. Christians can be as immoral as infidels; 'My native BRITAIN cou'd produce as Barbarous and Sordid wretches, as I ever met with in my Conversation with the Infidels'.[33] As Gerrard notes, Hill 'is undoubtedly more interested in projecting himself into the picture as an adventure hero than in attempting a serious synthesis of political, religious and geographical observation'.[34] Despite his sensationalist agenda and opportunistic motivation, Hill's *Full and Just Account* has a lot to say about contemporary British opinion regarding Ottoman culture, history and politics. Hill admires the legendary military prowess of the Ottomans asserting that this once victorious nation is ripe for resurgence:

> Yet, notwithstanding the Inglorious reigns of several Modern Emperors, have added nothing to their Territories, they still continue in a full Possession of their former Acquisitions, and are not only able to Defend their own, but Conquer other Countries, shou'd the Warlike Spirit of some more Active Sultan once lead 'em out to Action. (4)

Hill's claim that if the Ottomans had 'active' leaders, they could regain their position as a world-dominating imperial power should not be construed as suggesting that his 'Serious Observation' is entirely commendatory of Turkish political and social customs. Hill repeatedly criticises Turkish morality and religious belief. However, his text defines a Turkish model of empire that offers an example to Britain and her empire-builders.[35]

Hill's *Full and Just Account* is not an isolated example of literary approbation of Ottoman culture. In *Letters from the Turkish Embassy* (1716–18),

Lady Mary Wortley Montagu frequently commends Turkish government, law and social etiquette.[36] Other lesser-known texts, such as David Jones's *A Compleat History of the Turks* (1701 reprinted, 1718), praise the Turks for their colonial prowess.[37] Joseph Morgan's 1725 translation of Mahomet Rabadan's *Mahometism Explained* attempts to diffuse Christian misconceptions of Islamic belief, drawing parallels between the moral and ethical dogma of Protestantism and 'Mahometism'.[38] These texts are certainly aimed at capitalising upon the British public's fascination with the Near East. The taste for Islam was at the very least a significant commercial motivation for the composition and publication of factual and fictional accounts of Ottoman culture. But within this commercially responsive trend in publication is a colonial discourse focused on a repeated conflation and comparison of British and Ottoman colonial activity. These texts are participating in political and social debates which go beyond a fashionable fascination with the exotic.

There is an intrinsic contradiction evident in all of these texts, arising from attempts to reconcile inherited accounts of Turkish atrocities with an admiration for Ottoman colonial policy and success. Although problematic, this contradiction is crucial to texts involved in the promotion of colonial policy modelled on the Ottoman Empire. The division between Briton and Turk, repeatedly positioning the Christian Britons as superior to the Muslim Turks, suggests that, unlike the dwindling Ottoman Empire, the developing British Empire has the potential not only to flourish but also to survive. British Protestantism and the patriotism of the nation are again brought as evidence of Britain's right over its dominions and her superiority over her colonial peers. Contemporary accounts of the Ottoman Empire, both narrative and dramatic, identify moral and political principles crucial to the success of the burgeoning British Empire. Such texts engage in a debate regarding the ideological foundations of British colonialism.[39] The Ottoman Empire, like the Roman Empire, is a valuable model despite its failings. The immediacy of the Ottoman model, its existence alongside modern colonial Britain and its complex image as a social/cultural adversary, economic ally and exotic other, problematises this model in a way which is resistant to the linguistic gloss achieved in the Roman plays. This negotiation of the Ottoman Empire as a colonial model, culturally and socially exoticised, morally abhorred, militarily threatening yet on the brink of disintegration forms the basis for the confused and contradictory public perceptions that the Scanderbeg plays of the 1730s both respond to and are embroiled in.

## Liberty and consent

William Havard's *Scanderbeg* (1733) and George Lillo's *The Christian Hero* (1735) provide their audiences with opposed interpretations of the Ottoman Empire and divergent constructions of Britain's ideological empire. What places these two texts, ostensibly concerned with the same moment in Ottoman history, on such opposed paths is not just the difficulties commentators faced in constructing a uniform interpretation of the Turk but also their obverse responses to the notions underpinning Britain's claim to colonial authority. Eighteenth-century colonial commentators had to navigate a myth based upon 'liberty, homogeneity, commerce and natural laws' which was repeatedly disrupted and undermined by 'the reality of dissenting politics, alterity, conquest and systematized exploitation'.[40] This fracture between the myth of empire and the facts of colonialism has much in common with the myths relating to national stability and the homogeneity of Britishness discussed in previous chapters, mythologies which Lillo's text upholds and Havard's deconstructs.

Lillo's version of idealised empire is carefully grounded in the patriotic rhetoric of liberty.[41] Lillo's Scanderbeg is characterised as a patriot fighting for the freedom of his nation. Paralleling contemporary Western European perceptions of rebellious Ottoman colonies, such as the Romanian principalities, which saw in the decline of the Ottoman Empire the opportunity for regaining their independence, Lillo's Scanderbeg accepts as his duty the liberation of Epirus from Turkish rule:[42]

> I arm'd my subjects for their common rights.
> The love of liberty that fired their souls,
> That made them worthy, crown'd them with success.
> I did my duty – 'Twas but what I ow'd
> To Heaven, an injured people and myself.[43]

Lillo makes significant moral distinctions between the Christians and the Turks. Whereas Scanderbeg is the restorer and guardian of liberty, the Sultan deprives both his colonised peoples and his fellow Turks of their freedom. Lillo's text leaves no space for anything but a British Christian version of liberty. In contrast, although Hill identifies the subject's lack of liberty as a flaw in the Ottoman model of empire, his laconic description of the Turk's consequent 'superior happiness' turns his commentary from disapproval of Turkish oppression to thinly disguised criticism of Britain's own political system:

> Depriv'd of that indulgent Liberty we taste in Britain, and sometimes sacrific'd to the mercenary Interest of a brib'd Decider, he [the Turkish subject] has yet this Happiness superiour to us, that he always loses a Cause before the melancholy Consequences of a tedious Controversy has disabled him to support that loss.[44]

In highlighting the corruption underlying British and Turkish politics Hill targets Britain's self-professed superiority. British liberty is here identified as one of the myths of Britishness, but Hill's account hints at more than a localised national mythology. 'Indulgent Liberty', overstated as an advantage within British society itself, is also the notion upon which British colonies were established, a promise made but gradually eroding. Hill's account not only blurs the distinction between British colonial benevolence and Turkish atrocities but also highlights those areas of domestic affairs where Turkish modes of governance can be interpreted as the superior system. For the Turk, justice is swift and decisive; for the Briton, justice is slow and its consequences are irrelevant in comparison to the resultant social infamy associated with lengthy judicial processes and a society hungry for salacious gossip. Placed in the context of Britain's colonial future Hill's comments seem somewhat prophetic. The notion that liberty acted as a governing value for colonial growth was of course untenable. Persuasive rhetoric was employed to 'reconcile the paradox of a mercantilist colonial system informed by post-revolutionary political ideology'.[45] Promises of liberty to the colonies were meaningless when followed by the systematic extraction of all economic productivity for the benefit of London. Government-supported theories for a mature colonial system based on assurances of liberty never came to fruition. Restricting the economic self-control of the colonies through inordinate taxation for the benefit of Britain inevitably undermined the myth of liberty.[46] In Lillo's play, however, liberty is crucial to the success of empire and forms the basis for Britain's superiority in comparison to her Ottoman counterpart. The Turks lose the territories they have conquered because the liberty of those colonised is infringed. Forced to adhere to Islam and terrorised by their Turkish masters, the Albanians rebel under the leadership of their rightful king.

Lillo identifies no parallel between the lack of liberty granted to Ottoman colonies and the empty promises of liberty made to British territories. Although in reality Britain's colonies received little benefit from the 'Protestant, commercial, maritime and free' principles upon which Britian's colonial expansion was purportedly based, Lillo's play clearly upholds this precept.[47] For Lillo, liberty is the foundation of empire and, as Christians, Britons should grant their colonised peoples the same rights as those enjoyed by free Englishmen.

Havard's *Scanderbeg* presents a very different construction of colonialism. Here the patriotic rhetoric of liberty is rejected as self-congratulatory mythologising. Havard's text reflects instead the facts of colonialism and, like Hill, Havard emphasises the points of contact between British and Ottoman national politics and colonial activity. In Havard's play liberty is an abused term which the tyrannical Vizier uses to coerce his followers into rebellion:

> How must the glorious Change transport us all,
> When into Freedom Tyranny is turn'd?
> When each may say his Fortune is his own,
> And sleep in Fullness of Tranquillity?
> Then shall we taste the Sweets of Life, and Ease,
> Which happier Climes have known: then, enjoy
> That Liberty, which *Britain*'s smiling Isle
> So long has boasted thro' a Length of Years.[48]

The Vizier is clearly well-versed in the application of patriot rhetoric. In his attempts to raise followers for his planned rebellion against the Sultan, the Vizier suggests that the Ottoman Empire, under his rule, would enjoy the benefits of a liberty synonymous with Britain. However, the Vizier's promises are empty; it is clear to the audience that his followers will never experience true liberty under his rule. His disingenuous use of the ideal of British liberty demonstrates the way in which patriot rhetoric can be abused. Not only does this have implications for party claims to patriotism but also casts doubt upon the notion of liberty itself. In terms of colonial jingoism liberty is a powerful rhetorical tool. In Havard's play patriotism is reduced to an empty construct of partisan rhetoric.[49]

Although Havard's Scanderbeg pursues the liberation of his country 'the double Cause of love and Liberty' (5), it is notable that he makes no promises of liberty and no offer of freedom to either his people or those he has conquered. Havard draws a link here between Britain and Albania by positioning Scanderbeg as the political leader of a developing colonial power. As such, rather than claiming to grant liberty, Scanderbeg's control over his new territory is secured by less ideological means, a strategy with clear resonance for British audiences engaging with the allegorical reference to their own country's empire-building. In Havard's version Scanderbeg's colonial activities are distanced from images of forced subjugation or empty ideological justifications based upon fantasy. His colonial strategy focuses instead upon voluntary consent, a notion I shall return to shortly. In searching for the political stability so obviously absent from the disintegrating Ottoman Empire and thus demonstrably crucial to successful colonial expansion, Britain, and Scanderbeg, must address the facts of colonialism. In the wake of the South Sea Bubble commentators began to acknowledge that colonial stability could only be achieved with 'enlightened, and responsible geo-politics'.[50] The subjugation of the colonised nations might be necessary for the economic benefit of the colonial power but should be carried out in proportion to that tangible benefit. The Ottoman Empire as model for British colonialism offers exemplary subjugation but lacks proportion in enforcing suppression.

In Havard's text, enlightened and responsible colonialism necessitates the consent of the colonised nation. To this end Deamira, 'the beauteous Cause of Ruin and Destruction' (5), is positioned as Scanderbeg's consenting conquest. Deamira is desired by representatives of the three political factions dominating the play; Scanderbeg, the Sultan and the seditious Vizier. All three parties fight to possess her, 'Why flows the Blood of Millions on the Plain / But all for thee?' (70). Deamira, the desired woman, becomes an analogy for the desired territory. She must be fought for and conquered. More importantly, Havard introduces the concept of consent through his portrayal of this desirable woman. All three parties demonstrate a concern for securing her consent, but only Scanderbeg is the fortunate possessor of her promise. Despite the common concern voiced by her pursuers for securing her consensually, various attempts are made to violate Deamira. The Sultan exercises restraint by limiting his sexual advances to verbal threats, stating that his violent conduct is curtailed by her gender:

> – tho' to Man the Sultan's Temper
> Be fierce, revengeful, terrible and bold;
> Yet to the Fair that Haughtiness subsides,
> And sinks in due Proportion to their Softness:
> He wou'd not rudely violate the Will,
> And force the Bondage of Constraint upon it:
> He scorns to take, what his Compulsion drags;
> The gentle Wing of tender Inclination,
> Reluctant, flies from Force: Nor wou'd the Sultan
> Barely possess her Person, not her Mind. (5–6)

The Vizier however, is persuaded that force is an acceptable and established route to conquest, 'to force her to your Arms – 'tis no new Doctrine' (48). Both he and his subordinate advisor Heli attempt to rape Deamira. Although the motives behind these attacks differ – Heli is driven by greed and envy, whereas the Vizier demands sex as payment for rescuing her from Heli, claiming to have, 'sav'd thee from a Slave's Pollution' (69) – both men are depicted as interpreting Deamira as a possession or commodity for exchange. But Havard's text does not allow this commodification to stand unchallenged and joins those other early eighteenth-century commentators who argued that, in terms of colonial endeavour, there was an alternative to sheer force.[51] In Havard's version of the Scanderbeg history such an alternative is established by the combining of consent and coercion.

In this sense, Havard constructs Scanderbeg as an allegorical representation of the ideal colonial power. The slippage of terms between the language of sexual and colonial conquest facilitates this representation. Deamira is desired by each centre of power but she is resistant to either coercion or force, and ultimately Scanderbeg takes possession of Deamira because she consents to his ownership. Having rescued her from the Vizier, and in effect succeeding where his opponent failed, Scanderbeg returns to battle with the promise that: 'The Care of thee / Shall be my first Concern, and Conquest next' (73). Here, love and colonial conflict collide. Before his conquest of Deamira, Scanderbeg must take care of his 'colony' and protect her from the remaining prospective invader. As an allegorical colonial power Scanderbeg must accept both the role of subjugator and protector. Havard's *Scanderbeg* demonstrates the 'vacillation between consent and coercion characteristic of colonizing power'.[52] Various attempts are made to coerce Deamira into accepting conquest but it is significant that the success of Scanderbeg's advocacy of Christian doctrine, his dogmatic coercion and her resultant conversion arm her against subsequent attempts made upon her virtue by the Turks. In order to secure consensual colonisation the colonial powers must employ coercion, but coercion based upon empty promises of 'liberty' and 'freedom,' as opposed to the tangible benefits of religious conversion, ultimately leads to instability and insurrection.

Of course, women are not the only objects of forced colonisation in these plays, although the gendered language of exchange and bargaining and the implicit hierarchy between coloniser and colonised are sustained irrespective of the object of colonisation. In Havard's version of the Scanderbeg history, the hero is on the brink of rebellion. Captured by the Turks, converted to Islam, subjected to physical and emotional abuse,

Scanderbeg finally turns against his nation's long-term oppressor.[53] In a dual assault on Albania and Deamira, Amurant attempts to persuade Scanderbeg to re-establish his native land as part of the Turkish Empire:

> Her Will, you must confess,
> Has the best Title to dispose her Person;
> Yet still to let you see how dear thou art,
> That I remember still what once you were;
> Take back your Kingdom, be the Second here. (29)

Although the Sultan shrouds his coercion behind an alledged concern for obtaining Deamira's consent, he barters for her by attempting to bribe his primary opponent. Scanderbeg's reply is dismissive of the Sultan's attempt to strike a bargain, he rejects the notion of compromise:

> Woud'st thou barter thus
> For Love and Justice – No, the Pow'r above,
> Who at one Look sees all the Riches here,
> Sees nothing that can equal the Exchange – (29)

Scanderbeg will not jeopardize his colonial ambition by accepting a territory considered inferior to his already consenting conquest. In matters of empire, compromise is not an option. The 'vacillation between consent and coercion' may be an alternative to 'sheer force' but the best interests of the colonising power cannot be compromised. In Havard's version Scanderbeg demonstrates that, in colonial terms, to strive for consent does not necessarily indicate willingness to compromise. The delicate balance between these two potentially contradictory notions is one of the instabilities inherent in Havard's text; if to seek consent is necessary on the part of the colonial power, what happens when that consent is denied? Havard proposes no model for such circumstances, and his representation of Scanderbeg makes the presumption that a colonial power of quality will always be accepted by its intending colony.

Lillo and Havard offered their audiences revised versions of earlier dramatic interpretations of the Ottoman Empire.[54] Reflecting a change in attitude towards Turkish culture, and rejecting the traditional characterisation of the Turk as fundamentally evil, these plays attempt to create a model for Britain's own colonial growth. Patriot ideologies of empire relied on the notion of liberty and consent as justification for the imposition of colonial authority. It is these ideological constructs which enable

Lillo to differentiate between Turk and Briton, British liberty signifies superiority and thus presupposes success. In Lillo's play, systematic colonialism is idealised by reiterating the myth of consenting liberation on the part of the colonised people. For Havard however, the instabilities underpinning this ideology are too prevalent to support such myths. With the liberty of Britons themselves under threat the idea of such benefits being extended to the colonies is, for Havard, pure fantasy. In Havard's play colonialism is demystified by fact; colonialism and liberty do not go hand in hand. But Havard's text does not categorically abandon the imperial fantasy so dominant in Lillo's text. As we shall see, for both playwrights, the eradication of political factionalism and instability – shown to be ultimately destructive to the Ottoman Empire – is necessary for the realisation of imperial fantasy in a British context. Both texts identify the need to redress party divisions and establish a unified strategy for the government of a *British* Empire if Britain is to fare better than the Ottomans.

## How to govern an empire: Briton turn'd Turk?

In this simplistic formulation Briton and Turk are placed in a comfortable opposition, one governed by political and personal freedom the other constrained by political and social tyranny. Britain will succeed due to the nation's defence of personal and political liberty. Of course this model does not hold under close scrutiny, both accounts being subject to reductive cultural essentialism. Havard's text demonstrates the instability of such assumptions whereas Lillo's more conventional pro-Christian anti-Turk rendering of the Scanderbeg history is undermined, even from within the confines of his own text, by the clear points of contact between British and Ottoman colonial engagement. Persistent and uncontrolled expansion, loss of political control and loss of legal and cultural identity were concerns shared by contemporary commentators, anxieties which could be evidenced in the Ottoman Empire seen to be, 'Weaken'd by the Natural Corruption and Infirmities of Age'.[55] Fears for the potential loss of control of the burgeoning British Empire were being realised in Ottoman politics, and were seen by some commentators as a direct warning to Britain and her political leaders. The shared fate of the ancient empires of Rome and Turkey, both doomed by internal faction resulting in the successful rebellions of their colonised peoples, could easily be extended to Britain whose colonial expansion proceeded against a backdrop of political factionalism and disquiet. Were Briton and Turk really all that dissimilar?

Of course, this ominous representation was but one interpretation and, in common with other contemporary accounts of the Turk, the Turkish history plays presented a number of positive interpretations of Ottoman culture. Many early eighteenth-century writers commended in particular Turkish government and law.[56] Towards the end of the seventeenth century, Sir Paul Rycaut wrote in *The Present State of the Ottoman Empire* of a Turkish government that was wise, judicious and profound.[57] In 1709 Aaron Hill described the Turkish government as a 'Tall Oak' with 'Rooted Depth'.[58] In 1718 Lady Mary Wortley Montagu asserts that 'the Turkish Law, to our shame be it Spoken, [is] better design'd and better executed than Ours'.[59] The Ottoman Empire both serves as a model for colonial governance and an example of the dangers and costs of maintaining an empire, a vacillation that often occurs within individual texts rather than being dictated by a particular partisan position or agenda.[60]

Just as the myth of empire and the facts of colonialism competed in the construction of an imperial fantasy, so too did opposing models for the appropriate governance of Britain's developing empire. Even the issue of how to finance colonial expansion generated concerns regarding the granting of such power and this became a controversy inextricable from the issue of governance, both at home and abroad. As Cain and Hopkins have suggested, the rise of the moneyed interest, which funded colonial expansion, was the subject of one of the principal controversies of British politics during the eighteenth century. Interpretations of the character and qualities held by 'commercial men' were divided. The moneyed-interest were represented either as patriots with economic aptitude which they put to use funding 'the defence of the realm, overseas expansion and domestic employment'; or, as a direct threat to the nation's political stability by bringing ' "avarice" into a world that depended on "virtue" to guarantee good government'.[61] How should the developing Empire be governed? Should British colonies be subject to 'avaricious' law based on the commercial and, in Whig terms, patriotic interests of Britain or should patriot ideals of political selflessness be adhered to in the government of empire? Certainly, there is an inherent difficulty in assimilating the theories of colonialism to the rhetoric of patriotism. The contradiction characteristic of 'factual' accounts of Ottoman government (such as Montagu's, Rycaut's and Hill's) and echoed in the 1730s Scanderbeg play, is further complicated by divided opinion with regard to acceptable modes of colonial government. So, how are these problems negotiated in the Turkish history plays and in what way does the legend of Scanderbeg contribute to, or alleviate, such anxieties?

Lillo's text engages in the debate about empire by offering national-ist libertarianism as a salve for moral concerns regarding the ethics of colonialism.[62] In terms of political commentary, the loss and restitution of liberty are at the centre of this play. In the prologue, Lillo deplores the 'declining art' of writing plays in which:

> Nations destroy'd revive, lost Empires shine,
> And Freedom glows in each immortal Line.
> In vain would Faction, War, or lawless Power,
> Which mar the Patriot's Scheme, his Fame devour;
> When Bards, by their Superior Force, can save,
> From dark Oblivion and defeat the Grave.
> Say, Britons, must this art forsake your isle,
> And leave to vagrant apes her native soil?
> Must she, the dearest friend that freedom knows,
> Driv'n from her seat, seek refuge with her foes?
> Forbid so great a shame, and save the age
> From such reproach, you patrons of the stage. (259)

The patriot hero who succeeds against all odds is, of course, a resolution for a far greater threat to British freedom than simply the loss of good patriot drama. The prologue toys with linguistic ambiguity between representations of the patriot on stage and the need for modern patriot models upon which to base such representation. Lillo's agenda is not however limited to the dearth of modern patriots worthy of the stage but extends to the place of sovereignty in a free nation. The 'art' forsaking Britain's Isle is true patriotism, devoid of factionalism and unhindered by arbitrary power. Lillo's Scanderbeg frequently takes tyranny and abuse of power as his topic:

> The abject Slave, to his Reproach, shall see,
> That such as dare deserve it, may be free:
> And conscious Tyranny confess, with Shame,
> That blind Ambition wanders from her Aim;
> While Virtue leads her Votaries to Fame. (259)

This version of colonial ideology identifies liberty as the reward of virtue. Slavery is acceptable (owing to its commercial benefits) and does not preclude liberty, as virtuous slaves will be rewarded with their freedom in heaven, if not before. Equally, only *conscious* or deliberate tyranny, motivated by personal ambition is inexcusable, unconscious tyranny is not presumed to be devoid of virtue and does therefore not necessarily constitute a threat to the liberty of citizens.

Scanderbeg's advocacy of absolute rule over conquered territories suggests an ideological connection between Ottoman and British colonial policy reflecting the contemporary British tolerance for and attempts to justify Turkish political tyranny. However, tyranny and ambition within government are recurrent themes in Lillo's play and subject to the contradiction so often characteristic of purportedly factual accounts of Turkish modes of government. In a later passage, Aranthes, hostage to the Turk, attacks Amurath's perceived abuse of power, 'The most accurs'd, perfidious and ungrateful, / Are those, who have abus'd the sovereign power' (269). Amurath's reply is clearly an avocation of divine right, 'The unprincely meanness of thy soul, / Who would by law restrain the will of kings' (269–70). It is the Sultan's unpatriotic closing assertion, 'I fight to reign and conquer for myself' (270), that indicates that the authoritative voice belongs to Aranthes, 'The name of Prince, of Conqueror and King, / Are gifts of fortune and of little worth' (275). The abuse of sovereign power, rather than absolute power itself, threatens liberty. It is the ambition of 'sordid Souls, who know no joy but wealth' (275), the use of tyranny in order to increase personal wealth, that is roundly condemned. However, left more ambiguous is the degree to which tyranny for the purpose of increasing the public wealth is acceptable. A clear distinction is made between the appropriate government of the colonies and the government of the colonial nation. In the colonies absolute government is appropriate. In the metropolis the liberty of subjects is a more pressing concern. Lillo establishes a hierarchy between the citizens of a colonial power and the colonised peoples. The liberty of Britons should not be threatened, but the liberty of the inhabitants of the territories may be constrained in the interests of the Empire as a whole.

Similarly Hill advocates the establishment of arbitrary government for the protection of an Empire which 'must be supported strongly by some uncommon Policy'.[63] Aranthes' warnings against unfettered sovereign ambition seem to cross Whig/Tory political agendas. The lack of partisan affiliation is reiterated in the epilogue. The Patriots (Tories) and Courtiers (Whigs) are criticised for their lack of moral principles. Britain is portrayed as a country in which ambition and financial gain are the only motivation for 'patriotic' duty: 'A statesman rack his brains, a soldier fight – / Merely to do an injur'd people right. / What! Serve his country, and get nothing by't?' (320). Britons are encouraged to emulate Scanderbeg's patriotism, relinquish their partisan affiliations and unite 'To do their king and injur'd country right' (320). This alignment with the patriotic principles of the liberating Scanderbeg does not necessitate a rejection of colonial ambition. Lillo's depiction of party politics and factionalism as morally destructive has broader significance when applied to the governance of Empire. Party politics and factionalism are depicted as morally destructive. As Hill observes, factionalism is fatal to an empire and the Ottoman Empire is a prime example of this, 'the daring Ambition of aspiring Princes, and the formidable violences of intestine Discords, would like some surprising Earthquake, break fiercely thro' the Bands of Duty, and by their factious Consequences involve the Empire in most inevitable Ruin.'[64] In common with Hill, Lillo's text is not anti-colonial; rather, it is concerned with the maintenance of empire and advocates a politically integrated approach to governing British territories. This distancing from Whig, Tory and Opposition Whig political agendas relates to Langford's notion regarding the lack of clear government-led colonial policy during the period. Lillo's play, written during a period in which colonial policy was fluid and lacking fixity, constructs colonial policy from an array of perspectives rather than a singular, formed partisan agenda. This is not to suggest that such a poly-partisan schema is sustained throughout the play. Whatever grandiose claims are made to incite the audience to a non-partisan patriotism, there are points at which overtly partisan politics emerge.

In Act V of *The Christian Hero* in accordance with the last request of the dying Hellena, Scanderbeg releases the captive Amurath:

> Heaven is heavy on thy crimes,
> And deals thee forth a portion of those woes,
> Which thy relentless heart, with lawless lust
> And never sated avarice of power
> Has spread o'er half the habitable earth. (274)

This reference to Turkish atrocities committed in the process of establishing the Ottoman Empire can be related to the economic and strategic policies promoted by Walpole and his administration. Accusations of an avaricious control of power maintained by his possession of key ministerial posts, coupled with a strengthening of power through the securing of parliamentary placemen and political favouritism, were repeatedly made against Walpole by Tories and Opposition Whigs. The spread of British power 'o'er half the habitable earth' was taking place along similar strategic lines, albeit instigated by the Chartered Trading companies. This merchant-led strategy governing Britain's economic development was indicative of an avaricious policy of imperial expansion not dissimilar to that which had once helped build and maintain the now disintegrating Ottoman Empire. It is here that Lillo's text reveals a tangible partisan agenda in a clear critical commentary on Walpole's exercise of power.

Lillo positions the Christian Scanderbeg as the antithesis of the political and moral policy of the Turkish Sultan. Although the Sultan's actual behaviour is not *always* represented as reprehensible, Scanderbeg is a faultless hero. Representative of ideal government, he is a patriot king dismissive of his father's disastrous policy of maintaining peace with the Turks at any cost, 'The amorous prince – I know his haughty soul / Ill brooks his subtle father's peaceful schemes' (281). Lillo's representation of Scanderbeg as the patriot champion of the Christian Near East points to Frederick Lewis, Prince of Wales, patriot champion of the British opposition. Critical of George II's co-operation with Walpole's policy of peace with Europe, Frederick Lewis, like Scanderbeg, 'ill brooks his subtle father's peaceful schemes'. Frederick, the text suggests, will rescue Britain from those elements of Walpole's policy that are, like Turkish tyranny and avarice, unpatriotic and immoral. Of course, this does not necessitate the rejection of merchant-led colonial expansion, merely a re-adjustment of the rhetoric associated with the activities of the Chartered Trading companies, bringing such endeavours into line with patriot ideology.

Havard also makes claims for his text's non-partisan agenda. The prologue asserts:

> *I ask not any to espouse my Cause,*
> *For I shou'd blush at Party-made Applause:*
> *The Man who claps an undeserving Line,*
> *Betrays his Weakness in approving mine.*

Having drawn our attention to the problems of party affiliation, Havard uses the Scanderbeg history to demonstrate the shortcomings of British partisan politics. Mirroring the political structure of Britain, Havard introduces three factions to his play, first the Sultan Amurant, second the 'late revolted' Vizier, and third the 'dreaded' Scanderbeg. Such factionalism is ultimately dangerous, providing opportunities for traitors:

> But who shall tax successful Villany,
> Or call the rising Traitor to account?
> Sublimely seated in the Pomp of State,
> Greatly beyond the Malice of his Fate;
> He laughs at each Cabal and idle Jar,
> The Rage of Factions, and their Party-War;
> By Friends surrounded, happy, and unseen,
> Safely he rides, and drives the great Machine. (15)

The Vizier's criticism of the Sultan can be applied to the British political situation. Driving 'the great Machine' of British politics, Walpole, surrounded and protected by his parliamentary placemen, may, like the Sultan, be unaware of a treacherous threat to his power and the nation's stability. Factionalism promotes favouritism and self-interest. The ensuing political instability results in an inherently self-destructive government, unfit to control and maintain an empire.

Scanderbeg defends himself against accusations of unpatriotic self-interest in fighting to secure his possession of Deamira:

> Yet those who never felt what we describe,
> May censure us as Triflers, who wou'd waste
> The Hours of Action in a fond Discourse
> Of Love, and Softness – Idle Murmurers!
> Where strictest Virtue, softest Love unite,
> How fierce the Rapture! and the Blaze how bright!
> True Joys proceed from Innocence, and Love,
> Th'unsteddy by this Lesson may improve,
> Disclaim their Vices, and forget to rove. (20)

His assertion that his virtuous love for Deamira has elicited a constancy that others should observe and learn from has implications for my reading of Deamira as analogous to a colonised nation. Scanderbeg's professed constancy relates not only to love but also to government and religion. Engaged in 'fond discourse' rather than 'action', the Imperial power does not use force but governs by 'virtue'. The resultant relationship permits 'true joys' rather than hierarchical subjugation. Scanderbeg's perceived self-interest is therefore rhetorically transformed into virtuous patriotism governing both imperial and colonised nations. In contrast to these 'true joys' shared between Scanderbeg and Deamira, the hierarchical relationship between Scanderbeg and Amurath is destructive and commercial. Scanderbeg, denied Deamira by the enraptured Sultan, demands:

> Have I not led his Armies to the Field?
> How seldom have I fought without Success?
> Adorn'd his Crescent with so bright a Blaze,
> That it outshone the Sun that gaz'd upon it?
> And all to be despis'd: One Boon deny'd –
> Dismiss'd the Presence like the meanest Slave –
> These are such Wrongs, my Friend, as who can bear
> That owns Mortality: Our great Example
> Was sensible of Wrongs, tho' he forgave 'em. (25)

Scanderbeg sees the Sultan's detainment of Deamira as a denial of the 'debt' owed by the Turk. For Scanderbeg Deamira is recompense for his past services to Amurath. In figuring Deamira as reward, Scanderbeg's words, 'One Boon deny'd,' thus echo the Vizier's demand for 'payment' upon rescuing Deamira from her would-be rapist Heli. The contrast between these representations of the colonial relationship is significant. First, unlike Lillo's Scanderbeg, Havard shows the hero to be imperfect, affected by his position in the colonial hierarchy. Governed by an inconsiderate, commercially driven imperialist power, Havard's Scanderbeg, although self-liberated, resorts to commercial negotiation with the Sultan. As the governing power, however, Scanderbeg bases the political control of his own colonies on virtuous intent and mutual agreement.

This is not to suggest, however, that Havard unreservedly recommends patriotism as a political model for colonial government. Scanderbeg's success against the Turks is the result of a strategy of military scavenging:

> Tis as I wish'd; the Hand of Heav'n is in it,
> And points this easy Way to Victory;
> Wonder with me, *Lysander*, at the Pow'r,
> That turns th'injurious Stroke upon themselves;
> At once the Suff'rers, and our great Avengers. (62–3)

The Albanian troops have nothing to do but watch the Turks fight amongst themselves and then pick over the bones of their enemies once the heat of battle is over. Scanderbeg takes the 'easy way to victory' by allowing the two Turk factions to destroy themselves on the battlefield.[65] Havard's text suggests that by emulating such unpatriotic or conventionally un-heroic methods of warfare, the Tories could strengthen their position in the British government. The Tories, like Scanderbeg, have only to stand back and wait until the Whig factions destroy themselves thorough internal conflict. Havard's text goes some way towards rejecting patriotism in favour of a more predatory political and commercial policy. The words and actions of Heli, perhaps the most insidious character of the play, reflect the 'reality' of politics and commerce:

> How ignorant thou talk'st! what, Honesty!
> A Name, scarce Echo to a Sound: – Honesty!
> Attend the stately Chambers of the Great –
> It dwells not there, nor in the trading World:
> Speaks it in Councils? No; the Sophist knows
> To laugh if thence: Why shou'd we waste the Time

> In dull Discourse on nothing? – Come, no more –
> Let me not take what I wou'd have a Gift –
> Hence with Resistance – (67)

Heli's words are not exactly endorsed by Havard's text but the ironically 'honest' account of the realities of politics prevents the imposition of rhetorical falsities as justification for colonial activity.

In the search for a political model for the government of empire, these texts propose two very different strategies: Lillo reiterates the myth of empire, identifying liberty and patriotism as the primary concerns of an imperial government yet he condones the absolutist government of the colonial power over its territories. Conversely, Havard rejects liberty and patriot kingship, focusing rather on the balancing act between virtuous and immoral modes of governing an empire. Despite these political differences, however, both texts share an entrenched fear of, or concern regarding factionalism. For both texts, a stable imperial centre is imperative and the Ottoman Empire an appropriate warning against factionalism. For Havard, however, factionalism is a potential source of political gain. The ideologically divided Whig party is inherently unstable, Whig factionalism can be seen to provide opportunities for the Tories. Factionalism becomes a double bind, incorporating fears for the safety of the Empire and a desire to overturn the Whig supremacy. So, in political terms at least, Briton and Turk are subject to similar issues, internal conflict and divisions threaten both the disintegrating and the expanding Empires. Havard and Lillo position the Ottoman Empire as a dualistic example, on the one hand of successful colonial growth but on the other a clear demonstration of the need for political stability in governing an Empire.

These points of contact between Briton and Turk are however placed in sharp contrast when set alongside religious difference and it is these differences to which I would like to turn our attention next. In all of the texts, plays and factual accounts, Islam and Christianity sit uncomfortably alongside each other, augmenting the sense of conflict between approbation of and criticism of Turkish culture. With the Church acting as a site of resistance to pro-Islamic commentary during the early eighteenth century, could the Ottoman Empire offer anything but an anti-model for the role of religion in empire? Religious difference between Britain and her colonies is a significant problem in relation to an ideological conception that defined Britain and the British Empire as 'Protestant, commercial, maritime and free'.[66] Notions of British liberty and the supposed liberty of the colonies can be, as in Havard's text, debunked and exposed as empty rhetoric. However, despite their very different interpretations of liberty and patriot colonialism both plays engage with the imperial fantasy of Protestant superiority as a form of political and moral-justification aimed at creating a sense of stability and permanence for which there was little tangible evidence.

## Turk turn'd Christian: authorising Protestant colonialism

In *The Present State of the Ottoman Empire*, Rycaut rejects Islam as superstitious nonsense, 'the Tales of an old Woman'.[67] Sixteenth- and earlier seventeenth-century attitudes to Islam were even more extreme and lead to the widely-held belief that the success of the Ottoman Empire was not the consequence of wise and judicious government, but rather 'a divine chastisement or "scourge" to punish backsliding Christians'.[68] This rejection of the 'Mahometan Religion' as the heathen worship of false idols continued to influence eighteenth-century perceptions of Islam. The taste for the Near East was constrained by a history of religious antagonism that perpetuated the divisions between East and West.[69] Consequently, antagonism towards the Turks was expressed predominantly in religious rather than cultural terms, fuelled by the political threat perceived posed by the Ottomans.[70] Tolerance of secular aspects of Islamic life was one thing, acceptance or toleration of the religious doctrine of Islam was another.

Scanderbeg is particularly significant for anti-Islamic propaganda because his apostasy operates in direct contrast with the popular dramatic trope of Christian turned Turk.[71] Contemporary historical accounts of the life of George Castriota tell how, taken hostage at the age of eight by Amurath II and educated as a Turkish son, Scanderbeg, as the Turks named him, rebelled against his Muslim indoctrination and reconverted to Christianity, reclaiming his native land of Albania and fighting against the Turks who had enslaved him.[72] Scanderbeg was therefore represented as an almost unique figure, a complex amalgamation of Turkish and European culture.[73] He has experience of both Islamic and Christian mores, and the opportunity to adopt and practise the wisdom of both societies. In the Scanderbeg plays of the 1730s, audiences were offered a re-working of the familiar wise 'oriental', traditionally critical of Western society. Scanderbeg brings the wisdom of the East, acquired by his formative Islamic education, not just in the form of criticism but in terms of action. These texts therefore suggest the potential for a fusion of the best cultural elements from the Islamic and Christian worlds.

In Havard's play, criticism of Islam is expressed initially through the conventional Christian attack on Islamic ideas of paradise. Seventeenth-century dramatic texts identified the lascivious Muslim paradise as a threat to the more sedate Christian heaven.[74] Reported promises of unfettered sexual activity were the impetus, Christian commentators imagined, which must prompt their fellow men to convert to Islam. Such anxiety about apostasy is shared by Havard's text which highlights the falsity of Islamic doctrine, ironically through the words and actions of the Sultan. Amurant's repeated invocations of his 'Immortal Prophet' are interspersed with denouncements of his 'Ungrateful Prophet'. The Sultan's unanswered pleas contrast sharply with Deamira's prayer, 'Hear me, some Angel, wing to my Relief! – / Take my sad Life, but spare the Violation' (71). Scanderbeg's intercession on her behalf occurs directly after these lines. This 'divine intervention' in response to Deamira's display of Christian humility re-enforces the falsity of Islamic belief. However, representations of Islam and Christianity in Havard's text are complicated by the simultaneous criticism of both religions for their shared doctrinal intolerance of other systems of belief. Just as in Hill's *A Full and Just Account*, Havard demonstrates the Christian propensity for Turk-like tyranny and vengefulness. When Scanderbeg demonstrates forgiveness by freeing the captured Turks both his Christian followers and his Turkish enemies criticise his judgement. Amurant's desire for revenge dominates his response to Scanderberg's interim victory but he identifies 'the cool Measures of decisive Judgment, / And the weak patient Impotence of Reason' (56–7) as Scanderberg's weakness and a potential avenue for his revenge. Lysander also sees Scanderbeg's mercifulness as a sign of his infirmity of purpose:

> Tis god-like to forgive; yet oftentimes
> That Mercy sinks into a Weakness, as it gives
> A second Opportunity to those
> Who miss the first; and as the Wrong
> Was offer'd to your self – (16)

For Lysander, the Turks are not worthy of Scanderbeg's forgiveness as they are not trustworthy and will use their freedom to mount another attack on the Christians. However, Scanderbeg's reply, whilst maintaining contemporary notions of the moral superiority of Christianity, promotes a restrained religious tolerance:

> Shall I cut off the Means of their Repentance,
> As by their Deaths I shou'd? No, Heav'n forefend!
> Heav'n can again o'ertake them, if their Crimes
> Deserve a second Blow (16).

Scanderbeg's position is morally superior in comparison to both that of his fellow Christian Lysander and the Muslim Sultan. Lysander is intolerant and unforgiving. Amurant is vengeful. Scanderbeg demonstrates strength of religious conviction moderated by a toleration of the beliefs of others.

Although Havard's text does not deploy the trope of 'Christian turn'd Turk', conversion is significant to the establishment of a hierarchy between Christianity and Islam. Conversions and denouncements of religious belief are restricted to disillusioned Turks and the reconverting Scanderbeg. Deamira describes her conversion to Christianity with fervour:

> New Force inspires me, and my strengthen'd Soul
> Feels Energy divine: The fair Example
> Of steadfast Martyrs and of dying Saints,
> Has warm'd me into better Thoughts: I now
> Can with a Smile behold Misfortune's Face,
> And think the Weight of Miseries, a Trial.
> . . . .
> A Beam divine directs our Steps aright,
> And shews the Moral, in the Christian Light. (11)

This enthusiasm for her new faith seems to confirm the superiority of Christianity over Islam. However, Havard demonstrates the rhetorical subtlety of this hierarchy. Many of the experiences Deamira perceives to be derived from her conversion to Christianity are just those concepts that the Turks revile, 'not inclin'd, or able to resent, / Think'st Suff'ring meritorious' (26).

Deamira's conversion has obvious significance to her position as a disputed territory. Her rejection of Islam is symbolic of her acquiescence to Scanderbeg's Christian authority. In contrast, Heli pretends to convert in order to gain Scanderbeg's protection, 'think me as a Friend, a Friend convinc'd, / Who wonders at thy Virtues, and wou'd join 'em' (42). Although the thought of converting infidels appeals to Scanderbeg's sense of power, he is only momentarily deceived and quickly recognises Heli's falsity — only true converts are granted his protection. Havard's text updates seventeenth-century preoccupations with the conversion of Christians to Islam. His play does not focus on the conversion of Christians but reverses this trope to focus instead on the problem of the forced and false conversion of infidels, particularly as a consequence of colonial expansion. Although I wish to demonstrate a distinction between seventeenth- and eighteenth-century dramatic texts on the basis of this shift in focus from the conversion of Christians to the conversion of Muslims, I do not want to suggest that the conversion of Christians to Islam was of no concern to eighteenth-century audiences and commentators. However, the Scanderbeg plays are not the only examples of this shift.[75] Havard's text reveals new anxieties relating to the authority of the colonial power to impose conversion and the lack of religious tolerance signified by the justification of colonial expansion along the lines of Protestant superiority. Havard's text engages with a conflict between the ethical implications of the imposition of Protestantism on future British colonies and the tangible benefits to Britain's colonial power arising from ideological conformity resulting from conversion of the colonies.

Lillo's *The Christian Hero* establishes a clearer division between Christianity and Islam. In the opening scene, Hellena observes that by pursuing 'the ever victorious hero / Of Epirus' (262) her father will 'Provoke the malice of his adverse stars, / And urge his own destruction' (262). Echoing Rycaut's analysis of Islam, Lillo identifies superstition as the governing aspect of Islamic belief. The religious difference between the two protagonists is quickly established. Amurath follows a religion characterised by malice and cruelty; conversely, Scanderbeg's faith is not only represented as doctrinally superior but also indicative of the essential link between Protestantism and patriotism.[76] Protestant ethics such as selflessness and forgiveness were equally the staples of patriot rhetoric with its emphasis upon acting for the common good and national, not personal, ambition. Capitalising upon the common moral codes of patriotism and Protestantism, Lillo's play creates in Scanderbeg not just a Christian, but a Protestant hero. However, the identification of patriotism as a form of uniquely *Protestant* morality is not the only possible reading of the relationship between patriotism and religious doctrine in this play. It is possible to identify Turkish patriots, or at least to identify isolated acts of Turkish patriotism, such as the self-sacrificing Helena. However, these isolated occurrences do not diminish the superiority of Protestantism. In this sense Lillo's play engages with analogies drawn between Islam and Catholicism, thus narrowing the gap between moral codes and allowing space for Turkish patriotism. However, in the context of softening interpretations of Ottoman culture this overlap could equally be read in a non-allegoric form. In either reading however, the points of contact between Protestantism and Islam/Catholicism are gradually eroded as the play progresses. The focus for patriotic morality is undoubtedly Scanderbeg.

Lillo's hero utilises the propagandistic power of patriot rhetoric to motivate his troops before battle, 'You fight the cause of liberty and truth, / Your native land, Aranthes and Althea' (309). Lillo successfully appropriates patriot terminology to create a 'pious hero and a patriot king' (259). Although the love interest (Scanderbeg's passion for, in this instance, Althea) remains central to the action, it is not Scanderbeg's primary motivation for battle. As the play closes there is a notable increase in the hostility of representation of the Turks. Islam is denigrated and the resultant conservative reading of Turkish culture does not sit comfortably with earlier references to Turkish wisdom and patriotism. Most significant in this progressive vilification is Scanderbeg's assertion, 'Be witness, heaven! I pity and forgive him' (316). Forgiveness characterises the Christian hero; Scanderbeg becomes a representative of both idealised patriotic and idealised Christian behaviour without compromising either principle.

The Turks fail to emulate this patriotic and religious idealism. Lillo further enhances the distinction between Muslim and Christian through Amurath's bitter denouncement of his prophet 'false Mahomet' (317) and his vengeful attacks on those he holds responsible for his downfall. In contrast with Scanderbeg's Christian forgiveness, Amurath condemns the treacherous Amaise to death, 'See him impal'd alive, we'll let him know / As much of hell as can be known on earth, / And go from pain to pain' (317). Lillo's text clearly defines Islam as a false religion, based on spurious precepts and deceit, 'False or ungrateful prophet! Have I spread / Fell devastation over half the globe, / To raise thy crescent's pale, uncertain light, / Above the Christian's glowing crimson cross, / In hoary age to be rewarded thus!' (317). Amurath reaches a level of self-awareness that to some extent redeems his character. He renounces his religion and gains an awareness of the severity of his crimes and their consequent brutal punishment:

> Can this be true! Am I cast down from that
> Majestick Height, where like an earthly God,
> For more than half an Age, I sate enthron'd,
> To the abhor'd Condition of a Slave?
> A pardon'd Slave! What! live to be forgiven!
> And all this brought upon me by *Hellena*!
> Shou'd our Prophet return to Earth and swear it
> I'd tell him to his Face that he was perjured.
> Hell wants the Power and Heaven wou'd never curse
> To that Degree a doating, fond, old Man. –
> What make my Child! my loving, gentle Child!
> The Instrument and Author of my Ruin! (74)

However, not only does Amurath continue to place blame for his failure upon others, thus eliding his own responsibility; his concern for his own sovereign status suggests a failure to learn from Christian demonstrations of patriotic selflessness. In renouncing his religion Amurath merely identifies the 'falsities' of Islam; he blames his Prophet, his daughter and his followers, but does not recognise his own failings as an unpatriotic sovereign. Lillo's representation of Islam as a false and unforgiving faith does not permit the Sultan's redemption. Despite his earlier depiction as an astute observer of Christian culture, Amurath degenerates into an example of unpatriotic sovereignty whose private behaviour and political activities are reduced to tropes of anti-Islamic propaganda.

Havard's and Lillo's Scanderbeg plays can therefore be read as anti-Islamic. Both texts utilise dramatic conventions that emphasise the supposed falsity of Islam in contrast to the imagined truth of Christianity. However, this antagonistic polemic not only presents an anti-Islamic statement but also forms the basis of the texts' political agendas. For Lillo, Islam is a vehicle for demonstrating the consequences of colonial expansion unrestrained by patriotism. *The Christian Hero* espouses merchant-led colonial strategy, albeit modified by patriotic rhetoric. Lillo's text's pro-colonialism is based on the dominant merchant model, perceiving commercial gains as strengthening the good of the nation and evoking a patriot agenda in order to transpose British colonial endeavour away from the 'depravity' of the Ottoman model. For Havard, the atrocities committed by colonising Ottomans in the name of Islam are mirrored in the British Protestant myth of empire. Havard's *Scanderbeg* rejects current practice and challenges colonial propaganda as part of a broader mythology. Havard's text locates the fallacy of existing models; the commercial imperative for expansion is challenged, as are patriot claims for mutual beneficence. Only the tangible benefits of religious conversion, infidel to Christian, are espoused. Anti-Islamic rhetoric is therefore evident in both plays, yet it contributes to differing perspectives on a shared agenda – the negotiation of imperial fantasy which authorises colonial activity by asserting Britain's Protestant supremacy. However, like the fantasies based on notions of liberty and patriot colonialism, British Protestantism's justification of colonial authority tends towards instability. Lillo's model fails to reconcile the disparity between cultural endorsement of the Turk and the doctrinal vilification necessary to conclude his play satisfactorily. In Havard's version the hierarchies between Christian and Muslim are blurred and confused, the points of contact between Briton and Turk too frequent to allow a clearly defined model of consistent doctrinal superiority. Like the fantasies of liberty and patriot colonialism, Protestant superiority cannot hold back the encroaching realities of colonialism. This notion is taken further in the final play of this Scanderbeg trilogy, Whincop's *Love and Liberty*, in which colonialism, greed and arbitrary power are fused.

## Penitent Turks/libidinous Christians

Thomas Whincop's *Scanderbeg; or, Love and Liberty* offers a third approach to the issues of empire, government and religion. Written some time after the South Sea Bubble in 1721 and before Whincop's death in 1730, the play was completed by his widow Martha Whincop and finally published in 1747.[77] Whincop's *Scanderbeg; or Love and Liberty* contains perhaps the most transparent and unrefined political commentary of the three Scanderberg plays. The prologue is largely concerned with the 'tragic' history of the playwright himself, making an 'appeal to Britons' on behalf of his widow:

> He sunk, when young, beneath the Weight of Cares,
> By that full Scheme, that ruin'd half the Land:
> When robbed of all, Death lent his friendly Hand.[78]

The 'Scheme' referred to is of course the South Sea Company in which Whincop invested and subsequently lost a considerable sum of money. The financial devastation caused by the South Sea Bubble, is a concern explored in Whincop's text through the theme of liberty, 'The Cause of

Liberty his Muse inspir'd, / And by chaste love her warmest Thoughts were fir'd' (xix). Loss of liberty is significant to the Scanderbeg history both figuratively and literally. The various combinations of hostages and the battles for Albanian freedom are linked to a spiritual repression experienced in turn by both Christians and Muslims. Whincop's *Scanderbeg* not only highlights the significance of liberty by using the term in the title of the play, but also transposes the struggle for literal and figurative freedom onto the aftermath of the South Sea Bubble. After the stock market crash concerns grew regarding the dangers of speculation, which commentators such as George Berkley saw essentially as a form of gambling.[79] The artificiality of the stock market was dangerous, a threat to real tradesmen and merchants. The financial independence of these citizens had implications for public liberty. By not submitting to slavery as peasants (financially dependent upon the good will of their masters), or adopting tyranny, as aristocracy (financially dependent upon the industry of their vassals), commercial men were protecting British liberty. In rejecting the mutual financial dependency of this outdated feudal model of society, tradesmen and merchants formed the firmest base for public liberty. The South Sea Bubble stripped honest men, such as Thomas Whincop, of their funds, leaving them destitute and desperate, deprived of the freedom that their modest fortunes had secured.

In Act V, Scanderbeg compares the Ottoman Empire and the Turks with Bedlam and its inmates, 'Such a sad abject view of human greatness / (Now in this high tide of our prosperous fortune) / May check our pride, and teach us we are men.' (82). Without proper care for their liberty, Britons will succumb to further financial temptations. Inevitably this would result in the degeneration of the nation and the burgeoning Empire. For Whincop's *Scanderbeg*, the Turks represent something to be feared by Britons, not a fear arising from a religious or military threat but from the concurrent fall of this once great Empire and the loss of trade signified by such a fall. This was a fate that the experiences of speculation that resulted in the South Sea Bubble had demonstrated Britain could all too easily replicate.

In common with Lillo's *The Christian Hero*, liberty is utilised in Whincop's *Scanderbeg* as a patriotic trope. However, despite its titular significance, liberty is given only cursory attention in the action of the play itself. It is personal not political liberty that dominates the protagonist's concerns. The rhetoric inspired by patriotic notions of liberty is condensed into a mechanism of defence against bribery. Ariant refuses to command his daughter to comply with the Sultan's demands in return for a share in the Ottoman Empire because 'Slavery's liberty / Whilst the free mind's unfetter'd' (37–8). The Turks are the restrainers of liberty, but also the tools by which the patriotic concept of freedom is challenged. Ariant's words unwittingly reveal the benefit to Arianissa of continued slavery. As the Sultan's concubine she would enjoy more liberty than as a Christian daughter or wife. This predicament is played out when she evades her Turkish oppressors and places herself under the protection of Scanderbeg, both literally and figuratively silencing herself. Although she unsettles homosocial relations by becoming the site of inter-factional political and religious conflict, Arianissa is responsible for her own loss of liberty.[80] An inverted Turk/Christian hierarchy transforms liberty as a patriotic term. When controlled by the Turks, Arianissa has no actual freedom, but is at liberty to choose her fate. Controlled by the Christians, she is ostensibly free but her personal liberty is limited by cultural constraints.

Thus, Whincop's text disrupts conventional Christian/Muslim religious and cultural hierarchies. In *Scanderbeg; or, Love and Liberty*, the hero appears initially as a patriot warrior defending his country from Turkish barbarians: 'Behold me first, never to sheath the sword / Till Albany shines forth in all its pristine glory' (2). Conversely, his Turkish enemy Amurath, is portrayed by the Christian princes as a foul creature, guilty of the avaricious murder of Scanderbeg's brothers: 'justice will not spare / His monst'rous crimes, tho' for a while it sleeps' (3). This explicit Christian-dominated hierarchy is quickly reversed. Despite repeated calls from the Christians for 'justice' in reaction to Turkish barbarities, in reality Scanderbeg's chief concern is not his country or his defiled religion but his beloved Arianissa: 'O! were I *sure* to find that charming maid, / .../ I'd rush *impetuous* on the tyrant's camp' (6, my emphasis). This passage demonstrates Scanderbeg's unpatriotic priorities. His private anguish overwhelms his sense of public duty, which requires a rational and considered response to the Turkish threat. This is further emphasised by the discovery of an intercepted letter containing orders for Arianissa's execution. The letter confirms that she has not yielded to the Sultan's sexual demands and, assured of her constancy, Scanderbeg cries for vengeance, 'Seize, tear him, rend him, drag him, headlong drag him / To dungeons, tortures, racks' (10) and is assured by his advisors that, 'Just is thy wrath, and righteous is thy vengeance' (12). Despite this endorsement of Scanderbeg's desire for revenge, it is clear that Whincop's Scanderbeg is driven to action by desire and personal anguish.

Further undermining notions of British liberty and the broader significance of political freedom, the newly emancipated Christians are irrelevant in comparison to Scanderbeg's joy at being reunited with

Arianissa. Indeed, the death of Amurath, rather than becoming the focus of a celebrated Christian victory, is a non-event and has no bearing on the denouement of the play which is entirely concerned with Scanderbeg's happiness who 'lives unhurt, aveng'd on all his foes' (79). Scanderbeg's lust for revenge has been satiated and, importantly, Arianissa is returned to his keeping, 'Conquest and love to bless my reign combine, / Albania free, and Arianissa mine' (86). During the course of the play liberty is progressively divorced from patriotic rhetoric. Scanderbeg's motivations lack patriotism. He is driven by selfish desires; and Arianissa is his trophy, 'behold my Arianissa's beauty / The price of dangers, and the pay of war' (85). This denigration of Scanderbeg's status as a patriot is inflected in his own use of rhetoric. When leading his troops to fight against the Turks, Scanderbeg's battle speech imposes a hierarchy of terms completely at odds with patriot rhetoric, 'Love, honour, justice, liberty, revenge / All call aloud, and spur us on to Victory'. A true patriot leader, such as Lillo's Scanderbeg, would not evoke such self-serving sentimental rhetoric, placing justice and liberty beneath love and acting not for the benefit of his country but for revenge. Whincop divests Scanderbeg of the patriotism conventionally associated with this Christian hero in order to prioritise a sentimental rendering of this staple of anti-Islamic Christian history.

What Whincop's Scanderbeg lacks in terms of patriotism is offset by his religious fervour. Whincop's use of religious rhetoric is striking. Scanderbeg is repeatedly represented with near divine characteristics. He expresses dissatisfaction with the inaction of the 'coercive; but recording heav'ns' (13) and relates this lack of divine intervention to his own defeatist followers, 'The daring foe / Too long already arrogantly vain, / By our delay, hath triumphed o'er your valour' (17). Scanderbeg's response is to adopt the role of avenger and he becomes the administer of divine vengeance. Scanderbeg, the patriot saviour of his homeland, has a divine purpose that transcends the usual boundaries of religious morality. Again, however, Scanderbeg's words are shown to be mere rhetoric, his dedication to Christian concepts has little tangible impact on the events of the play. The threatened murder of Arianissa, so crucial to the opening scenes of Whincop's play, never takes place and her reprieve is secured not as a result of Christian intervention but due to Amurath's penitent compunction. Rather than being integral to his representation of Christian doctrine, guilt becomes a fundamental concept in Whincop's version of Islamic culture. The Sultan and Scanderbeg are both characterised by their desire for personal revenge, but the Christian fails to demonstrate any subsequent feelings of remorse. In terms of conventional Christian rhetoric, Amurath's feelings of guilt and his rueful conduct are morally superior to Scanderbeg's thirst for revenge. This inversion of the expected religious hierarchy in favour of Islam echoes the simultaneous inversion of the expected patriotic hierarchy.

Justification for Scanderbeg's actions is offered by his sense of divine purpose. He experiences what appears as divine assistance on the battlefield. Despite the greater strength of the Turkish troops Scanderbeg is victorious, with little loss of life on the Christian side. Conversely, Amurath is repeatedly thwarted in his attempts to avenge himself. In Act III, having vowed vengeance against Ariant, the Sultan is again beset by guilt and self-doubt:

> Destiny
> Hath mark'd me out, inevitable fate
> Still drives me on: my shipwreck'd soul is lost
> Amid the billows of outrageous passions;
> Whilst hope, despair, love, grief, rage and remorse
> By turns distract me. (39)

Amurath's rage is simultaneously a distraction from and the cause of his 'shipwrek'd soul'. As if to further his own destruction, Amurath rejects the humbling sentiment of this soliloquy and threatens Arianissa with the death of her father if she does not comply with his sexual advances. Whincop's representation of Islam is confusing and contradictory. The seemingly subversive inversion of the expected Islamic/Christian hierarchy created by positioning Amurath as a Christian-like penitent in contrast to the anger-driven unpatriotic Scanderbeg is counteracted by Amurath's repeated inability to apply his own wisdom. Whincop positions the Turks and the Christians in a battle of libidinous rather than religious purpose. Arianissa is the trophy of this war, not the more conventionally sought freedom of Albania or protection of the Christian faithful from the tyranny imposed by the Ottoman Empire. Whincop brings together versions of Christianity to contrast with versions of Islam and play out an extended battle of morality. Whatever his doctrinal failings Scanderbeg is victorious and the Christians remain unharmed; Christianity, in its diverse forms, supplants Islam. The deaths of both Amurath and his heir Chanhassen leave the Turks leaderless and in disarray. The Turks experience guilt, but are unable to restrain their behaviour. In keeping with the inconsistencies of other contemporary accounts of Islamic culture, Whincop creates Turks who demonstrate an admirable religious zeal whilst at the same time a fundamental lack of morality.

Each of the Scanderbeg plays approaches the negotiation of an ideology of empire from a distinct perspective. Repeated claims made in all three texts for a non-partisan political agenda align these plays with Langford's notion of the lack of explicit, government-directed colonial policy during this period. The variations in the representation of the Scanderbeg history allow each text to present models for the maintenance and/or strengthening of the burgeoning British Empire that negotiate conflicts between the claimed economic benefits and feared economic dangers of colonial expansion, as well as the possibilities for the dissemination of Protestantism that arise from colonial endeavour. The plays suggest through their figuration of Turkish politics, government and culture a reading of aspects of British colonial policy. The representation of the Turk is central to this comparative analysis, especially through the Muslim/Christian model of Scanderbeg. In comparing these two religions, the texts participate in contemporary discussions evolving out of encounters with Islamic culture in which the Turk is seen to be simultaneously part of yet distanced from Western European cultural, economic and political experience.

Whincop rejects patriotism as an appropriate model for successful colonialism. Equally, his text does not promote non-partisan politics as a pre-requisite for the formation of sound imperial government. In contrast to Havard's and Lillo's versions of the Scanderbeg history, and in answer to Candace in *The Fall of Saguntum* Whincop's text depicts the arbitrariness of colonial success. Scanderbeg is, at times, unpatriotic and Christianity is not morally superior to Islam. Both sides are skilled in battle and the Christians win merely as the result of good fortune not religious, moral or military superiority. Here, colonialism takes on the same speculative characteristics as stock-jobbing, dangerously unregulated, ungoverned and disastrously unpredictable. Whincop's *Scanderbeg; or, Love and Liberty* not only rejects the notion of a model for successful colonialism; but it also denies any morally acceptable motivation for empire-building. Scanderbeg acts primarily on personal inclination rather than in his nation's best interest. The Turks use morally reprehensible methods of colonialism and Amurath shares Scanderbeg's libidinous motivation. Liberty cannot be secured through colonialism and the liberty of both citizens and colonised peoples is threatened by the pursuit of empire. Colonialism 'undermines the established social order', the building of an empire can only result in the increased 'avarice' of government, entirely to the detriment of good citizens.[81] Reflecting the author's own investment losses, Whincop's text dwells on the futility and transient nature of empire building, disengaging from the conventional moral, economic, social and religious justifications for colonial endeavour which the other Scanderbeg plays manipulate. Here, even the trade incentives for colonial expansion are discounted, people are bartered for but the exercise is futile and no tangible economic benefit is shown for either the colonial power or the colony. Whincop rejects such notions of mutual beneficence which even a colonial sceptic such as Havard presumes to be present in the tangible benefits of religious conversion.

The Scanderbeg history is appropriated for the promotion of widely differing perspectives on empire. The dramatists manipulate the 'factual' history, disseminated by writers such as Rycaut, Jones, Hill and Montagu to suit their own political motivations. The chronological proximity of these plays and their shared historical subject-matter provide a clear example of the pliability of history for political appropriation. This is not, however, the most significant aspect of these texts. The Turkish history plays demonstrate three disparate versions of colonial engagement constructed on an Ottoman model but envisioned for a British, Protestant context. Contemporary concern for the welfare of the developing British Empire and the sustainability of religious and political ideals within this emergent imperial ideology are heightened by the geographic and temporal proximity of a declining empire. Informing these multivalent models for colonial expansion are a host of fantasies; imagined Turks, patriot ideology, notions of liberty, economic prosperity, mythologies of Britishness and imperialism itself. What these plays demonstrate therefore is not simply a change in dramatic interpretations of the Turk but the instability and alterity of colonial identity during the early eighteenth century. The Scanderbeg plays share a political immediacy that distinguishes them from the thematically similar Roman histories. Here colonialism is shown in a more brutal, less theoretical light. Whereas the Roman and English histories discussed in this book are 'governed by simple and dramatic oppositions, the Turkish history plays engage with a more complex relationship between Briton and 'Other', a relationship in which 'appropriative traffic' is not only two-way but directly challenges notions of national self-hood.[82] The precarious nature of fantasies constructed on the impossible conflation of imperialism and patriotism, liberty and Protestant supremacy gives these texts political currency as contributions to an ongoing negotiation of the nature of Britishness in an imperial context.

# Conclusion: History, Fantasy and the Staging of Britishness

> *Concord*, whose Myrtle Wand can steep
> Ev'n *Anger's* blood-shot Eyes in Sleep:
> Before whose breathing bosom's Balm,
> *Rage* drops his Steel, and Storms grow calm;
> Her let our Sires and Matrons hoar
> Welcome to *Britain's* ravag'd Shore,
> Our Youths, enamour'd of the Fair,
> Play with the Tangles of her Hair,
> Till in one loud applauding Sound,
> The Nations shout to Her around,
> O how supremely art thou blest,
> Thou, Lady, Thou shalt rule the West!
>
> William Collins, *Ode to Liberty* (1746)

The endorsement of 'concord' in Collins's *Ode to Liberty* (1746) has much in common with the patriot rhetoric produced for the early eighteenth-century London stage. Collins's poem reflects upon the cabinet divide over the Breda peace negotiations which saw Pelham suing for peace whilst Newcastle and George II called for war.[1] As a nation Britain was all too familiar with such conflict in the highest echelons of government, with faction and party divisions being the defining characteristics of the previous administration. The diverging agendas of the first minister, secretary of state and the monarch echoed the mounting pressure put on Walpole during the 1720s and 1730s for war with Spain. Nevertheless, this manifestation of a popular desire to maintain national pride through aggressive political posturing is not the only point of contact between Collins's *Ode* and the history plays produced in the preceding decades.

Prior to Collins's call for the soothing effects of 'concord', commentators had proposed a number of solutions to the lack of political unity during the Walpole administration. Bolingbroke advocated the abolition of party favour as the route to political concord, as his imagined 'patriot king' would resolve the nation's disquiet. Earlier in the century another call for concord was made in *Cato's Letters*. Gordon and Trenchard created a Cato who demanded, 'Frequent parliaments and frequently rotating ministries,' and a 'party system which was free from faction and purged of the opinions which distorted a true understanding of the public interest'.[2] Concord, therefore, was a repeatedly evoked fantasy – although, whether this fantasy took the form of an idealised female muse or a manly patriot, it was a fantasy that was never achieved. The grubbier realities of contemporary politics – factionalism, political placemen, favouritism and ministerial self-interest – rendered 'agreement' within parties, let alone across party divides, practically impossible. However, a form of concord did exist in the language of politics, particularly the rhetoric of patriotism and party appropriations of notions of liberty. The language of patriotism, as it relates to notions of patriot kingship, was, as Gerrard asserts, 'messianic' and consequently pervaded political rhetoric irrespective of conventional divides. All sides could benefit from representing their leaders, members and followers as patriot liberators.[3]

If the language of patriotism and associated notions of liberty could be appropriated cross-party, could agreement be reached over the nature of a specifically British patriotism? When commentators evoked the image of the patriot did they have recourse to a homogenous notion of British identity and, therefore, did concord also exist in the form of a unified version of Britishness? Certainly the plays discussed in this book reveal a diverse array of historical precedents that offered audiences model patriots, but these historical figures were the product of a mythology, no more tangible as models for actual governance than Bolingbroke's fantasy of a patriot king. However, a degree of concord is again realised in the dramatic iconography of these images and if it is not unity then it at least reveals a commonality in terms of the representation of these past heroes and heroines as idealised Britons.

The diversity in the range of historical periods and the variety of political agendas engaged with in the plays discussed in this book, despite providing an abundant scope for literary interpretation, problematises any attempt at reading these plays as a body of texts engaging in the negotiation of and promotion of a shared notion of British identity. If, as I have argued, these texts engage in such a discourse, why do the historical themes range from ancient British to English to European to ancient Roman and even Islamic pasts? Similarly if the political foci are so varied – party politics, favouritism, domestic politics, politics of colonialism – how can these diverse agendas be seen as offering representations of a homogonous notion of British identity? Given the multiplicity of historical themes and political agendas these plays engage with, it seems unlikely that they would provide any evidence for a partisan concord regarding Britishness. However, if a definitive version of British identity had not been formed, who *were* the BRITONS so frequently addressed in the prologues and epilogues of eighteenth-century history plays?

## Histories of Britishness

A number of modern scholars have identified patterns in eighteenth-century versions of Britishness. Murray Pittock summarises multifarious interpretations of what it was to be an eighteenth-century Briton and asserts the tenacity of resistance to the term, particularly amongst those Britons who felt themselves most disenfranchised from what was perceived to be the nation's centre – London.[4] Linda Colley has defined Britishness as a notion that existed in opposition to perceptions of cultural 'others' deemed as 'morally and politically defective and/or oppressive', an attitude that was 'as much a defence mechanism as an expression of serene superiority'.[5] Certainly, many of the plays discussed in this book represent non-Britons as politically defective or oppressive but this in itself does not guarantee a communal notion of homogenous national identity and is not a universal interpretation to be applied to every dramatic representation of a non-Briton. Some texts, such as *The Fall of Mortimer*, fit Colley's contention well, others, such as Aaron Hill's *Henry the Fifth*, merely substitute British for English and thus, as Pittock's model suggests, reveal a degree of dismissal regarding the myriad of cultural identities subsumed within the one nation, particularly amongst those commentators who were not the inhabitants of, or migrants from, the non-dominant nations of Britain.

Both of these critical models represent eighteenth-century notions of Britishness residing within a melting-pot of cultural influences, some of which originate from within the nation itself; others, the result of intercultural contact from further afield. In addition, perceptions of Britishness were informed and shaped by partisan agendas, trade interests and Enlightenment shifts in the ways in which 'Briton's' conceptualised their world. What finally unites the various cultures and regions of Britain during this period, are the shared histories that are re-produced, and in some cases, re-invented in narrative, scholarly and literary forms. These histories are subject to political bias, varied interpretation and are often more subject to fantasy than fact. But it is not the veracity of these historical accounts that is pertinent to their intersection with notions of British identity and the part played by the history plays in promoting various fantasies associated with Britishness, such as liberty and patriotism. Indeed, it is the very 'shared' nature of these fantasies that connect the plays discussed in this book and from which a sense of concord regarding

British national identity can be derived. That is, the defining characteristics of Britishness are the fantasies of liberty and patriotism endorsed by the history plays. These British character traits are deemed so central a component of a uniquely British code of conduct that they can be traced back to the nation's most distant ancestors.

The diversity of themes in these historical narratives and the diversity of political agenda for which these narratives are appropriated suggests that Britishness was an unstable term. Although patriotism and liberty are the defining characteristics of the Britons on stage and the projected Britons in the imagined audiences who gather to watch representations of their cultural, political or religious ancestors, this apparently homogenous version of British identity is undermined by the varied attempts to appropriate Britishness. On the stage, Britons re-enact the nation's past, in the face of various political, religious and ideological opponents – Catholics, Jacobites, predatory Islamic nations – a foe suited to every potential xenophobic agenda.

To some degree British was merely a term by which Britons could define themselves in opposition to one or more of these imagined or real threats. Irrespective of political agenda or national or regional allegiance, Britishness itself was, to appropriate Colley's assertion, a sort of 'defence mechanism', an umbrella term of self-definition that provided an imagined barrier, guaranteeing, imaginatively at least, that Britons could defend their island from any potential aggressor. However, such a variety of appropriations of the defining characteristics of Britishness lead to rhetorical instabilities. Qualities deemed to be definitively British could be used to promote any number of political agendas and this lack of stability was self-perpetuating. In order to prove their party's patriot credentials, or superior qualities, commentators had to resort to denigrating their opponents in opposition to themselves, a perpetuation of factionalism, itself deemed unpatriotic and un-British.

In contrast to such political instabilities, by capitalising upon contemporary feelings of nationalism evoked in response to various threats from abroad, the London theatres perpetuated and sustained notions of Britishness and a sense of communal identity. Such identity was, of course, mere fantasy existing only within the politicised cultural spaces of the theatres and having little, if any, value beyond those confines. So, notions of Britishness, in this sense, comprised of various fantasies and mythologies that underpinned not only imagined communities but also politics, trade, theology, fashion, art and literature; encompassing all aspects of British cultural and political life. So why was the theatre so successful in creating a homogonous version of Britishness with which to address its audiences? The theatre had a distinct advantage over other forms of literary representation, due to its unique ability to draw upon and manipulate familiar 'short-hand' as part of a visually immediate mode of communication. In this way, dramatic texts could access and evoke communal experience derived from the shared interpretations of visual clues, often pre-filtered by the production itself, either by way of assigning types of role to specific actors and actresses or, by deploying familiar props as visual tropes or, in manipulating audience expectations by transgressing or subverting such anticipated norms. The eighteenth-century theatre occupied a unique space in terms of its engagement with contemporary political and cultural debates. Able to draw together the various ideological strands that fed into conceptions of Britishness and by appealing to audiences as 'Britons', evoking politically universal codes of patriotism and liberty, the theatre was able to impose a unified notion of national identity that was all but fantasy outside the theatrical space.

## Staging Britishness

One strategy for identifying the ways in which such a diverse group of texts as the history plays could be seen to contribute to a debate that generated an homogenous conceptualisation of national identity is to consider these texts in relation to the types of threat they depict. If the theatrical representation of history is the key to identifying a homogenous, although fantastical account, of early eighteenth-century notions of Britishness, then some degree of concord must be reached across these plays, beyond that achieved by reading these texts in thematic clusters based upon a shared historical focus. Do the history plays, when placed in juxtaposition with each other, outside the confines of the shared histories they re-appropriate, demonstrate common characteristics in the idealised versions of Britishness they hold-up for the audience to emulate. Given Colley's contention that Britishness existed as a way in which Briton's could linguistically categorise themselves in contrast to 'others' then the representation of such opponents, the historical and allegorical threats to Britain that these plays re-enact, becomes one route to the Identification of any concordant image of Britishness pervading these texts.

### Foreign incursions

Many of the plays discussed in this book focus on the origins of British culture, the foundation of modern British society and politics. Such references suggest a need to connect contemporary political action with a return to a purer version of the British nation – a Britain that preceded the Norman conquest and was therefore devoid of the corrupting influences of institutionalised Catholicism. To some extent these plays produce a mythologised version of the state, a fantasy outlining what Britain lost as a result of successive foreign incursions. The plays position Britain as a site of conflict, preyed-upon by foreign foes either explicitly in the form of military invasion, or more covertly in the form of physical and personal incursions directed at the site of power.

In the history plays aggressors were manifest in a variety of forms, such as Vikings, Danes, barbarians, infidels, Catholics, women, even the insurgent residents of Britain's own non-dominant nations. The threat posed to Britain by Catholic European neighbours is repeatedly the subject of the medieval English history plays. In these plays the dangers of factionalism and favouritism to modern British liberty are compared with the threat posed to England by favourites such as Mortimer, Catholic nations such as France and Spain, and the combined misogynistic and religious prejudice evidenced by the seemingly universal hatred of foreign queens. In many of these texts, particularly the adaptations of Shakespeare's history plays, there is a move away from the characteristic 'manliness' of Britishness demonstrated in the ancient British history plays. In the adaptations by Aaron Hill, Ambrose Philips and Theophilus Cibber, British women are represented as the patriotic equals of characteristically British men. Women participate in politics and have the power to influence the public sphere both negatively and positively. These texts make a cross-gender call to all Britons. Men *and* women have responsibility for maintaining the liberty of their nation. However, despite this all-hands depiction of a particularly Protestant patriotism, these texts continue to struggle with the instability of Britishness in this historical context.

Despite the common focus on liberty and patriotism, these texts lack a clearly defined notion of the British national character. These histories have little to offer but idealised versions of events, mythical interpretations of the past. They persistently evade the fact that, however patriotic, however hard their struggle for liberty, and however ardently they strive to protect their own freedom, these British ancestors ultimately lose to foreign incursions. Repeatedly these plays attempt to assert the stability of the nation; Shakespeare and Protestant heroes are drawn upon to demonstrate a lineage from the nation's most ancient histories to modern times, an attempt at imposing order upon a mutable identity.

The myths of stability, ironically, are shored-up by texts that demonstrate Britain's past encounters with foreign aggressors, the very episodes from British history which best illustrate the vulnerability of a small island nation to incursion and uprising. Thus, notions of Britishness are distilled into what these aggressors are not; patriotic, Protestant and secure in their own land.

Britishness is thus represented here as a shared identity based on the patriotism and liberty of the British people and their desire to protect their freedom. However, this identity is also shown to be evasive and exclusionary. Where, for example, are the Scottish Britons? Why are women's roles in the articulations of national identity so varied? Why are British Catholics so frequently ignored? The reality of Britain's varied history is elided in order to promote Britishness in a positive light; key cultural components of the nation are sidelined, ignored or even vilified as a threat to the nation's illustrious ancestors and modern, political and social order. Thus the notion of Britishness is destabilised and undermined by the very histories that purport to validate and demonstrate the national character.

Ironically, therefore, representations of Britishness in the history plays are further destabilised by inconsistencies in their insistence upon the nation's political, dynastic and cultural stability. Whether favourites represented as patriots, women represented as political activists, Caesar, as a model for patriot colonialism, Turk as a model for overseas trade, all such representations falter because they are at odds with normative or conventional appropriations. In addition, broader anxieties resonate throughout the plays regarding religion, taste, speculation and dynastic uncertainties. Irrespective of repeated claims that Britain's dynasty was by the 1720s and 1730s fixed and settled, many commentators continued to see the need for reiterations of the nation's dynastic stability. The spectre of the Jacobites on the continent was thus an ever-present threat in the British imagination. Yet again, in attempting to establish the superiority of the British and the homogeneity of Britishness, these texts reveal the inherent conflicts within this nationalistic image.


## Otherness and superiority

Britishness is also described against a background of emergent imperialism and it is in this context – as Colley argues – that the image of Britishness reaches its most stable form. In these plays, desire for and fear of empire frequently coexist. Black has argued that Britain's sense of its own imperial value re-enforced notions of the nation's cultural, religious and political superiority in comparison to its European neighbours:

> Thanks to a burgeoning economy, an apparently successful political system, and a great and powerful world empire, there was less of a general sense of inferiority than there had been in the seventeenth century and more of a sense of an elect nation.... it appeared that the country of Newton and Sloane, Reynolds and Watt, had little to learn from the Continent.[6]

But even within this conceptualisation of Britain as the 'elect' nation, British colonialism was itself subject to seemingly contradictory accounts. The rhetoric utilised by commentators engaged in discourses relating to British colonial endeavour oscillates in its focus between concern for trade interests and desire for military expansion. This dichotomy has a tangible impact upon the representation of national identity. British colonialism is represented either as a liberating, improving, cultural and political development or, alternatively, as a scourge, a direct threat to British liberty and the nation's economic and political stability. Thus, the representation of Britishness, loses stability when placed in context with the myths of colonialism, becoming little more than empty political rhetoric encouraging a tottering belief in self-aggrandizing notions of British supremacy.

The history plays discussed in this book challenge the notion of British imperialism by drawing comparisons between contemporary Britain and her colonial predecessors or counterparts. The audience is assured that, inevitably, the qualities of Britishness will either allow Britain to attain similar successes or will protect Britain from similar failures. However, the gap between the British colonial myth, the realities of colonialism and the definitive characteristics of Britishness – patriotism and liberty – is too wide to support a version of British identity that can be applied to Britons variously dispersed across a developing maritime empire. British imperialism therefore results in ideological and linguistic fracture. The fantasy of imperialism is set against cultural fears regarding national instability and disintegration that can only be resolved by nationalistic jingoism.

## Modern fantasies

Ultimately, the history plays discussed in this book all demonstrate a limited degree of concord regarding British identity. In all of these texts liberty and patriotism define the British. This definition is not limited to modern Britons but is an inheritance traceable to their recent, medieval and ancient ancestors. Even foreign heroes such as Frederick, Duke of Lunenburgh or Scanderbeg are endowed with such qualities to the extent that they themselves take on the attributes of Britishness – how else could their histories be pertinent to eighteenth-century British audiences? Whatever the political or ideological agendas of these history plays, the representation of Britishness rests upon these simple defining characteristics. At this basic level, notions of Britishness are stable and fixed. However, it is only at this level that concord resides. Throughout the varied attempts at appropriating the characteristics of Britishness to promote partisan agendas, these core characteristics remain untouched and constant, and it is only once commentators move beyond these simple principles that contention abounds. Whether Britishness is perceived broadly or narrowly, deemed to include the entire population of the British Isles or simply substituted for Englishness, liberty and patriotism are central and immovable characteristics. Protestantism, trade and commercial interests, colonial endeavour – even gender and cultural difference – are more fluid concepts that engender a myriad of interpretations when integrated into notions of Britishness.

Mythology is the factor that unites these varied accounts of Britishness. A shared notion of innate superiority and the assumption that the British national character is located in the nation's past and that contemporary politics (history in-the-making) can be validated or discredited by reference to Britain's history. Thus, these plays demonstrate the pervasive attractiveness of the modern fantasy of Britishness, arising from a mythologised British past. Britons, thanks to their patriotism and their tenacious protection of their liberty, were, are, and will be free. This myth is, of course, easily countered by Britain's own history, but, nevertheless it remained part of a powerful and compelling fantasy of supremacy that history was to prove, from some perspectives at least, would serve this burgeoning maritime empire very well indeed.

# Notes

## Introduction: Dramatising Britain – Nation, Fantasy and the London Stage, 1719–1745



1. Bertrand A. Goldgar, *Walpole and the Wits: The Relation of Politics to Literature 1722–1743* (Lincoln: University of Nebraska Press, 1976), p. 220.
2. Hume has argued that 'drama is topical enough that one can trace its response to history closely from decade to decade, and even at times from year to year'. Robert D. Hume, *The Rakish Stage: Studies in English Drama, 1660–1800* (Carbondale: Southern Illinois University Press, 1983), p. 21.
3. Loren Kruger, ' "Our National House": The Ideology of the National Theatre of Great Britain', *Theatre Journal* 39 (1) 1987, 36–48.
4. Jean I. Marsden, 'Female Spectatorship', Jeremy Collier and the Anti-Theatrical Debate's *English Literary History* 65 (1998), p. 881. See also Robert D. Hume, 'Jeremy Collier and the Future of the London Theater in 1698', *Studies in Philology* 4 (1999), 480–511.
5. Writing on the literary reverberations of Bolingbroke's *Patriot King* (1738), David Armitage notes, 'the *Patriot King* had sprung from the soil of patriot poetry and plays in the 1730s and patriot kingship returned to the English stage in response to increased Anglo-Irish tension in the mid-1770s and to the possibility of Franco-Spanish attack during the American War' (David Armitage, 'A Patriot for Whom?', 'The Afterlives of Bolingbroke's Patriot King' *Journal of British Studies* 36 (1997), p. 408).
6. Brean S. Hammond, *Professional Imaginative Writing in England, 1670–1740 'Hackney for Bread'* (Oxford: Clarendon Press, 1997), p. 65.
7. Hammond describes Henry Fielding's plays in these terms. My somewhat less salubrious example is James Ralph, whose personal political agenda shifted as a reflection of his financial needs. For my discussion of Ralph see Chapter 2. For Hammond's discussion of Fielding see, *Professional Imaginative Writing*, Chapter 7.
8. Hume, *The Rakish Stage*, p. 67.
9. D. R. Woolf, *The Idea of History in Early Stuart England: Erudition, Ideology, and 'The Light of Truth' from the Accession of James I to the Civil War* (Toronto: University of Toronto Press, 1990), p. xv.
10. Christine Gerrard, *The Patriot Opposition to Walpole: Politics Poetry and National Myth 1725–1742* (Oxford: Clarendon Press, 1994), pp. 101–2.
11. Ibid., p. 101.
12. J. B. Kramnick, *Making the English Canon: Print-Capitalism and the Cultural Past, 1700–1770* (Cambridge: Cambridge University Press, 1999), p. 24.
13. Woolf, op. cit., p. 16.
14. Ibid., p. 172.
15. Karen O'Brien, *Narratives of Enlightenment: Cosmopolitan History from Voltaire to Gibbon* (Cambridge: Cambridge University Press, 1997), p. 5.
16. Ibid., p. 7.

17. Gerrard, op. cit., p. 102.
18. Brean S. Hammond, *Pope and Bolingbroke: A Study of Friendship and Influence* (Columbia: University of Missouri Press, 1984), p. 160.
19. O'Brien, op. cit., p. 16.
20. Ibid., p. 18.
21. Laurence Echard is one example of an historian rejected by the public. The popularity of his *History of England* (1707–1718) waned as a reflection of the decreasing popularity of his politics. For further discussion of Echard see Chapters 4 and 5.
22. J. G. A. Pocock, *Virtue, Commerce and History: Essays on Political Thought and History, Chiefly in the Eighteenth Century* (Cambridge: Cambridge University Press, 1985), p. 247.
23. Hugh Cunningham, 'The Language of Patriotism', in *Patriotism: The Making and Unmaking of British National Identity* (London: Routledge, 1989), vol. 1, p. 58.
24. Gerrard, op. cit., p. 102.
25. Ibid., pp. 102–3.
26. The fact that at least some of these 'staple icons' were not from English dynasties either was a detail that historians, playwrights and political commentators frequently struggled to hide and a recurrent problem that I shall return to.
27. Linda Colley, *Britons Forging the Nation, 1707–1837* (London: Vintage, 1996). pp. 4–7.
28. David Armitage, 'A Patriot for Whom?, p. 36.
29. Cunningham, op. cit., p. 58. Bolingbroke's version of patriotism, Brean Hammond contends, was grounded in the 'ancient constitution' that preserved 'the traditional political liberties of the English nation as long as it is respected by the government whose duty is to put it into practice'. See, Hammond, op. cit., p. 132.
30. Hammond has argued that 'under Walpole's management, parliamentary institutions stabilized but did not develop'. See, op. cit., p. 130.
31. Pocock, op. cit., p. 243.
32. Hammond, op. cit., p. 130.
33. Alexander Pettit, *Illusory Consensus: Bolingbroke and the Polemical Response to Walpole, 1730–1737* (Newark: University of Delaware Press, 1997), p. 20.
34. Goldgar, op. cit., p. 8.
35. Some critics have gone as far as to suggest that the Walpole administration was destitute of literary support. See, for example, Goldgar, op. cit., p. 218.
36. Goldgar, op. cit., p. 218.
37. Hammond, op. cit., pp. 129–30.
38. Pocock, op. cit., p. 234.
39. Anne M. Cooke, 'Eighteenth-Century Acting Styles' *Phylon* 5 (3) 1944, 220.
40. George Sherburn, 'The Fortunes and Misfortunes of "Three Hours After Marriage"', *Modern Philology* 24 (1) 1926, 91–109.
41. In reaction to the success of Gay's *Beggar's Opera*, both the *Craftsman* and the *Weekly Journal* were prosecuted in 1728/29 whilst subsidies awarded to government journals increased. See John Loftis, *The Politics of Drama in Augustan England* (Oxford: Clarendon Press, 1963) p. 97.
42. For example, Pettit claims that the Stage Licensing Act virtually abolished politically suggestive drama. See Pettit, *Illusory Consensus*, p. 21. Loftis notes that although only plays making the 'grossest kind of political allusion were

banned' was a result of the failure of the development of drama as the mono-
polistic provisions of the Licensing Act. See John Loftis, op. cit., pp. 150–3.
Hume contends that the 'London theatre of the 1730s was hardly a hotbed of
partisan political activity'. See Robert D. Hume, 'Henry Fielding and Politics
at the Little Haymarket, 1728–1737' in Hume (ed.) *The London Theatre World
1600–1800* (Carbondale: Southern Illinois University Press, 1980), p. 104.

43. Louise D. Mitchell, 'Command Performances During the Reign of George I,
*Eighteenth-Century Studies* 7 (3) 1974, p. 348.

44. Nicoll identifies Addison's *Cato* (London: J. Millar, 1731) as one of a limited number of literary successes due to the absence of a love interest in
favour of a more fittingly tragic subject. Nicoll describes Addison's hero as
a philosopher 'whose nature and problems could be revealed appropriately
in rhetorical dialogue, certainly more so than the natures and problems of
violently passionate lovers and their mistresses'. According to Nicoll, this
type of 'pseudo-classic' tragedy was the best that the eighteenth-century
London stage had to offer. For the rest, Nicoll has little positive comment
to make. He assigns five categories to eighteenth-century drama, pseudo-
classic or pathetic tragedy, ballad-opera, pantomime, sentimentalism, and
domestic drama. Nicoll asserts that plays that adopted historical themes can
be grouped as a 'cognate species of drama, often with echoes of Shakespeare
and Otway'. I would agree with this statement but not his assessment of
eighteenth-century history plays as universally poor. See, Allardyce Nicoll,
*British Drama* (London: Harrap, 1978), pp. 130–45.

45. Arthur H. Scouten & Robert D. Hume, ' "Restoration Comedy" and its
Audiences, 1660–1776', *Yearbook of English Studies* 10 (1980), 57–69.

46. Loftis, *The Politics of Drama*, p. 153.


# 1   Ancient Britons and Liberty

1. For example Linda Colley in *Britons* argues for an increasingly inclusive and
dominant British identity. Murray Pittock in *Inventing and Resisting Britain:
Cultural Identities in Britain and Ireland 1685–1789* (London: Macmillan Press,
1997) and Jim Smyth in *The Making of the United Kingdom, 1660–1800* (London: Longman, 2001) identify within such a unified model varying levels
of regional dissent and dissatisfaction with this dominant identity. Overall
the scholarly consensus is that some form of uniquely British identity was
formed post-1707 but opinion is varied as to the strength and persistence
of the national characteristics of Welsh, Irish and Scottish Britons, and the
regional identities of the English themselves.

2. Nicholas Phillipson, 'Politeness and politics in the reigns of Anne and the
early Hanoverians' in J. G. A. Pocock (ed.) *The Varieties of British Political Thought, 1500–1800* (Cambridge: Cambridge University Press, 1993)
211–45. As I shall discuss later in this chapter Linda Colley also identifies
this post-1688 idealisation of British politics as the best in Europe.

3. Colley, *Britons*, pp. 10–58.

4. Pittock, op. cit., p. 54.

5. Smyth, *The Making of the United Kingdom, 1660–1800* (London: Longman,
2001), pp. 153–4.

6. Gerrard, *The Patriot Opposition to Walpole*, p. 142.

7.  Phillipson, 'Politeness and politics', p. 235. Phillipson suggests Defoe, Hoadly, Addison and Steele as such writers.
8.  There are other examples of plays which take ancient Britain as their setting, such as Delariviere Manley's *Lucius the First Christian King of Britain* (1717).
9.  David Armitage (ed.), *Bolingbroke: Political Writings* (Cambridge: Cambridge University Press, 1997); 'A Dissertation upon Parties', Letter XII (*Craftsman* 436, 9 November 1736), p. 113.
10. Armitage (ed.), *Bolingbroke*, p. 114.
11. Barthes, *Mythologies* (London: Vintage, 1993), p. 67.
12. Ibid., p. 102.
13. Phillipson, op. cit., p. 244.
14. Armitage (ed.), op. cit., p. 114.
15. Ibid., pp. 114–15.
16. Phillipson argues that it was not until the 'historical age' of George III that Whigs began to recover 'the Saxon past for Whiggery'. See, Phillipson, op. cit., p. 244.
17. Gerrard, op. cit., p. 104.
18. David Mallet and James Thompson, *Alfred* (London: A. Millar, 1740), p. 35.
19. Pettit, *Illusory Consensus*, p. 166.
20. Blair Worden, *Roundhead Reputations: The English Civil Wars and the Passions of Posterity* (London: Penguin Press, 2001), p. 65.
21. Hammond, *Pope and Bolingbroke*, p. 132.
22. George Jeffreys, *Edwin* (London: Woodward, Walthoe, Peele, and Wood, 1724), pp. 35–6.
23. Pettit, op. cit., pp. 96–7.
24. Pittock, op. cit., p. 128.
25. William Philips, *Hibernia Freed* (London: Jonah Bowyer, 1722), p. 25.
26. Aaron Hill, 'Athelwold' in *The Dramatic Works of the late Aaron Hill, Esq* (London: T. Lownds, 1760), vol. i, p. 358.
27. Hammond, op. cit., pp. 94–5.
28. Phillipson, op. cit., p. 244.
29. Armitage (ed.), op. cit., p. 112.
30. Worden, op. cit., p. 67.
31. Ibid., p. 67.
32. Pettit, op. cit., pp. 96–7.
33. Ibid., p. 97.
34. Hammond, op. cit., p. 133.
35. Aaron Hill, 'To Dear Sir, Sept. 25, 1731', in *The Works of the Late Aaron Hill Esq* (London, 1753), vol. 1, p. 77.
36. Hill describes Leolyn as 'a Briton', 'Leolyn, because a Briton, ought not to have his habit Saxon; all the rest have the authority of Verstegan's Antiquities, for the ground-work of their appearance; only I need not observe to you, that some Heightenings were necessary, because beauty must be join'd to propriety, where the decoration of the stage, is the purpose to be provided for' (To Mr Wilks, Oct. 28, 1731 in *The Works*, vol. 1, p. 89).
37. Hill, *Athelwold*, pp. 35–40. In Jefferys's *Edwin*, Leolin is the captive of the King of Britain, and although his cultural background is not mentioned, his name suggests the same Welsh link.

38. Pittock, op. cit., p. 13.
39. Ibid.
40. Smyth, op. cit., p. 138.
41. Ibid.
42. Ibid.
43. Smyth goes on to suggest that, as they came to think of themselves as 'the Irish nation', Irish Protestants began to appropriate the Gaelic past'. See, ibid., p. 142.
44. Pittock notes that even those in support of the Union were conscious of this conflicting interpretation. See, Pittock, op. cit., p. 56
45. For examples of eighteenth-century representations of the Scottish characteristic see Smyth, op. cit., pp. 153–5.
46. Pittock, op. cit., p. 59.
47. Michèle Cohen, 'Manliness, Effeminacy and the French: Gender and the Construction of National Character in Eighteenth-Century England', in Tim Hitchcock and Michèle Cohen (eds), *English Masculinities 1660–1800* (London: Longman, 2001), p. 47.
48. Ibid., p. 49.
49. Ibid., p. 60.
50. Michael Mangan, *Staging Masculinities: History, Gender, Performance* (London: Palgrave Macmillan, 2003), p. 166.
51. See, for example, Smyth's analysis of xenophobic representations of Welsh, Scottish and Irish characteristics in Smyth, op. cit., pp. 153–5.
52. Ibid., p. 155; Pittock, op. cit., p. 55.
53. Armitage (ed.), op. cit., p. 115.
54. Barthes, op. cit., p. 72.
55. Colley, op. cit., p. 52.
56. Ibid., p. 52.
57. Ibid., pp. 53–4
58. Ibid., p. 53.
59. Worden, op. cit., p. 67.
60. Ibid., p. 154.
61. Armitage (ed.), op. cit., p. 111.
62. Worden, op. cit., p. 168.
63. Armitage (ed), op. cit., pp. 111–12.
64. Worden, op. cit., p. 168.
65. Ibid., p. 163.
66. Pettit, op. cit., p. 20.

## 2 Kings, Ministers and Favourites: the National Myth in Peril

1. Blair Worden, 'Favourites of the English Stage', in L. W. B. Brockliss & J. H. Elliott (eds.), *The World of the Favourite* (New Haven: Yale University Press, 1999), pp. 159–83. Worden cites Christopher Marlowe's *Edward II* as the earliest example of a dramatic representation of a favourite.

2. Terms commonly associated with the favourite include; false, ungrateful, unhappy, base, upstart, greedy. Worden argues for a continuity of language from the earliest stage representations of favourites until their demise during the first half of the eighteenth century. See Worden, op. cit., p. 159.

3. I. A. A. Thompson, 'The Institutional Background to the Rise of the Minister-Favourite', in Brockliss & Elliott (eds), *The World of the Favourite*, p. 14.

4. Thompson, 'The Institutional Background to the Rise of the Minister-Favourite', p. 14.

5. Thompson identifies the first sixty years of the sixteenth century as the high point of this phenomenon. See 'The Institutional Background to the Rise of the Minister-Favourite', p. 14.

6. Worden, 'Favourites on the English Stage', p. 161.

7. Thompson, 'The Institutional Background to the Rise of the Minister-Favourite', pp. 15–16.

8. See Gerrard, *The Patriot Opposition to Walpole*, pp. 20–5.

9. See the wealth of favourites discussed in Brockliss & Elliott (eds), *The World of the Favourite*. Early examples include Robert de Vere (1362–92), favourite of Richard II. Opposition commentators appropriated the history of De Vere as a reflection of Walpole's position as favourite to the Hanoverians. For an example of such parallels see, *The Norfolk Sting, or the history and fall of evil Ministers including the lives of Roger Mortimer, Earl of March and R. de Vere, Earl of Oxford – in covert reference to Sir Robert Walpole* (London, 1732).

10. For example, Queen Anne's 'bed-chamber women', see Rachel Weil, *Political Passions: Gender, the Family and Political Argument in England 1680–1714* (Manchester: Manchester University Press, 1999). For Queen Elizabeth I's array of favourites, see Paul E. J. Hammer, 'Absolute Sovereign Mistress of her Grace? Queen Elizabeth I and her Favourites, 1581–1592', in Brockliss & Elliott (eds), *The World of the Favourite*, pp. 38–53. Other infamous examples include Piers Gaveston and of course Roger de Mortimer.

11. For a more detailed analysis of Walpole's relationship with George I and George II, and his policies during this period, see J. M. Black, *Robert Walpole and the Nature of Politics in Early Eighteenth Century Britain* (London: Macmillan, 1990).

12. Mark Hallett, *Hogarth* (London: Phiadon, 2000), p. 272.

13. Anon., 'Ready Money the Prevailing Candidate, or; the Humours of an Election' (1727) in Hallett, *Hogarth* (London: Phaidon, 2000), p. 272.

14. For example, George Sewell, 'Walpole', in *Posthumous Works* (London: E. Curl, 1728); Joseph Mitchell, 'The Alternative', in *Poems on Several Occasions* (London, 1732); William Pattison, *The Poetical Works* (1728). For a critical discussion of anti-Walpole poetry, see Gerrard, *The Patriot Opposition to Walpole*.

15. Joseph Mitchell, *A Familiar Epistle to the Right Honourable Sir Robert Walpole; concerning poets, poverty, promises, places &c.* (London, 1735).

16. Anon., *The Norfolk Sting*, p. 34.

17. Ibid. p. 34.

18. Pocock, *Virtue, Commerce and History*, p. 234.

19. Anon., *The Norfolk Sting*, p. 34.

20. For further discussion of Gravelot's *A Devil Upon Two Sticks* see, Hallett, op. cit., pp. 274–5.

21. Worden, 'Favourites of the English Stage', p. 162.
22. Ibid., p. 7.
23. George Sewell, *The Tragedy of Sir Walter Raleigh* (London: John Pemberton, 1719), prologue.
24. Gerrard, op. cit., p. 157.
25. Ibid., p. 158.
26. I use the term 'conduct play' because Haywood's text is reminiscent of the increasingly popular genre of women's conduct books which she later satirised in *The Female Spectator* (1744–46). In *Frederick*, Haywood sets out an idealised mode of patriotic conduct that, the epilogue suggests, Frederick Lewis should follow in order to rid Britain of political corruption at his anticipated ascension to the throne. For discussion of Haywood's periodical writing, see Ros Ballaster *et al.*, *Women's Worlds: Ideology, Femininity and the Woman's Magazine* (London: Macmillan, 1991); Helene Koon, 'Eliza Haywood and the *Female Spectator*', *Huntington Library Quarterly* 42 (1978–79), 43–55.
27. Anon., *The History of Mortimer Being a Vindication of the Fall of Mortimer Occasioned By its having been Presented as a Treasonable libel* (London: J. Millar, 1731), p. 5.
28. In March 1731, in accordance with the Anglo-Spanish Peace (1728), the Austrian emperor Charles VI agreed to allow Spain to occupy Parma and Piacenza (Tuscany). The resultant Treaty of Vienna offered Charles British and Dutch guarantees of the Pragmatic sanction – to secure the prior succession to the Austrian Habsburg dominions (Austria, Hungary, southern Netherlands and territories in Italy) in his future children, male or female, rather than in the two surviving children of his brother Joseph I. In addition (a further condition of the Anglo-Spanish Peace), British and Dutch commercial considerations required Charles VI to terminate his profitable Ostend Company. See J.M. Black, *The Rise of the European Powers 1679–1793* (London: Edward Arnold, 1990). Hoadly's references to the Treaty of Vienna are based on the publication of the Provisional Treaty (1729).
29. Benjamin Hoadly, *Observations on the conduct of Great-Britain with regard to the Negotiations and other transactions abroad* (London: J. Roberts, 1729), p. 3.
30. Hoadly, op. cit., p. 30.
31. Ibid., p. 30.
32. Ibid., pp. 60–1.
33. In fact, George II openly supported the army (although he did favour compromise and stability in domestic affairs). Given how significant the King's patronage was for Walpole's career, the period of peace from the end of the Spanish war (1728) to the outbreak of the War of Jenkins Ear with Spain (1739) was a significant achievement for the minister. George II did not lead an army until Dettingham in 1743. See J. Brooke (ed.), *Horace Walpole: Memoirs of King George II* (Harvard: Yale University Press, 1985).
34. Hoadly, op. cit., p. 56.
35. Frederick Lewis was electoral prince of Brunswick-Lunenburg.
36. Eliza Haywood, *Frederick Duke of Brunswick Lunenburg* (London: W. Mears & J. Brindley, 1729), p. 4.
37. William Havard, *King Charles the First, written in imitation of Shakespeare* (London: J.Watts, 1737), prologue.

38. Tobias Smollett, *The Regicide: or, James the First of Scotland* (London: J. Osorn and A. Millar, 1749), p. 43.
39. Anon., *The Norfolk Sting*, p. 4.
40. See Milton Percival, *Political Ballads Illustrating the Administration of Sir Robert Walpole* (Oxford: Oxford University Press, 1916), pp. 200–4; Loftis, *The Politics of Drama*, p. 105; Goldgar, *Walpole and the Wits*, pp. 108–9; Lance Bertelsen, 'The Significance of the 1731 Revisions to *The Fall of Mortimer*', *Restoration and Eighteenth Century Theatre Research* (2) 1987, 12–13.
41. For a detailed account see Bertelsen, op. cit.
42. Gerrard notes that the play continued to be staged in its original as well as in its revised form throughout the 1730s. See, Gerrard, op. cit., p. 165. Dobson and Watson suggest that a persistent and largely apocryphal anecdote appended to the execution of Essex in 1601 formed the basis for John Banks's immensely successful *The Unhappy Favourite: or, The Earl of Essex* (London: Richard Bentley and Mary Magnes, etc., 1681). In Banks's version Essex sues for mercy but the Queen, due to treachery, does not receive his message. Ralph's *The Fall of the Earl of Essex* (London: W. Meadows, S. Billingsley *et al.*, 1731) Henry Jones's *The Earl of Essex* (1753) and Henry Brooke's *Earl of Essex* (1761) follow similar patterns to Banks's original. Dobson and Watson note the 'flagrant fictionality' of some aspects of these versions of the Essex history for example, the secret wife – Essex's real spouse was Frances Walshingham, widow of Sidney; the unwarranted claim that the Countess of Nottingham was a spurned ex-mistress; and the frequent strategic 'forgetting' of the Essex Rebellion. See Michael Dobson and Nicola J. Watson, *England's Elizabeth: An Afterlife in Fame and Fantasy* (Oxford: Oxford University Press, 2002), pp. 89–90.
43. Bertelsen, 'The Significance of the 1731 Revisions to *The Fall of Mortimer*', p. 10.
44. Paul E. J. Hammer, 'Absolute Sovereign Mistress of her Grace? Queen Elizabeth I and her Favourites, 1581–1592', in *The World of the Favourite*, p. 49.
45. For discussions of the events surrounding the banning of *The Fall of Mortimer* see Bertelsen, op. cit., p. 8; Arthur H. Scouten *et al.* (eds), *The London Stage 1660–1800* (Carbondale: University of Illinois Press, 1961), Part 3 Vol 1, pp. xlix, 148.
46. See Hume, 'The London Theatre From the *Beggar's Opera* to the Licensing Act', in *The Rakish Stage*, pp. 270–311.
47. Worden, *Favourites on the English Stage*, p. 34.
48. Robert D. Hume, 'Henry Fielding and Politics at the Little Haymarket 1728–1737', in John M. Wallace (ed.) *The Golden and Brazen World: Papers in Literature and History 1650–1800* (L.A.: University of California Press, 1985), p. 96.
49. Ibid., p. 104.
50. For a more detailed discussion of Caroline's role in British politics and her relationship with Walpole see, R. L. Arkell, *Caroline of Ansbach* (Oxford: Oxford University Press, 1939).
51. Anon., *The Fall of Mortimer* (London: J. Millar, 1731), p. 2.
52. Gerrard, op. cit., p. 150.
53. Dobson and Watson, op. cit., p. 97. Dobson and Watson also note that in eighteenth-century versions of the Essex history the two years between Essex's execution and Elizabeth's death were usually made into a much

shorter period. The Queen's death construed as a response to Essex's execution secured her 'sentimental femininity'. See, Dobson and Watson, op. cit., p. 94.

54. I describe Isabella and Mortimer as 'seemingly allied' because Mortimer cannot truly be described as an ally. His relationship with Isabella is purely formed out of his own self-interest. He has no concern for her other than for her role in his own advancement.

55. Anon., *The Fall of Mortimer*, p. 21. This statement could equally apply to Ralph's Essex. His 'failure' is a direct result of his Queen's withdrawal as his protector.

56. Gerrard notes that 'Gibson attempted to ensure that advancement was given only to clerics who could prove both their theological orthodoxy and their total loyalty to the Hanoverians and the Whig government'. See, Gerrard, op. cit., p. 25.

57. J. C. D. Clark, *English Society 1660–1832: Religion, Ideology and Politics During the Ancien Regime* (Cambridge: Cambridge University Press, 2000), p. 99.

58. See, for example, George Sewell, 'Walpole; or, the Patriot', in *Posthumous Works* (London, 1728), pp. 43–56. Sewell identifies Walpole as a moral minister without personal ambition. In pursuing a policy of peace Walpole denies himself military glory. In contrast, Sewell suggests Walpole's critics would, 'riot in Blood, / Unpeopling Nations for Another's Good' (lns. 172–3, p. 55). As I discuss in chapter four, Colley Cibber makes a similar observation with regards to Julius Cæsar in *Cæsar in Ægypt* (1724).

59. The *Dictionary of National Biography* notes that Ralph was a hack writer. Amongst other enterprises he acted as co-editor for Fielding's anti-ministerial paper the 'Champion' in 1741. However, there is evidence that prior to this period, Ralph attempted to gain Walpole's patronage. Horace Walpole's *Memoirs of George II*, (book iii) 345, claims that Walpole rejected Ralph. Pope insisted in the 1743 edition of the 'Dunciad' that Ralph deserted Walpole in 1742.

60. J. G. A. Pocock, *The Machiavellian Moment, Florentine Political Thought and the Atlantic Republican Tradition* (Princeton: Princeton University Press, 1975), pp. 462–505.

61. There is of course a certain irony here; Ralph's play is written in an attempt to gain Walpole's patronage – Ralph's motives are purely financial and hence self-interested. He wants to contribute to the body of propaganda created to secure Walpole's position – exactly the sort of opposition accusation he defends Walpole from in his play.

62. Bertelsen, op. cit., p. 19.

63. It is worth noting that *The Fall of Mortimer* is a significantly better play, more engaging and dynamic than Ralph's *Essex*. Characterisation in *Mortimer* is not necessarily more sophisticated but clearly more alluring and the text traverses genre boundaries, with comic scenes and the inclusion of an underclass in the sub-plot.

64. Clark, op. cit., p. 105.

# 3   Shakespeare, the National Scaffold

1. Jean I. Marsden, 'Re-written Women: Shakespearean Heroines in the Restoration', in *The Appropriation of Shakespeare: Post-Rennaisance Reconstructions of*

the Works and the Myth, ed. Jean I. Marsden (Hemel Hempsted: Harvester Wheatsheaf, 1991), p. 43.

2. Anne K. Mellor, 'Joanna Baillie and the Counter-Public Sphere', *Studies in Romanticism* 33 (1994), 561.
3. Hume has argued that drama's topicality provides readers with a contemporary response to historical events. See Hume, *The Rakish Stage*, p. 21.
4. Loftis, *The Politics of Drama*, p. 81.
5. Dobson, *The Making of the National Poet: Shakespeare, Adaptation and Authorship, 1660–1769* (Oxford: Oxford University Press, 1994), pp. 96–7.
6. As Judith Milhous asserts, this play is unlikely to be the work of Betterton, but the text has been repeatedly identified as his work due to playbills and advertising assigning the text to him. This was, presumably, a managerial ruse intended to capitalise upon Betterton's name and reputation as an adapter of Shakespeare. See, Judith Milhous, 'Thomas Betterton's Playwriting', *Bulletin of the New York Public Library* 77 (1974), 375–92.
7. In addition, John Sheffield, Duke of Buckingham published *The Tragedy of Julius Caesar* (London: J. Barber, 1722) and *The Tragedy of Marcus Brutus* (London: J. Barber, 1722), a two-part revision of Shakespeare's *Julius Caesar*. For a brief discussion of these plays see Michael Dobson, op. cit., p. 95.
8. Pettit, *Illusory Consensus*, p. 188.
9. Pocock, *Virtue, Commerce, and History*, p. 245.
10. Nicholas Rogers, 'Riot and Popular Jacobitism in Early Hanoverian England' in Eveline Cruickshanks (ed.), *Ideology and Conspiracy: Aspects of Jacobitism, 1689–1759* (Edinburgh: John Donald, 1982), p. 82.
11. Daniel Szechi, *The Jacobites: Britain and Europe, 1688–1788* (Manchester: Manchester University Press, 1994), p. 33.
12. Colley, *Britons*, pp. 83–4.
13. Ibid., p. 49. For a more favourable reading of the early Hanoverians, see R. Hatton, *George I: Elector and King* (Cambridge, Mass.: Harvard University Press, 1978); see also Brooke (ed.), *Horace Walpole*.
14. After his coronation George I visited Hanover five times and was buried there. Similarly George II visited Hanover frequently. In 1741 he intervened in foreign policy by breaking his alliances and making Hanover neutral without consulting the British ministry. As Linda Colley notes, neither king visited Wales, Scotland, the Midlands or the north of England. See Colley, op. cit., pp. 216–19; John Brewer comments upon the lack of allegorical and heroic representations of George I and II as an indication not only of the two kings' personal tastes in art but also the images they projected to their people. See John Brewer, *The Pleasures of the Imagination* (London: Harper Collins, 1997), pp. 21–2.
15. Howard Erskine-Hill, 'Literature and the Jacobite Cause: Was there a Rhetoric of Jacobitism?', in Cruickshanks (ed.), op. cit., p. 56.
16. Szechi, op cit., pp. 89–90.
17. Cibber, *King Henry the Sixth*, prologue, p. iii.
18. Ambrose Philips, *Humfrey Duke of Gloucester* (London: J. Roberts, 1723), p. i.
19. Katherine West Scheil, 'Early Georgian Politics and Shakespeare: The Black Act and Charles Johnson's *Love in a Forest* (1723)', *Shakespeare Survey* 51 (1998), 51.

20. The political analogy is explored further in Goldgar, *Walpole and the Wits*, pp. 29–32.
21. Erskine-Hill, op. cit., p. 52.
22. Ibid., p. 51.
23. Lewis Theobald, *The Tragedy of King Richard III* (London: G. Straham, 1720), p. 9.
24. Szechi, op. cit., p. 86.
25. Colley, op. cit., p. 216.
26. Nicholas Rogers, op. cit., p. 72.
27. Szechi, op. cit., p. 137.
28. Jeremy Black, *A System of Ambition? British Foreign Policy 1660–1793* (London: Longman 1991), p. 155.
29. Murray Pittock, *Jacobitism* (London: Macmillan, 1998), p. 81.
30. Marsden asserts that whereas Shakespeare's women are often represented as monstrous versions of femininity, the women of the adaptations are meek and passive – repeatedly represented as the inverse of Shakespeare's originals. See Marsden, op. cit., p. 46. My reading of the female characters discussed in this chapter does not altogether support Marsden's claim.
31. Christine Gerrard, *Aaron Hill the Muses' Projector, 1685–1750* (Oxford: Oxford University Press, 2003), p. 154. Gerrard asserts that, 'Hill equates King Harry's victory over France with his own hoped-for dramatic victory over French and Italian imports'. He was interested in 'cultural' not 'military conquest'. See Gerrard, *Aaron Hill*, p. 154. Katherine West Scheil makes a similar argument. See 'Early Georgian Politics and Shakespeare: The Black Act and Charles Johnson's *In A Forest* (1723)', 45–56. For my comment see p. 107.
32. Philips, *Humfrey Duke of Gloucester* (London: J. Roberts, 1723), p. 55.
33. For example, Kristina Straub, *Sexual Suspects: Eighteenth-Century Players and Sexual Ideology* (Princeton: Princeton University Press, 1992), p. 5.
34. See Jean I. Marsden, 'Daddy's Girls: Shakespearian Daughters and Eighteenth-Century Ideology', *Shakespeare Survey* 51 (1998), pp. 17–26.
35. Straub, op. cit., p. 128.
36. This is of course not limited to the adaptation. For further discussion of the commercial importance of the actress and of women as the 'stars' of the theatre see Elizabeth Howe, *The First English Actresses* (Cambridge: Cambridge University Press, 1992), p. 171.
37. Ros Ballaster, *Seductive Forms: Women's Amatory Fiction from 1684 to 1740* (Oxford: Clarendon Press, 1992), p. 115.
38. Nicoll, *British Drama* (London: Horrap, 1978), p. 132. Later in his career, according the Nicoll, Thomson loses this edge, reverting to the more popular dramatic theme of love in *Edward and Eleonora* (1739) and *Trancred and Sigismunda* (1745).
39. Marsden, op. cit., p. 43.
40. Colley, op. cit., p. 253.
41. Weil, op. cit., pp. 162–4.
42. Pittock, op. cit., p. 78.
43. For example, Straub asserts that 'the cross-dressed actress came into a fashion that lasted, not without changes, throughout the century. Whereas obvious travesty was crucial to the acceptance of male cross-dressing on the early

eighteenth-century stage it seems to have become so for female cross-dressers only in the second half of the century' See Straub, op. cit., p. 127.

44. Aaron Hill, *King Henry the Fifth; or, The Conquest of France by the English* (London: W. Chetwood, 1723), p. 18.

45. Straub, op. cit., p. 127.

46. Joan Riviere, 'Womanliness as a Masquerade', in Victor Burgin, James Donald and Cora Kaplan (eds), *Formations of Fantasy* (London: Methuen, 1986), p. 35.

47. Riviere, op. cit., p. 42.

48. Crossdressing in eighteenth-century adaptations of Shakespeare's history plays is not limited to plot-furthering disguises – female characters adopting male dress as a form of concealment. The Dramatis Personae of the 1745 edition of Colley Cibber's *Papal Tyranny* lists the part of Arthur played by Miss J. Cibber. It could be argued that the role of the youthful and patriotic Arthur is feminised in order to achieve a realistic representation, but why not simply cast a young man? Nepotistic opportunism aside, cross-dressing in order to signify an exchange of gendered character traits was relatively common. As Emmet L. Avery states in his introduction to *The London Stage*, men often played the more vulgar female roles in comedy and for a brief time plays performed entirely by a female cast were popular. However, in these cases, cross-dressing has less significance in terms of the politicisation of women's roles and therefore supports my assertion that Harriet's real political agency is achieved through her patriotism rather than her cross-dressing. See Emmet L. Avery (ed.), *The London Stage* (Carbondale: Southern Illinois University Press, 1962), part 2, vol. i, p. cxxiv.

49. Marsden, 'Daddy's Girls', p. 26.

50. Pittock, op. cit., p. 80.

51. Straub, op. cit., p. 21.

52. Colley Cibber, *Papal Tyranny in the Reign of King John* (London: J. Watts, 1745), pp. 8–9.

53. Some obvious examples are the representations of Elizabeth I and Mary Queen of Scots and the allegorical representations of women created by Aphra Behn, Delariviere Manley and Eliza Haywood.

54. Marsden, op. cit., p. 20.

55. Pittock, op. cit., p. 8

56. Ibid., p. 80. Pittock cites as an example a print showing Jacobite women 'being attacked by British army soldiers with drawn swords at Culloden, apparently in a spirit of self-congratulation'.

57. 'To Mr Philips, on his *Humphrey Duke of Gloucester*, by a Gentleman of the House of Commons' *The British Journal* No. XXV, March 9th 1723, pp. 2–3. This is again contrary to Marsden's argument that women who participate in the political realm face scathing criticism, see Marsden, 'Daddy's Girls', p. 20.

58. Marsden, op. cit., p. 20.

59. Clark, *English Society*, pp. 114–15.

60. Ibid., p. 118.

61. Rachel Weil argues for a similar cross-gendered perception of monarchs in relation to criticism levied at Anne. Despite being perceived as a weak and pliable monarch, Anne's failings, Weil contends, were never considered to be the result of her sex. See Weil, op. cit., pp. 162–70.

62. Lewis Theobald, *King Richard II*, preface. Peter Seary describes Theobald's *Richard II* as 'a relatively unpopular play'. It ran for seven performances in 1720 and three more in 1721. In reference to Theobald's alteration of Shakespeare's original text Seary notes that, 'Theobald, like Dryden, was prepared to believe that observance of the rules might intensify dramatic impact'. I would suggest that if Theobald's alterations 'intensify dramatic impact' the heightening of Aumerle's and Piercey's roles play a significant part in this intensification. See Peter Seary, *Lewis Theobald and the Editing of Shakespeare* (Oxford: Oxford University Press, 1990), pp. 39–40.

63. Rather unconvincingly, Katherine West Scheil limits the political purpose of Hill's adaptation to an attempt to discourage his audience from attending French entertainments. See Scheil, op. cit., 45–56.

64. Goldgar, *Walpole and the Wits*, pp. 32–3.

65. Cibber, *Papal Tyranny*, dedication to Philip, Earl of Chesterfield, p. i.

66. See Helene Koon, *Colley Cibber: A Biography* (Lexington: University of Kentucky Press, 1986), pp. 142–4. *Papal Tyranny* was abandoned twice. At first 'disagreeable apprehensions of a first day' (p. 142) prevented its production. Then in 1737 Cibber withdrew his text from rehearsal due to public criticism of his endeavours. Emmett L. Avery cites some interesting examples of Cibber's attempts to quell this attack in 'Cibber, King John, And the Students of the Law', *Modern Language Notes* 53 (1938), 272–75.

67. Clark, op. cit., p. 102.

68. Pittock, op. cit., p. 81.

69. Weil, op. cit., p. 231.

70. Howard Erskine-Hill, 'Literature and the Jacobite Cause: Was there a Rhetoric of Jacobitism?' in Cruickshanks (ed.), op. cit., p. 59.

71. Bruce Lenman, *Britain's Colonial Wars 1688–1783* (Harlow: Longman, 2001), p. 77.

72. For an overview of eighteenth-century criticism and theory concerning Shakespeare and the adaptation of his plays for the 'modern' stage, see Catherine M. S. Alexander 'Shakespeare and the Eighteenth Century: Criticism and Research', *Shakespeare Survey* 51 (1998), 1–15.

73. Jean I. Marsden, op. cit., p. 17.

74. The Temple of British Worthies was home to sixteen busts depicting exemplary Britons – fourteen historical and two contemporary. Included were, Alfred, Edward the Black Prince, Elizabeth I, William III, Raleigh, Drake, Hampden, Bacon, Newton, Locke, Shakespeare, Milton, Inigo Jones, and Thomas Gresham. See, Dobson, op. cit., pp. 135–46.

75. Elizabeth Montagu, *An Essay on the Writings and Genius of Shakespeare* (New York: Augustus M. Kelley, 1970), p. 58.

76. Anon., *The History of Mortimer* (London: J. Millar, 1731), p. 4. Montagu was just one of a group of female commentators whose contributions to the field of Shakespeare criticism reflected both contemporary approaches to Shakespeare (as playwright and cultural icon) and to the function of drama more generally, such as that outlined in *The History of Mortimer*. Montagu's fellows included Margaret Cavendish whose 'Sociable Letter' (1664) is held to be the first published critical essay on Shakespeare, Charlotte Lennox, Elizabeth Griffith and Elizabeth Inchabald. For further discussion see, Ann

Thompson & Sasha Roberts (eds), *Women Reading Shakespeare 1660–1900: An Anthology of Criticism* (Manchester: Manchester University Press, 1997).
77. Benedict Anderson, *Imagined Communities* (London: Verso, 1991), p. 36.
78. For a more detailed discussion of the rise of bardolatry during the eighteenth century see J. B. Kramnick, *Making the English Canon: Print-Capitalism and the Cultural Past, 1700–1770* (Cambridge University Press: Cambridge, 1999).
79. Lenman, op. cit., p. 77.
80. Marsden op. cit., p. 17.


## 4   Britain, Empire and Julius Caesar

1. Woolf, *The Idea of History*, p. 172.
2. For example, Howard D. Weinbrot, 'History, Horace and Augustus Caesar: Some Implications for Eighteenth-Century Satire' *Eighteenth Century Studies* 4 (1974), 395–6; Bridget Orr, *Empire on the English Stage* (Cambridge: Cambridge University Press, 2001); Philip Ayres, *Classical Culture and the Idea of Rome in Eighteenth-Century England* (Cambridge: Cambridge University Press, 1997).
3. Ayres, *Classical Culture and the Idea of Rome*, p. 1. Ayres also notes that Court Whig, dissident Whig, opposition, Tory and Jacobite commentators appropriated the discourse of patriotism and liberty.
4. Phillipson, 'Politics and Politeness', p. 231.
5. Orr emphasises the political range of such perspectives on Rome 'from Tory celebrations of Augustan absolutism to classical-republican critiques of Tyranny'. See, op. cit., p. 253. Ayres makes a similar point by contending that political drama of the period was one of the dominant participants in a debate in which connections were continually made between contemporary political events and ancient Rome. See, ibid., p. 6.
6. Kathleen Wilson, *The Sense of the People: Politics, Culture and Imperialism in England, 1715–1785* (Cambridge: Cambridge University Press, 1995), p. 153.
7. Wilson, *The Sense of the People*, pp. 140–1.
8. Howard D. Weinbrot, *Britannia's Issue: The Rise of British Literature from Dryden to Ossian* (Cambridge: Cambridge University Press, 1993), p. 244. Critics such as Norman Vance depict a dominant body of literature that was explicitly anti-imperial Rome, see Vance, 'Imperial Rome and Britain's Language of Empire, 1600–1837', *History of European Ideas* 26 (2000), p. 2. Ayres observes that the majority of political commentators until the mid-century were anti-Caesarean, particularly anti-Julian, see Ayres, op. cit., p. 18.
9. Bolingbroke, Locke, Berkley and Hume, for example, all aligned their political philosophies with the Roman Republic.
10. Dean and Knapp describe Cibber's play as a failure but its existence an indication of the opera's success. Certainly the six performances of *Cæsar in Ægypt* compare unfavourably with *Giulio Cesare's* impressive initial run and subsequent revivals (to date *Giulio Cesare* remains part of the standard operatic repertoire) but the play was not an unmitigated disaster. See, W. Dean and J. M. Knapp, *Handel's Operas 1704–1726* (Oxford: Clarendon Press, 1987) p. 501.

11. Dean and Knapp describe Caesar's reaction to 'The gift of Pompey's severed head' as a denouncement of Tolomeo's barbarity 'full of angry scales and burst of that prolonged coloratura, narrow in compass, low in pitch, and intensely energetic'. For a detailed interpretation of Handel's score and a full plot summary of *Giulio Cesare*, see Dean & Knapp, op. cit., pp. 483–526.
12. Colley Cibber, *Cæsar in Ægypt* (London: J. Watts, 1725), p. 30.
13. Weinbrot, op. cit., p. 244. Weinbrot provides a brief analysis of the play concluding that Cibber concurs with the growing consensus regarding Caesar's tyranny. Weinbrot bases his interpretation on the words of Decius, 'If Cæsar is oppos'd, he knows his Course, / 'Tis forward; thro' your Walls, with Wasteful War' (21). This anti-war sentiment is unfortunately taken out of context. Firstly is it not curious that Decius, one of Caesar's Lieutenants, adopts such pacifist terminology? Secondly, Decius' warning is followed by an aside, 'How will the Heart of Godlike Cæsar glow, / Folding his Arms around the vanquish'd Pompey!' (21).
14. Wilson, op. cit., pp. 155–7.
15. O'Brien, *Narratives of Enlightenment*, p. 19.
16. Michael Wilding (ed.), *John Sheffield, Duke of Buckingham The Tragedy of Julius Cæsar and The Tragedy of Marcus Brutus* (London: Cornmarket, 1970), pp. i–ii. Wilding claims that Mulgrave's alterations detract from Shakespeare's political themes in favour of rationality, decorum and orderliness. Although I would not dispute this notion of a neo-classical revamp, I feel that Wilding misjudges Mulgrave's political agenda.
17. Dobson, *The Making of the National Poet*, pp. 94–5. See also Michael Dobson, 'Accents Yet Unknown: Canonisation and the Claiming of Julius Cæsar', in Marsden (ed.), *The Appropriation of Shakespeare*, 11–28.
18. Ayres, op. cit., p. 19.
19. In reference to Echard's *Roman History*, Joseph Levine comments , 'the work was very popular, judging by the number of editions that were quickly printed'. Levine also cites John Tomlinson's opposing opinion. Tomlinson suggests that the work was not usually applauded, although the first two volumes were thought better than the rest. Echard's *History* ran to five volumes in total, the last three of which were published anonymously. This suggests the validity of Tomlinson's analysis of the perceived inferiority of the later volumes however, as Levine notes the rapid re-printing of the first two volumes suggests a positive reception. See Joseph Levine, *The Battle of the Books History and Literature in the Augustan Age* (New York: Cornell University Press, 1991), p. 345.
20. Weinbrot cites Fielding as one of Echard's most prominent critics. Fielding attacked Echard's *Roman History* in *Voyage from This World to the Next* (1743). By 1771 *Roman History* was labelled 'a tasteless, hurriedly composed work', 'lame and defective'. See Weinbrot, 'History, Horace and Augustus Caesar', 395–6.
21. Laurence Echard, *The Roman History*, vol. I, p. 366.
22. See O'Brien, op. cit., pp. 17–20. O'Brien emphasises the text's Whig credentials. Rapin was a Huguenot lawyer and fought for William of Orange at the Battle of the Boyne. For his services he was granted a pension from the King.

23. Paul Rapin-Thoyras, *The History of England, as well Ecclesiastical as Civil. By Mr De Rapin Thoyras, ed*. Nicholas Tindal (London: James and John Knapton, 1726), vol.1, prologue.
24. O'Brien, op. cit., p. 18.
25. Rapin, op. cit., vol. 1, p. 31. Colley Cibber makes an opposing observation in his play by devising a scene in which Caesar is seen to reward his troops with military honours and the spoils of their battle, keeping only the glory of military achievement for himself. William Philips creates a similar image of Belisarius as a beneficent leader.
26. Ibid., vol. 1, p. 40.
27. As O'Brien suggests, Rapin's popularity 'could be regarded today as a complicating factor in our understanding of national self-awareness in this period'. Rapin's success is, 'not easily reconciled to this modern narrative of emergent national awareness except, perhaps, as evidence for the persistence of older elite, cosmopolitan ways of characterising the nation's history'. See, O'Brien, op. cit., p. 18.
28. Aaron Hill *The Works of the Late Aaron Hill Esq*., 'To Lord Bolingbroke, June 25, 1738' (London, 1753) vol. 1, p. 284.
29. Ibid., 'To my Brother, Oct. 3, 1737' vol. 2, p. 57.
30. Ibid., 'From Lord Bolingbroke, July 21, 1738' vol. 2, p. 417.
31. For a further example of the representation of Caesar as pro-republican see, Gio Battista Coniazzi, *Political Observations on the Moral Characters of the Roman Emperors, Commencing from the Reign of C. Julius Cæsar, and finishing with that of Constantius Chlorus* (London, 1755). Coniazzi defends Caesar's moral character, identifying his downfall as the result not of ambition or greed but his misplaced trust in his so-called friends and supporters.
32. Joseph Addison, *Cato* (London: J. Tonson *et al*., 1713) I.i.
33. Ibid., IV.i.
34. For example, Plutarch offers a complex portrayal of Julius Caesar, emphasising his heroic qualities but condemning his ambition.
35. Even Rapin's account of the Roman Invasion of Britain suggests some level of military achievement on the part of Caesar.
36. Ayres, op. cit., p. 24.
37. Hill, *The Works of the Late Mr Aaron Hill Esq*., 'To My Brother, Oct. 3, 1737' (London, 1753) vol. 2, p. 57.
38. For further discussion of Hill's *Cæsar* which premiered as *The Roman Revenge* in 1747 see Gerrard, *Aaron Hill*, pp. 191–2.
39. Ayres has argued in relation to the rhetoric of patriotism that, like all post-1688 political discourses, it was about power and self-promotion and these central terms led to patriotism being assimilated by all the major parties. This was at once a benefit but also a flaw, in that patriotism was effective spin that any party could make use of. See, Ayres, op. cit., p. 19.
40. William Shakespeare, *Julius Cæsar* (London: Penguin, 1991) I.ii. 241–6, p. 62.
41. As Ayres has suggested, 'The Court Whigs under Walpole, desirous of presenting themselves as the defenders of liberties their party had secured, liked to picture the English as slaves until 1688. . . . Their party, they insisted, had created the balanced constitution with the Glorious Revolution, and their models and analogies were generally classical'. See, Ayres, op. cit., p. 5.

42. Although Belisarius was successful in returning the city of Rome to the Roman Empire (albeit an Eastern Empire) Justinian's plan to retake the Western Roman states never came to fruition.

43. William Philips, *Belisarius, a Tragedy* (London: T. Woodward, 1724), p. 2.

44. Echard, op. cit., p. 365.

45. Orr, op. cit., p. 271.

46. O'Brien, op. cit., p. 4.

47. Weinbrot, *Britannia's Issue*, pp. 250–1.

48. Ayres suggests that 'As Britain's power increased abroad, analogies with the classical world became less and less deferential, developing a strongly expansionist aspect'. See, Ayres, op. cit., pp. 14–19.

49. Weinbrot, op. cit., p. 275.

50. Philip Frowde, *The Fall of Saguntum* (London: W. Feales, 1727) pp. 13–14.

51. As Kathleen Wilson suggests, the St. Lucia fiasco reverberated throughout the decade continuing to be an issue for political debate well into the 1730s. See Wilson, op. cit., pp. 137–205.

52. Philips dedicates his text to 'the Honourable General Webb'. Webb was apparently shot at Wincanton in Somerset and, according to Philips's dedication, is secured, 'A victory which gave Preservation to the whole Confederate Army, added Glory to Your Country, and confers on You immortal Reputation'. Given the circumstances of Belisarius's demise I am not sure how flattering this comparison is meant to be.

53. O'Brien, op. cit., p. 19.

54. Kathleen Wilson notes that the imperial project, 'was immensely attractive to domestic publics, who seemed fervently to subscribe to its view of the essentially fair-minded, just and paternalistic nature of the British, as opposed to the French or Spanish, empire, and the formers ability to "Tame the fierce and polish the most savage", civilizing the world through commerce and trade'. See, Wilson, op. cit., p. 157.

55. For a detailed account of the level of investment in colonial activities during the period see, ibid., p. 160.

56. Gerrard, op. cit., pp. 132–3.

## 5  Turks, Christians and Imperial Fantasy

1. See, Mita Choudhury, *Interculturalism and Resistance in the London Theater, 1660–1800* (Lewis, Pa., and London: Bucknell University Press; Associated University Presses, 2000).

2. As Samuel Chew has noted, records of eighteenth-century theatre properties show that the 'Turk's head' was a common theatrical prop during this period. See Samuel C. Chew, *The Crescent and the Rose: Islam and England during the Renaissance* (New York: Oxford University Press, 1937), pp. 469–490.

3. See, Daniel J. Vitkus (ed.), *Three Turk Plays From Early Modern England* (New York: Columbia University Press, 2000), p. 6 and Orr, *Empire on the English Stage*, p. 66.

4. Vitkus identifies the key characteristics of the Turk as, 'aggression, lust, suspicion, murderous conspiracy, sudden cruelty masquerading as justice, merciless violence rather than "Christian Charity", wrathful vengeance instead of turning the other cheek'. See Vitkus, *Three Turk Plays*, p. 2. Later in this chapter I shall consider the ways in which the 1730s plays use these familiar characteristics in representing Turks yet also challenge such stereotypes.

5. John Sweetman, *The Oriental Obsession: Islamic Inspiration in British and American Art and Architecture 1500–1920* (Cambridge: Cambridge University Press, 1988), p. 61. Some prominent examples of the literary interest in the near and far east include, John Ogilby, *Asia Atlas* (1673); Antoine Galland's French translation of *The Arabian Nights*, (1704–7); Simon Ockley, *History of the Saracens* (1708–18); Thomas Shaw, *Travels in Barbary and the Levant*, (1737); Richard Pococke *Description of the East* (vol. I, 1743; vol. II, 1745); Frederick Lewis Norden, *Travels Through Egypt and Nubia* (1755 – French; 1757 – English). Colley has asserted that captivity, commerce and Christian scholarship combined to inform, or mis-inform, British curiosity about Islam. See, Linda Colley, *Captives: Britain, Empire and the World, 1600–1850* (London: Jonathan Cape, 2002), p. 106.

6. Scanderbeg or George Castriota (1405–68) gained fame for leading Albania in rebellion against the Turks.

7. It should be noted that these were not the earliest examples of plays concerning the history of Scanderbeg. An entry for E. Allde in the *Statione's Register* dated July 3, 1601 cites '*The True historye of George Scanderbarge* as yt was lately playd by the right honorable the Earle of Oxenforde his servants.' The text has not survived. See E. K. Chambers, *The Elizabethan Stage*, 4 vols. (Oxford: Oxford University Press, 1923, repr. 1945), vol. iv, p. 400; and, Samuel C. Chew, *The Crescent and the Rose*, pp. 475–78. Chew dismisses suggestions that Marlowe was the author.

8. Whincop died in 1730 at which time, according to his widow Martha, his play was unfinished. Martha herself is credited with completing her husband's work. See introduction to Thomas Whincop, *Scanderberg; or Love and Liberty* (London: W. Reeve, 1747).

9. See, David Armitage, *The Ideological Origins of the British Empire*, (Cambridge: Cambridge University Press, 2000) p. 170 and, Ros Ballaster, *Fabulous Orients: Fictions of the East in England, 1662–1785* (Oxford: Oxford University Press, 2005) p. 18. This is, of course, in many ways an oversimplification of the complex underpinnings of British imperialism during the period although, for the purposes of this discussion, the shift in balance between political and trade imperatives for colonial expansion is pertinent.

10. Vitkus, *Three Turk Plays* p. 8.

11. Chew, *The Crescent and the Rose* p. 541.

12. For example, J. L. Steffensen has asserted that Lillo's *Christian Hero* has no political significance. Whilst I am willing to concede that if read in isolation the political commentary shared by these texts may not be so immediate, I do not find Steffensen's asertion wholly convincing. See, J. L. Steffensen & Richard Noble (eds) *The Dramatic Works of George Lillo* (Oxford: Clarendon Press, 1993), p. 278.

13. As Ballaster has noted, heroic drama 'deployed oriental models as both analogue and opposite'. See, *Fabulous Orients: Fictions of the East in England, 1662–1785* (Oxford: Oxford University Press, 2005) p. 55.
14. Richard Knolles, *The generall historie of the Turkes* (London, 1606).
15. Annemarie Schimmel, *Pain and Grace: A Study of Two Mystical Writers of Eighteenth-century Muslim India* (Leiden: E. J. Brill, 1976), pp. 1–27.
16. Colley asserts that 'although the Ottoman empire was now increasingly condescended to in prose, western European governments remained diffident about challenging it in any more substantial fashion, and early modern Britain never seriously contemplated doing so'. Colley, *Captives*, p. 66.
17. Colley, *Captives*, p. 66. Colley suggests that this attitude remained dominant even after the Battle of Waterloo in 1816 when Britiain's 'European and global primacy seemed assured'.
18. Christine Woodhead, '"The Present Terrour of the World" Contemporary Views of the Ottoman Empire c.1600' *History* 72 (1987) p. 37.
19. Colley, *Captives*, p. 101.
20. Woodhead, 'The Present Terrour of the World', p. 37.
21. It is worth noting however that fears for the safety of Britons were certainly not imagined, although the exact source of this aggression was often misinterpreted. In only one year, 1711, North African privateering was directly responsible for British losses amounting to £100,000 in ships and cargo. Increasing pressure, particularly from the Church, to redeem slaves led to the release and procession through London of 150 British captives in 1734. This high-profile acknowledgement of the very real threat posed to Britons involved in trade in the Mediterranean coupled with the role of the Church in disseminating an antagonistic view of Islam resulted in a paradoxical conflation of interest in and fear of the Islamic nations. Linda Colley, 'Britain and Islam 1660–1760: Different Perspective on Difference', BSECS Annual Lecture (Oxford, January 1999). See also, Colley, *Captives*, pp. 65–72.
22. Colley, *Captives*, p. 69; p. 103.
23. Paul Langford, *A Polite and Commercial People: England 1727–1783* (Oxford: Oxford University Press, 1989) p. 166.
24. Robert Jones, *Gender and the Formation of Taste in Eighteenth-Century Britain; The Analysis of Beauty* (Cambridge: CUP, 1998) p. 34.
25. Jones, *Gender and the Formation of Taste*, p. 60.
26. Cf. the fall of St Lucia into French hands and parallels drawn in *The Fall of Saguntum* between Britain and Rome discussed in the previous chapter.
27. Langford, *A Polite and Commercial People*, p. 171.
28. Ibid. Langford goes on to argue that the British government and public had little interest in establishing a coherent economic or administrative policy for the colonies arising from any clear sense of the utility of the colonies but rather as part of a broader picture in terms of Britain's place in the hierarchy of European nations (pp. 172–4).
29. Geoff Quilley, ' "All ocean is her own": the image of the sea and the identity of the maritime nation in eighteenth-century British art' in Geoffrey Cubitt (ed.) *Imagining Nations* (Manchester: Manchester University Press, 1998), p. 136.
30. Gerrard describes Hill's *Ottoman empire* as 'a luxury publication designed to establish its author's social and literary credentials'. See, Gerrard, *Aaron Hill*, p. 22.

31. Aaron Hill, *A full and just account of the present of the Ottoman Empire in all its branches: with the Government, and Policy, Religion, Customs and Way of living of the Turks in General*, (London: John Mayo, 1709), p. 338.
32. Hill, *A full and just account*, p. 3.
33. Ibid., p. i.
34. Gerrard, *Aaron Hill*, pp. 22–4.
35. In her study of dramatic representations of the Ottomans, Orr contends that oriental despotism 'served as a negative exemplar not simply of statehood but of empire.' This might suggest that Hill's admiration for Turkish colonialism, however limited, was unusual so early in the century. Alternatively Orr may be placing too much emphasis on the widespread acceptance of a connection between oriental tyranny and British colonialism. See Orr, *Empire on the English Stage*, p. 66.
36. For example, letter xxvii, 1 April 1717, Montagu's description of the Bagnio at Sophia favourably compares Turkish women with their European counterparts; letter xxxix, 4 January 1718, 'I am also charm'd with many points of the Turkish Law, to our shame be it spoken, better design'd and better executed than Ours'. See Malcolm Jack (ed.), *Lady Marty Wortley Montagu: Turkish Embassy Letters* (London: Pickering, 1993), p. 108.
37. For other examples see, Daniel Defoe, *The history of the wars, of his late majesty Charles XII King of Sweden, from his first landing in Denmark, to his return from Turkey to Pomerania* (1720); Edmund Shishull, *Travels in Turkey and back to England* (1747).
38. Joseph Morgan, (ed.), *Mahomet Rabadan, Mahometism Explained*, 2 vols. (London, 1723–25).
39. Armitage, *The Ideological Origins of British Empire*, pp. 170–98.
40. Bruce McLeod, *The Geography of Empire in English Literature, 1580–1745* (Cambridge: Cambridge University Press, 1999), p. 218.
41. In this sense Lillo utilises the same patriot themes identifiable in the English histories. As in adaptations of Shakespeare's histories and the anonymous *The Fall of Mortimer* (1731) and James Ralph's *The Fall of the Earl of Essex* (1731), Lillo adopts patriotic rhetoric that historicises liberty as an ancient and lamentably diminishing right of all Englishmen.
42. See for example, Defoe, *The history of the wars, of his late majesty Charles XII*. For an Islamic, anti-Turk account see, Dimitrie Cantemir, *The History of the Ottoman Empire* (1714–16).
43. James L. Steffensen & Richard Noble (eds), *The Dramatic Works of George Lillo* (Oxford: Clarendon Press, 1993), p. 278.
44. Hill, *A full and just account*, p. 16.
45. Armitage, *The Ideological Origins of the British Empire*, p. 176.
46. This is evidenced for example by the New England Colonies described by John Morgan Dederer as 'the hotbed of sedition and revolutionary foment in the 1760s and 1770s' and the infamous Boston Tea Party in 1773. See John Morgan Dederer, *War in America to 1775* (New York: New York University Press, 1990); B. W. Labaree, *The Boston Tea Party* (New York: Oxford University Press, 1964).
47. Armitage, *The Ideological Origins of the British Empire*, p. 182.
48. William Havard, *Scanderbeg* (London, 1733), p. 12.

49. Havard's text is particularly significant in relation to my discussion of the partisan appropriation of patriotic rhetoric, in that here patriotism is overtly applied for an un-patriotic purpose.
50. McLeod, *The Geography of Empire*, p. 215.
51. McLeod attributes this assertion to Trenchard and Gordon who, in *Cato's Letters*, wrote in support of the type of empire endorsed by Swift in *Gulliver's Travels* and Defoe in *Robinson Crusoe*, as well as later commentators such as Samuel Johnson. See McLeod, *The Geography of Empire*, p. 218.
52. McLeod, *The Geography of Empire*, p. 218.
53. Scanderbeg histories relate the murder of his brothers by Amurath and the Sultan's dismissal of the treaty between Turkey and Albania, which secured Scanderbeg and his siblings as successors to the Albanian throne upon the death of their father.
54. It is important to note that in modern histories of Scanderbeg and in versions available to eighteenth-century readers, Scanderbeg rebels against the Ottoman Empire but does not liberate Albania from Turkish rule. See for example, Richard Knolles, *Historie* (1606), and Dimitrie Cantemir, *The History of the Ottoman Empire* (1973).
55. Hill, *A full and just account*, p. 338.
56. The image of 'oriental despotism' so often associated with early modern representations of the Turk requires qualification when applied to eighteenth-century factual and dramatic accounts of Ottoman colonialism. See, Vitkus, *Three Turk Plays*, p. 21.
57. Sir Paul Rycaut, *The Present State of the Ottoman Empire* (London: 1668) p. 117.
58. Hill, *A full and just account*, p. 5.
59. Isobel Grundy, *Lady Mary Wortley Montagu: Selected Letters* (London: Penguin, 1997), p. 168.
60. For example, Montague's admiration of Turkish law contrasts with her observation in an earlier letter that, 'There is no possibility for a Christian to live easily under this Government but by the protection of an Ambassador, and the richer they are the greater their Danger'. See Grundy, *Selected Letters*, p. 158. Obviously as the Ambassador's wife, Montagu may have had a self-interested motive in making this statement.
61. P. J. Cain and A. G. Hopkins, *British Imperialism: Innovation and Expansion 1688–1914* (London: Longman, 1993) p. 65.
62. Steffensen fails to recognise the way in which Lillo's *Christain Hero* participates in the debate on empire, asserting that the play has no real political significance. See, Steffensen and Noble (eds), *The Dramatic Works of George Lillo*, p. 214.
63. Hill, *A full and just account*, p. 5.
64. Ibid., p. 5.
65. Havard's Scanderbeg can be compared to William Philips's Irish heroes in *Hibernia Freed*, discussed in chapter one. Philips's heroes also defeat their enemies using conventionally un-heroic means yet their struggle against a militarily superior but pagan (and hence religiously inferior) opponent ensures that their patriotism is not questioned.
66. Armitage, *The Ideological Origins of the British Empire*, p. 173.
67. Rycaut, *The Present State of the Ottoman Empire*, p. 117.

68. Vitkus, *Three Turk Plays*, p. 10.
69. John Sweetman has argued that cultural interchange between Europe and Turkey in the early eighteenth century points to a lowering of the cultural barriers that had previously divided the two. To some extent his assertion is valid. However, I think it is important to distinguish European acceptance and occasional approval of Islamic cultures from attitudes towards religious practices. See Sweetman, *Oriental Obsession*, p. 60.
70. For more detailed discussion of anti-Islamic propaganda in English see Chew, *The Crescent and the Rose*, pp. 402–6, 441. It was widely known that from 1710 the entourage of George I included two captured and, importantly, *converted* Turks. Linda Colley asserted in, 'Britain and Islam 1660–1760 that anti-Islamic polemic was disseminated by the church. Colley has argued that British Catholics were more antagonistic towards Islam than British Protestants because they identified with the European Catholic states often at war with the Ottoman Empire. Conversely she suggests that the Quakers were particularly sympathetic towards the Turks because of their shared experience of persecution for religious difference.
71. Christian men were repeatedly depicted as turning Turk in response to the financial and lascivious attractions of Turkish culture. See Vitkus (ed.), *Three Turk Plays from Early Modern England*.
72. See for example, 'The Life of Scanderbeg' – inscribed to the spectators of *The Christian Hero*; Richard Knolles, *The generall historie of the Turkes* and David Jones, *A Compleat History of the Turks, from their Origin in the Year 755, to the Year 1718* (London: J. Darly, 1718).
73. In this way the 1730s representations of Scanderbeg can be seen to echo earlier dramatic representations of the Christian renegade – another cocktail of European and Turk.
74. See, for example, Vitkus (ed.), *Three Turk Plays*, p. 12.
75. For example, John Edwards, *The Christian indeed: described in a letter from Gaifer on his conversion to Christianity in English to Aly-Ben-Hayton, his friend in Turkey* (1757), had reached its seventh edition by 1767.
76. This division is nowhere made more evident than in the Turkish attempts to agree a bargain for the safety of the Christian hostages. Amurath demands that Scanderbeg relinquish his newly reclaimed control of Albania and recognise the Sultan's conquered provinces in Europe. The hostage motif has powerful implications for a British audience. The growing threat to Europeans posed by the Barbary pirates in the Mediterranean was a prevalent concern. The association by religion of Turkish and North African Muslims allowed this real threat to extend beyond its actual geographic limits. The Muslim pirates of the Barbary States renowned for their hostage taking are conflated with the Muslim Turks who become tarred with the same brush.
77. A degree of scandal was caused by Martha Whincop's claim that Lillo's *The Christian Hero* was a plagiarised version of her husband's text. Martha claimed that she took her deceased husband's unfinished manuscript to Lillo and asked if he would finish the piece. Lillo refused the offer, but some time later wrote *The Christian Hero* instead. See Thomas Whincop's *Scanderberg; or, Love and Liberty* (London, W. Reeve, 1747), introduction.

78. Thomas Whincop, *Scanderberg; or Love and Liberty* (London, W. Reeve, 1747), p. xviii.
79. George Berkeley, *An Essay towards preventing the ruine of Great Britain* (London: J. Roberts, 1721).
80. Mark Breitenberg, *Anxious Masculinity in Early Modern England* (Cambridge: Cambridge University Press, 1996).
81. See Cain & Hopkins, *British Imperialism*, p. 65.
82. Ballaster, *Fabulous Orients*, p. 57.


## Conclusion: History, Fantasy and the Staging of Britishness

1. For further discussion of Collins's poem see David Fairer & Christine Gerrard (eds), *Eighteenth-Century Poetry: An Annotated Anthology* (Oxford: Blackwell, 1999), pp. 349–353.
2. Phillipson, 'Politics and Politeness', p. 231.
3. Gerrard, *The Patriot Opposition to Walpole*, p. 107.
4. Pittock, *Inventing and Resisting Britain*, pp. 54–59.
5. Linda Colley, *Captives*, p. 105.
6. Jeremy Black, *A Subject for Taste: Culture in Eighteenth-Century England* (London: Hambledon & London, 2005), pp. 215–6.

# Bibliography


'To Mr Philips, on his Humphrey Duke of Gloucester; by a Gentleman of the House of Commons' in *The British Journal* XXV March 9th 1723, pp. 2–3.

*The Norfolk Sting: or, The History and Fall of Evil Ministers including the lives of Roger Mortimer, Earl of March and R. De Vere, Earl of Oxford – in covert reference to Sir Robert Walpole* (London: T. Dormer, 1732).

*The History of Mortimer Being a Vindication of the Fall of Mortimer Occasioned by its having been Presented as a Treasonable Libel* (London: J. Millar, 1731).

*The Fall of Mortimer* (London: J. Millar, 1731).

Addison, Joseph, *Cato* (London: J. Tonson *et al.*, 1713).

Alexander, Catherine M., 'Shakespeare and the Eighteenth Century: Criticism and Research' *Shakespeare Survey* 51 (1998) 1–15.

Anderson, Benedict, *Imagined Communities* (London: Verso, 1991).

Arkell, R. L., *Caroline of Ansbach* (Oxford: Oxford University Press, 1939).

Armitage, David, 'A Patriot for Whom? The Afterlives of Bolingbroke's Patriot King' *Journal of British Studies* 36 (4) 1997, 397–418.

——, *The Ideological Origins of the British Empire* (Cambridge: Cambridge University Press, 2000).

—— (ed.), *Bolingbroke: Political Writings* (Cambridge: Cambridge University Press, 1997).

Atherton, Herbert M., *Political Prints in the Age of Hogarth: A Study in the Ideographic Representations of Politics* (Oxford: Oxford University Press, 1974).

Avery, Emmett L., 'Cibber, King John and the Students of the Law', *Modern Language Notes* 53 (1938), 272–75.

Ayres, Philip, *Classical Culture and the Idea of Rome in Eighteenth-century England* (Cambridge: Cambridge University Press, 1997).

Ballaster, Rosalind, *Seductive Forms Women's Amatory Fiction from 1684 to 1740* (Oxford: Clarendon, 1992).

——, *Fabulous Orients: Fictions of the East in England, 1662–1785* (Oxford: Oxford University Press, 2005).

——, *et al.*, *Women's Worlds: Ideology, Femininity and the Woman's Magazine* (London: Macmillan, 1991).

Banks, John, *The Unhappy Favourite, the Earl of Essex* (London: Richard Bentley and Mary Magnes etc., 1682).

Barthes, Roland, *Mythologies* (London: Vintage, 1993).

Bate, Jonathan, *Shakespearean Constitutions: Politics, Theatre, Criticism: 1730–1830* (Oxford: Clarendon Press, 1989).

Berkeley, George, *An Essay Towards Preventing the Ruine of Great Britain* (London: J. Roberts, 1721).

Bertelsen, Lance, 'The Significance of the 1731 Revisions to *The Fall of Mortimer*' *Restoration and Eighteenth Century Theatre Research* 2 (1987), 8–25.

Betterton, Thomas, *The Sequel to King Henry the Fourth* (London: W. Chetwood etc., 1721).

Black, Jeremy (ed.), *Britain in the Age of Walpole* (London: Macmillan, 1984).

—— (ed.), *Knights Errant and True Englishmen: British Foreign Policy, 1660–1800* (Edinburgh: John Donald, 1989).

——, *Robert Walpole and the Nature of Politics in Early Eighteenth Century Britain* (London: Macmillan, 1990).

——, *The Rise of the European Powers, 1679–1793* (London: Edward Arnold, 1990).

——, *A System of Ambition? British Foreign Policy 1660–1793* (London: Longman, 1991).

——, *A Subject for Taste: Culture in Eighteenth-Century England* (London: Hambledon, 2005).

Bradley, James E., *Religion, Revolution, and English Radicalism: Nonconformity in Eighteenth-Century Politics and Society* (Cambridge: Cambridge University Press, 1990).

Braverman, Richard, *Plots and Counterplots: Sexual Politics and the Body Politic in English Literature 1660–1730* (Cambridge: Cambridge University Press, 1993).

Brewer, John, *The Pleasure of the Imagination: English Culture in the Eighteenth Century* (London: Harper Collins, 1997).

Breitenberg, Mark, *Anxious Masculinity in Early Modern England* (Cambridge: Cambridge University Press, 1996).

Brockliss, L. B. W., & Elliott, J. H. (eds), *The World of the Favourite* (New Haven: Yale University Press, 1999).

Brooke, Henry, *The Earl of Essex: A Tragedy* (London: To Davies, 1761).

Brooke, J. (ed.), *Horace Walpole: Memoirs of King George II* (Harvard: Yale University Press, 1985).

Burgin, Victor, Donald, James & Kaplan, Cora (eds), *Formations of Fantasy* (London: Methuen, 1986).

Burrows, Donald, *Handel* (Oxford: Oxford University Press, 1994).

—— (ed.), *The Cambridge Companion to Handel* (Cambridge: Cambridge University Press, 1997).

Cain, P. J. & Hopkins, A. G., *British Imperialism: Innovation and Expansion, 1688–1914* (London: Longman, 1993).

Cambini, Andrea, *Two Commentaries* (New York: Da Capo Press, 1970).

Cassels, Lavender, *The Struggle for the Ottoman Empire 1717–1740* (London: John Murray, 1966).

Chambers, E. K., *The Elizabethan Stage* 4 vols (Oxford: Oxford University Press, 1923 repr. 1945).

Chew, Samuel C., *The Crescent and the Rose: Islam and England During the Renaissance* (New York: Oxford University Press, 1937 reprint 1956).

Choudhury, Mita, *Interculturalism and Resistance in the London Theater, 1660–1800* (Lewis, PA., London: Bucknell University Press; Associated University Presses, 2000).

Cibber, Colley, *Cæsar in Ægypt* (London: J. Watts, 1725).

——, *Papal Tyranny in the Reign of King John* (London: J. Watts, 1745).

Cibber, Theophilus, *King Henry the Sixth* (London: W. Chetwood etc., 1724).

Clark, J. C. D., *English Society 1660–1832: Religion Ideology and Politics During the Ancien Regime* (Cambridge: Cambridge University Press, 2000).

Colley, Linda, *Britons Forging the Nation, 1707–1837* (London: Vintage, 1996).

——, *Captives: Britain, Empire and the World, 1600–1850* (London: Jonathan Cape, 2002).

Coniazzi, Gio Battista, *Political Observations on the Moral Characters of the Roman Emperors, Commencing from the Reign of C. Julius Cæsar, and finishing with that of Constantius Chlorus* (London, 1755).

Conolly, L. W., *The Censorship of English Drama 1737–1824* (San Marino: The Huntington Library, 1976).

Cooke, Anne M., 'Eighteenth-Century Acting Styles', *Phylon* 5 (3) 1944, 219–24.

Crawford, Rachel, 'English Georgic and British Nationhood', *A Journal of English Literary History* 65 (1998) 123–58.

Cronin, Mike, *A History of Ireland* (London: Palgrave, 2001).

Cruickshanks, Eveline (ed.), *Ideology and Conspiracy: Aspects of Jacobitism, 1689–1759* (Edinburgh: John Donald, 1982).

——, *The Glorious Revolution* (Basingstoke: Macmillan, 2000).

Cubitt, Geoffrey (ed.), *Imagining Nations* (Manchester: Manchester University Press, 1998).

Cunningham, Hugh, *Patriotism: The Making and Unmaking of British National Identity*, vol. 1 (London: Routledge, 1989).

Davis. Thomas (ed.), *George Lillo, Dramatic Works with Memoirs* (London: W. Lowndes, 1810).

Dean, Winton, *Handel and the Opera Seria* (London: Oxford University Press, 1970).

Dean, Winton & Knapp, John Merrill, *Handel's Operas, 1704–1726* (Oxford: Clarendon Press, 1987).

Dederer, John Morgan, *War in America to 1775* (New York: New York University Press, 1990).

Dennis, John, *The Invader of His Country* (London: J. Pemberton & J. Watts, 1719).

Dobson, Michael, *The Making of the National Poet: Shakespeare, Adaptation and Authorship 1660–1769* (Oxford: Oxford University Press, 1994).

Dobson, Michael, & Watson, Nicola J., *England's Elizabeth: An Afterlife in Fame and Fantasy* (Oxford: Oxford University Press, 2002).

Dutu, Alexandru & Crenovodeany, Paul (eds) *Dimitrie Cantemir, Historian of South East European and Oriental Civilizations: Extracts from the History of the Ottoman Empire* (Bucharest: Association Internationale d'Études du Sud-Est Européen, 1973).

Echard, Laurence, *The Roman History: from the Beginning of the City to the Prefect Settlement of the Empire by Augustus Cæsar* (London: Bonwick, Tonson *et al.*, 1707–14).

Ellison, Julie, 'Cato's Tears' *English Literary History* 63 (1996) 571–601.

Fairer, David & Gerrard, Christine (eds), *Eighteenth-Century Poetry: An Annotated Anthology* (Oxford: Blackwell, 1999).

Frowde, Philip, *Philotas a Tragedy*, (London: A. Miller, 1731).

——, *The Fall of Saguntum* (London: W. Feales, 1727).

Genest, John, *Some Account of the English Stage from the Restoration in 1660 to 1830* (Bath: H. E. Carrington, 1832).

Gerrard, Christine, *The Patriot Opposition to Walpole: Politics Poetry and National Myth 1725–1742* (Oxford: Clarendon Press, 1994).

——, *Aaron Hill the Muses' Projector, 1685–1750* (Oxford: Oxford University Press, 2003).

Gibb, H. A. R. & Bowen, Harold, *Islamic Society and the West: A Study of the Impact of Western Civilization on Moslem Culture in the Near East*, vol. 1, 'Islamic Society in the Eighteenth Century' (London: Oxford University Press, 1950).

Gibbon, Edward, *Gibbon's Story of Constantinople from the Decline and Fall of the Roman Empire* (London: J. M. Dent & Sons Ltd., 1921).

Goldgar, Bertrand A., *Walpole and the Wits: The Relation of Politics to Literature 1722–1743* (Lincoln: University of Nebraska Press, 1976).

Grundy, Isobel, *Lady Mary Wortley Montagu: Selected Letters* (London: Penguin, 1997).

Hallett, Mark, *Hogarth* (London: Phaidon, 2000).

Hammond, Brean S., *Pope and Bolingbroke: A Study of Friendship and Influence* (Columbia: University of Missouri Press, 1984).

——, *Professional Imaginative Writing in England, 1670–1740 'Hackney for Bread'* (Oxford: Clarendon Press, 1997).

Hatton, R., *George I: Elector and King* (Cambridge: Harvard University Press, 1978).

Haydon, Colin, *Anti-Catholicism in Eighteenth-Century England, c.1714–80: A Political and Social Study* (Manchester: Manchester University Press, 1993).

Havard, William, *King Charles the First, written in imitation of Shakespear* (London: J. Watts, 1737).

——, *Scanderbeg* (London, 1733).

Haywood, Eliza, *Frederick Duke of Brunswick Lunenburg* (London: W. Mears & J. Brindley, 1729).

Highfill, Philip H., *A Biographical Dictionary of Actors, Actresses, Musicians, Dancers, Managers and Other Stage Personnel in London, 1660–1800* (Carbondale: Southern Illinois University Press, 1973–c.1993).

Hill, Aaron, *A Full and Just Account of the Present of the Ottoman Empire in All Its Branches: with the Government, and Policy, Religion Customs and Way of Living of the Turks in General* (London: John Mayo, 1709).

——, *King Henry the Fifth* (London: W. Chetwood, 1723).

——, *The Works of the Late Aaron Hill Esq. in Four volumes* (London, 1753).

——, *The Dramatic Works of the Late Aaron Hill Esq.*, 2 vols (London: T. Lownds, 1760).

Hitchcock, Tim & Cohen, Michèle (eds), *English Masculinities 1660–1800* (London: Longman, 2001).

Hoadly, Benjamin, *Observations on the Conduct of Great-Britain with Regard to the Negotiations and Other Transactions Abroad* (London: J. Roberts, 1729).

Howard, Alfred (ed.), *The Beauties of Thompson Consisting of Selections from His Poetic and Dramatic Works* (London: Thomas Tegg, 1826).

Howe, Elizabeth, *The First English Actresses: Women and Drama 1660–1700* (Cambridge: Cambridge University Press, 1992).

Hughes, John, *The Siege of Damascus* (London: John Watts, 1720).

Hume, Robert D. (ed.), *The London Theatre World 1660–1800* (Carbondale: Southern Illinois University Press, 1980).

——, *The Rakish Stage: Studies in English Drama, 1660–1800* (Carbondale: Southern Illinois University Press, 1983).

——, 'Before the Bard: "Shakespeare" in Early Eighteenth-Century London', *English Literary History* 64 (1997), 41–75.

——, 'Jeremy Collier and the Future of the London Theatre in 1698' *Studies in Philology*, 4 (1999), 480–511.

Inglesfield, Robert, 'James Thomson, Aaron Hill and the Poetic Sublime' *British Journal for Eighteenth Century Studies* 13 2 (1990), 215–22.

Jack, Malcolm, (ed.), *Lady Mary Wortley Montagu: Turkish Embassy Letters* (London: Pickering, 1993).

Jeffreys, George, *Edwin* (London: Woodward *et al.*, 1724).

Jelavich, Barbara, *History of the Balkans: Eighteenth and Nineteenth Centuries* (Cambridge: Cambridge University Press, 1984).

Jones, David, *A Compleat History of the Turks, from Their Origin in the Year 755, to the Year 1718* (London: J. Darly, 1718).

Jones, Henry, *The Earl of Essex: A Tragedy* (London: R. Dodsley, 1953).

Jones, Robert, *Gender and the Formation of Taste in Eighteenth-Century Britain; The Analysis of Beauty* (Cambridge: CUP, 1998).

Knolles, Richard, *The generall historie of the Turkes* (London: A. Islip, 1606).

Koon, Helene, 'Eliza Haywood and the *Female Spectator*', *Huntington Library Quarterly* 42 (1978–79), 43–55.

——, *Colley Cibber: A Biography* (Lexington: University of Kentucky Press, c.1986).

Kramnick, Isaac (ed.), *Lord Bolingbroke: Historical Writings* (Chicago: University of Chicago Press, 1972).

Kramnick, J. B., *Making the English Canon: Print-Capitalism and the Cultural Past, 1700–1770*, (Cambridge University Press: Cambridge, 1999).

Kruger, Loren, ' "Our National House": The Ideology of the National Theatre of Great Britain' *Theatre Journal* 39 (1) 1987, 35–50.

Labaree, B. W., *The Boston Tea Party* (New York: Oxford University Press, 1964).

Langford, Paul, *A Polite and Commercial People: England 1727–1783* (Oxford: Oxford University Press, 1989).

Lenman, Bruce, *Britain's Colonial Wars, 1688–1783* (London: Longman, 2001).

——, *The Jacobite Risings in Britain, 1689–1746* (London: Methuen, 1980).

Levine, Joseph M., *The Battle of the Books: History and Literature in the Augustan Age* (New York: Cornell University Press, 1991).

——, *Between the Ancients and the Moderns: Baroque Culture in Restoration England* (London: Yale University Press, 1999).

Loftis, John, *The Politics of Drama in Augustan England* (Oxford: Clarendon Press, 1963).

Loftis, Southern *et al.* (eds), *The Revels History of Drama in English vol. v, 1660–1750* (London: Methuen, 1976).

Lucas, John, *England and Englishness Ideas of Nationhood in English Poetry 1688–1900* (Iowa City: University of Iowa Press, 1990).

Lund, Roger D., 'The Bite of *Leviathan*: Hobbes and Philosophic Drollery', *English Literary History* 65 (1998), 825–55.

Lynch, James J., *Box Pit and Gallery: Stage and Society in Johnson's London* (Berkeley & Los Angeles: University of California Press, 1953).

Mace, Nancy A., 'Fielding, Theobald, and *The Tragedy of Tragedies*', *Philological Quarterly* 66 (1987) 457–72.

Maclean, Donald, Landry, Donna *et al.* (eds), *The Country and the City Revisited: England and the Politics of Culture, 1550–1850* (Cambridge: Cambridge University Press, 1999).

Mainwaring, John, *Memoirs of the Life of the Late George Frederic Handel* (London: R. & J. Dodsley, 1760).

Mallet, David & Thomson, James, *Alfred* (London: A. Millar, 1740).

Mangan, Michael, *Staging Masculinities: History, Gender, Performance* (London: Palgrave Macmillan, 2003).

Marsden, Jean I. (ed.), *The Appropriation of Shakespeare: Post-Renaissance Reconstructions of the Works and the Myth* (Hemel Hempstead: Harvester Wheatsheaf, 1991).

——, 'Daddy's Girls: Shakespearian Daughters and Eighteenth-Century Ideology', *Shakespeare Survey* 51 (1998), 17–26.

——, 'Female Spectatorship, Jeremy Collier and the Anti-Theatrical Debate', *English Literary History* 65 (1998) 877–93.

Matar, N. I., 'The Renegade in English Seventeenth-Century Imagination', *Studies in English Literature* 33 (1993) 489–505.

McLeod, Bruce, *The Geography of Empire in English Literature 1580–1745* (Cambridge: Cambridge University Press, 1999).

Mellor, Anne K., 'Joanna Baillie and the Counter-Public Sphere' *Studies in Romanticism* 33 (1994), 559–67.

Mikalachki, Jodi, *The Legacy of Boadicea: Gender and Nation in Early Modern England* (London: Routledge, 1998).

Milhous, Judith, 'Thomas Betterton's Playwriting' *Bulletin of the New York Public Library* 77 (1974), 375–92.

Mitchell, Joseph, *Poems on Several Occasions* (London, 1732).

——, *A Familiar Epistle to the Right Honourable Sir Robert Walpole; Concerning Poets, Poverty, Promises, Places &c.* (London, 1735).

Mitchell, Louise D., 'Command Performances During the Reign of George I' *Eighteenth-Century Studies* 7 (3) 1974, 343–49.

Montagu, Elizabeth, *An Essay on the Writings and Genius of Shakespear Compared with the Greek and French Dramatic Poets* (New York: Augustus M. Kelley, 1970).

Morgan, Joseph, (ed.), *Mahomet Rabadan, Mahometism Explained*, 2 vols (London, 1723–25).

Nicoll, Allardyce, *British Drama* (London: Harrap, 1978).

O'Brien, Karen, *Narratives of Enlightenment: Cosmopolitan History from Voltaire to Gibbon* (Cambridge: Cambridge University Press, 1997).

Orr, Bridget, *Empire on the English Stage* (Cambridge: Cambridge University Press, 2001).

Patterson, Annabel M., *Reading Holinshead's Chronicles* (London: University of Chicago Press, 1994).

Pattison, William, 'To Mr. Mitchell, Upon His Poetical Petition to the Honourable Sir Robert Walpole, in *The Poetical Works* (London: H. Curll, 1728).

Percival, Milton, *Political Ballads Illustrating the Administration of Sir Robert Walpole* (Oxford: Oxford University Press, 1916).

Pettit, Alexander, *Illusory Consensus: Bolingbroke and the Polemical Response to Walpole, 1730–1737* (Newark: University of Delaware Press, 1997).

Philips, Ambrose, *Humfrey Duke of Gloucester* (London: J. Roberts, 1723).

——, *The Briton* (London: B. Lintot, 1722).

Philips, William, *Hibernia Freed* (London: Jonah Bowyer, 1722).

——, *Belisarius, a Tragedy* (London: T. Woodward, 1724).

Pittock, Murray G. H., *Jacobitism* (London: Macmillan, 1988).

——, *Inventing and Resisting Britain: Cultural Identities in Britain and Ireland 1685–1789* (London: Macmillan, 1997).

Pocock, J. G. A., *Virtue, Commerce and History: Essays on Political Thought and History, Chiefly in the Eighteenth Century* (Cambridge: Cambridge University Press, 1985).

——, *The Machiavellian Moment, Florentine Political Thought and the Atlantic Republican Tradition* (Princeton: Princeton University Press, 1975).

—— (ed.), *The Varieties of British Political Thought 1500–1800* (Cambridge: Cambridge University Press, 1996).

Ralph, James, *The Fall of the Earl of Essex* (London: W. Meadows, S. Billingsley etc., 1731).

Richards, Sandra, *The Rise of the English Actress* (London: Macmillan, 1993).

Ritchey, David, 'An Index to the Theatrical Materials in the English Theatre Journals published between 1700 and 1750', *Restoration and Eighteenth Century Theatre Research* 31 (1988), 34–63.

Rivers, Isabel, *Reason, Grace, and Sentiment: A Study of the Language of Religion and Ethics in England, 1660–1780*, 2 vols (Cambridge: Cambridge University Press, 1991–2000).

—— (ed.), *Books and Their Readers in Eighteenth-Century England: New Essays* (London: Leicester University Press, 2001).

Rycaut, Paul, *The Present State of the Ottoman Empire* (London: J. Starkey & H. Brome, 1668).

Samuel, Ralph (ed.), *Patriotism: The Making and Unmaking of British National Identity* (London: Routledge, 1989).

Sawyer, Paul, 'The Popularity of Shakespeare's Plays 1720–21 through 1732–33' *Shakespeare Quarterly* 29 (1978), 427–30.

Scheil, Katherine West, 'Early Georgian Politics and Shakespeare: The Black Act and Charles Johnson's *Love in a Forest* (1723)', *Shakespeare Survey* 51 (1998), 45–56.

Schimmel, Annemarie, *Pain and Grace: A Study of Two Mystical Writers of Eighteenth-Century Muslim India* (Leiden: E. J. Brill, 1976).

Schoenbaum, S., *Shakespeare's Lives* (Oxford: Clarendon Press, 1970).

Scouten *et al.* (eds) *The London Stage 1660–1800* (Carbondale: Illinois University Press, 1960–62).

Scouten, A. H. & Hume, Robert D., ' "Restoration Comedy" and its Audiences, 1660–1776', *Yearbook of English Studies* 10 (1980), 45–69.

Seary, Peter, *Lewis Theobald and the Editing of Shakespeare* (Oxford: Oxford University Press, 1990).

Sewell, George, *The Tragedy of Sir Walter Raleigh* (London: John Pemberton, 1719).

——, *Posthumous Works* (London: E. Curll, 1728).

Shaw, Stanford J., *History of the Ottoman Empire* (Cambridge: Cambridge University Press, 1990).

Sherburn, George, 'The Fortunes and Misfortunes of "Three Hours After Marriage"', *Modern Philology* 24 (1) 1926, 91–109.

Smith, Ruth, *Handel's Oratorios and Eighteenth-Century Thought* (Cambridge: Cambridge University Press, 1995).

Smollett, Tobias, *The Regicide: or, James the First of Scotland* (London: J. Osorn and A. Millar, 1749).

Smyth, Jim, *The Making of the United Kingdom, 1660–1800* (London: Longman, 2001).

Steffensen, James L. & Noble, Richard (eds), *The Dramatic Works of George Lillo* (Oxford: Clarendon Press, 1993).

Stone, Lawrence (ed.), *An Imperial State at War: Britain from 1689 to 1815* (London: Routledge, 1994).

Straznicky, Marta, 'Restoration Women Playwrights and the Limits of Professionalism', *English Literary History* 64 (1997), 703–26.

Straub, Kristina, *Sexual Suspects: Eighteenth-Century Players and Sexual Ideology* (Princeton: Princeton University Press, 1992).

Strohm, Reinhard, *Essays on Handel and Italian Opera* (Cambridge: Cambridge University Press, 1985).

Swedenberg, H. T. (ed.), *England in the Restoration and Early Eighteenth Century: Essays on Culture and Society* (Berkeley: University of California Press, 1972).

Sweetman, John, *The Oriental Obsession: Islamic Inspiration in British and American Art and Architecture 1500–1920* (Cambridge: Cambridge University Press, 1988).

Szechi, Daniel, *The Jacobites: Britain and Europe 1688–1788* (Manchester: Manchester University Press, 1994).

Theobald, Lewis, *The Tragedy of King Richard III* (London: G. Straham, 1720).

——, *Orestes: A Dramatic Opera* (London: John Watts, 1731).

Thompson, James, *Edward and Eleonora: A Tragedy* (London: Millar, 1739).

Thompson, Ann & Roberts, Sasha (eds.), *Women Reading Shakespeare 1660–1900: An Anthology of Criticism* (Manchester: Manchester University Press, 1997).

Tindal, Nicolas (ed.), *The History of England, as well Ecclesiastical as Civil by Mr De Rapin Thoyras* (London: James & John Knapton, 1726).

Vance, Norman, 'Imperial Rome and Britain's Language of Empire, 1600–1837', *History of European Ideas* 26 (2000), 211–24.

Varey, Simon (ed.), *Lord Bolingbroke: Contributions to the 'Craftsman'* (Oxford: Clarendon Press, 1982).

Vitkus, Daniel J. (ed.), *Three Turk Plays from Early Modern England* (New York: Columbia University Press, 2000).

Wallace, John (ed.), *The Golden and the Brazen World* (LA: University of California Press, 1985).

Weil, Rachel, *Political Passions: Gender, the Family and Political Argument in England 1680–1714* (Manchester: Manchester University Press, 1999).

Weinbrot, Howard D., 'History, Horace, and Augustus Cæsar: Some Implications for Eighteenth-century Satire', *Eighteenth Century Studies* 7 (4) (1974), 391–414.

——, *Britannia's Issue: The Rise of British Literature from Dryden to Ossian* (Cambridge: Cambridge University Press, 1993).

Wheeler, David, 'Eighteenth-Century Adapations of Shakespeare and the Example of John Dennis', *Shakespeare Quarterly* 36 (1985), 438–49.

Whincop, Thomas, *Scanderberg; or Love and Liberty* (London, W. Reeve, 1747).

Wilding, Michael (ed.), *John Sheffield, Duke of Buckingham, The Tragedy of Julius Cæsar and the Tragedy of Marcus Brutus* (London: Cornmarket, 1970).

Wilson, Kathleen, *The Sense of the People: Politics, Culture and Imperialism in England, 1715–1785* (Cambridge: Cambridge University Press, 1995).

Womersley, David (ed.), *Augustan Critical Writing* (London: Penguin, 1997).

Woodhead, Christine, ' "The Present Terrour of the World"? Contemporary Views of the Ottoman Empire c1600', *History* 72 (1987), 20–32.

Woolf, D. R., *The Idea of History in Early Stuart England: Erudition, Ideology and 'The Light of Truth' from the Accession of James I to the Civil War* (Toronto: University of Toronto Press, 1990).

Worden, Blair, *Roundhead Reputations: The English Civil Wars and the Passions of Posterity* (London: Penguin Press, 2001).

# Index

Breinigsville, PA USA
14 August 2010
243610BV00003B/24/P